NINETY-NINE MORE NEWFIES

73	Nana and the Old Guy - Nana & Moses	318
74	My Heart and Soul - Mojo	323
75	Turned Around By Love - Leia	329
76	Faux Motherhood - Maple	333
77	My Veteran Show Dog - Dante	337
78	Days With Dundee - Dundee	342
79	A Swedish Teddy Bear - Nalle	346
80	A Cautionary Tale - Ellie	351
81	Welcome Home - Miska	356
82	Jude Takes Manhattan - Jude	361

The Ninety-nine MORE Newfies   365
Acknowledgements   367

57	Rising to the Occasion - Kayla	251
58	The Laird of Drumnaguie - Seamas	255
59	Weird But Wonderful - Benny	259
60	The Power of a Dog, My Dog - Jake Doyle	263
61	A Lesson in Diversity - Izzy & Elsie	267
62	The Long Road Home - Moses	271
63	Miss Mild Meets Miss Mayhem - Taylor & Splash	276
64	He Sent Us Sam - Sam	281
65	Lex - Lex	285
66	Trust—In the Midst of Chaos - Halo	288
67	Circe's Birds - Circe	294
68	Natural Born Lifesaver - Finnegan	297
69	A Life Lived on the Edge - Zulu	301
70	Chief Companion - Chief	305
71	A Life in the Limelight - Pirate	309
72	Alaska Luke - Luke	314

| 42 | The Nature of Norman - Norman | 179 |
| 43 | Run Free, My Rudy, Run Free - Rudy | 183 |

Photos — 187

44	Wild At Heart - Lily	194
45	The Nutburger - Lexi-Bear	198
46	Our Penny from Heaven - Penny	202
47	Learning to Live for the Moment - Sage	206
48	Wild Child and the Lamb - Juno & Miley	211
49	Practically Perfect - Pinkerton	217
50	My Watchful Shepherd - Maxine	222
51	A Rescue From Above - Bear	226
52	Generations of Furry Comfort - Thunder & Tank	230
53	A Special Day - Sioux Pooh	236
54	My Almost Too Embarrassing Dog Moment - Leroy	240
55	Boulder Bear, Promoter Extraordinaire - Boulder	243
56	Almost Famous - Deacon	247

27	Contagious Love - Gummy Bear	105
28	An Indoor Pool and A Bank Job - River & Malcolm	110
29	Alaskan Life Savers - Cassiopeia	116
30	Jeter's Journey - Jeter	122
31	First Day At Doggie School - Taz	126
32	Who Do You Call? - Wendell & Shadow	131
33	Life Changer - Gabriel	135
34	A Newfy and His Pig - Gus	140
35	A True Easter Bunny Tale - Brandy, Mercedes & Maverick	144
36	Henry the Therapy Dog - Henry	148
37	Happy Accidental Kona Bear - Kona	153
38	Wonder Girl - Cheyenne	159
39	My Good Boy - Angus	165
40	Tourist Attractions - Duchess, Jackson Brown & Maggie Mae	169
41	To Yogi with Love - Yogi	174

12	Monsters in the Morning - Seamus	49
13	Finger Licking Good - Abra & Shiloh	53
14	The Dreaded Sucking Machine - Annie & Seven-of-Nine & Rowdy & Molly	57
15	Living and Laughing With Lulu - Lulu	61
16	First Responder - Shandy	65
17	Stick to the Script - Mandy	68
18	Conversing With Hoomans - Heffalump	72
19	Newf Sitting 101 - Jack & Cree	76
20	A Perfect Name - Bear	79
21	A Newfy Open Door Policy - Molly	83
22	A Bird in the Mouth Is Worth Two in the Bush - Kahlua	86
23	Losing Osa - Osa	89
24	Mamut's Camping Capers - Mamut	93
25	Celebrating Susy - Susy	97
26	Twice Blessed - Harley Bean & Coda	101

Contents

1	The Old Soul Who Rescued Me - Joey	1
2	Holy Cow - Murphy & Bailey	11
3	Blackie Trackie - Blackie	15
4	Landseer Horror Show - Ophie	19
5	Interstate Interlude - Scooter	22
6	The Christmas Dolly - Yogi & Noah	26
7	Beary, Beary Scary - Truffles	30
8	A Tale of Two Tails - Nana & Rosie	35
9	Remembering Ruggles, the ... Gentleman? - Ruggles	41
10	A Catholic Newf - Mariah	44
11	Mariah's Loveliest Song	48

Copyright © 2021 by Pat Seawell

All rights reserved. No part of this book may be reproduced in any manner whatsoever without written permission except in the case of brief quotations embodied in critical articles and reviews.

This book is designed to provide information and entertainment to our readers. It is sold with the understanding that the publisher is not engaged to render any type of professional advice. The content of each article is the sole expression and opinion of its author, and not necessarily that of the publisher. No warranties or guarantees are expressed or implied by the publisher's choice to include any of the content in this volume. Neither the publisher nor the individual author(s) shall be liable for any physical, psychological, emotional, financial, or commercial damages, including, but not limited to, special, incidental, consequential or other damages. Our views and rights are the same: You are responsible for your own choices, actions, and results.

Any Internet addresses (websites, blogs, etc.) printed in this book are offered as a resource. They are not intended in any way to be or imply an endorsement by the publisher, nor does the publisher vouch for the content of these sites and numbers for the life of this book.

ISBN: 9781736707302 (paperback)
ISBN: 9781736707319 (ebook)
ISBN: 9781736707326 (hardback)

Compiled and Edited: Pat Seawell

Interior and Cover Layout: Pickawoowoo Publishing Group

Front Cover Photo   Jake Doyle -*The Power of a Dog, My Dog*
Back Cover Photo   Maxine -*My Watchful Shepherd*

First Printing, 2021

Ninety-nine MORE Newfies

PAT SEAWELL

Chapter 1

The Old Soul Who Rescued Me - Joey

She was my first Newfoundland, a beautiful Landseer we named Bella. I had waited years for the time, money, and space needed to care for her. But at one year of age my precious puppy developed epilepsy, and after six months of valiantly trying to survive the monster that was claiming her, we allowed her to find rest and peace. Just two weeks before her death, I had also had to put down the collie/St. Bernard mix I had rescued almost thirteen years earlier. The loss of my two dogs was overwhelming. Although I attempted to carry out my normal routines, I could hardly breathe from the heartache.

I belong to an on-line group called Newf-L and it was there that I went to grieve. I poured my heart out on the keyboard and those who loved dogs understood my sorrow. One woman in particular watched and read all my words. She had spotted a Newfoundland in her neighborhood that was being neglected and mistreated. She feared that contacting the authorities would not make a difference because the laws at that time were not very strong; rather, she tried a more diplomatic approach.

She befriended the owners of the Newfoundland and learned that they had bought him with the idea of becoming backyard breeders.

The dog's owners were quick to tell her how much they hated the dog. He was bringing them nothing but work and trouble. As a pup they had taken him to a few dog shows but when he didn't place, they had thrown him outside with no shelter. They shoveled out a little dog food and poured his water, but gave him no other attention. Since they had no yard fence, he was left to roam the countryside. Intact. Although she offered to take him, the owners resisted because he was so "valuable." When they finally realized she would not buy him, they decided she could have him.

It was destiny. I had just announced on Newf-L that I had to have another Newf. The Christmas season was approaching and I knew I couldn't make it through the holidays without another huge face around.

Her email to me came immediately after I posted. She told me the neglected dog's story and offered him to me. She knew how much I loved my girls and how much my heart sorrowed for their passing. She believed I would give this old man a good home.

I didn't want a male. I didn't want a black. And I surely didn't want an older dog.

Then she told me about the car wash. This dog had a skin condition caused from poor nutrition and allergies. His prior owners had bragged about being able to bathe him without having to touch the ugly sores on his body. They told her they chained him to the pickup truck and pulled him through a car wash.

I went to get him the next morning.

It was a difficult five-hour trip. I had dislocated my shoulder and broken my humorous earlier in the year and when I pulled into her driveway, my shoulder was throbbing.

I don't know what I was expecting, but when I saw the dog that was to be mine I had to force a smile onto my face. He certainly wasn't the well bred, well groomed, well trained Newfoundland I had just had to put down. He was ragged, matted, covered with open sores, had blood-shot eyes, and was so skinny he looked like an Afghan rather than an adult Newf. I couldn't tell if he was longer than he was tall or taller than he was long. He was simply enormous and ... ugly. But it didn't matter. I needed him and he needed me.

I shook hands with the wonderful woman who rescued him and thanked her for helping both of us. We talked for a few more minutes, then she snapped a leash on the dog, handed him over to me, and we headed to my car. My head was swimming with pain and doubt. I didn't even know if he would fit into my car.

That's when he rose up and crashed down on my back, clubbing my still-healing shoulder. The pain was blinding. I almost passed out before someone pulled him down. I pasted that smile on my face again, caught my breath, and said I was okay.

I realized he had been left to his own devices for years and had no people manners. I hoped he wasn't any different from the Haflinger colts I raised. They were wild and wooly until halter training, but they all responded to my patience and skill. I clung to the hope that he, too, would respond to patience and skill.

We packed him into my car and he took up the entire back seat. I hadn't thought of the possibility of him not traveling well until that moment. I said a little prayer as I turned on the engine and headed back onto the highway.

I need not have worried. He was an angel on the way home. He slept the entire five hours. I look back on that car ride now and realize that was the first time he had slept "indoors" in years. He could finally relax. He felt safe.

When we arrived at our farmette, he slipped out of the back seat and on quivering legs took in the air. I took a good look at him as we stood under the pole light. In that quiet, gentle, alone moment, I bonded with him. I was home and he was home and our journey was about to begin. He had a name, but I changed it in that moment. He would have a new name for his new start in life. I christen him Joey, and under the stars he was no longer ugly. He became my beautiful boy and I was determined to change his life forever for the better. Little did I know then that he was to do the same for me, as well.

After he wobbled around a bit and surprised me by squatting to urinate instead of lifting his leg, I attempted to take him inside. By this time I was so tired I could hardly stand and I groaned as he balked going up the steps. His body was longer than my steps so I assumed at first that he couldn't figure out how to climb them. Then I realized he had probably been punished for trying to go into the house. I sat down on the steps and sighed. Doubt flooded me again and I began to cry.

You might expect that something magical happened at this moment, but it didn't. Joey just stood there with his huge head and jack-o'-lantern red eyes and watched me. He had no connection to humans at all. I had brought home a big, old, smelly, drooling mess of a dog who didn't know what to do with a crying two-legged. This was *not* what I had envisioned as a Newf-owner.

Eventually I wiped my face and tried again. This time I put his front paws on the steps and pushed him from behind. This was similar to what I did with the foals when I needed them to enter a place where they didn't want to go. Finally, with clumsy leaps, he made it up the steps and through the front door. I dropped his leash and headed for the bathroom.

When I returned to the living room I witnessed, to my horror, that he was lifting his leg and spraying my Christmas tree. He looked up at me as if to say, "Thank you, Missus, for putting a tree in here for me to pee on."

I did what any woman would do if she saw a big black dog peeing on her Christmas tree. I screamed!

And immediately I realized that was the worst thing I could have done.

Joey slunk to the floor. His entire demeanor changed. Up until then, he had just been a lug-head of a dog with not a care in the world. As soon as I yelled, he became a dog who feared. His body language told me he was waiting for the blows to arrive.

I rushed over to comfort him and he thought I was coming to hurt him. He crawled across the floor to escape me. I hurried after him. This all happened so fast that when I look back on it, I have to slow it down in my mind to capture the details. But once I realized that everything I had done had only made matters worse, I stopped, stood still, and waited.

Joey stopped trying to flee, but his shoulders and his hips were trembling. His fear was so obvious it made my heart hurt.

Quietly I went over to the couch in front of our picture window, sat down, and called for him. He had been taught to listen out of fear, and even though he was scared and in a strange home with a new two-legged, he came to me. When I beckoned to him to join me on the couch, those haggard eyes shied away from mine and his body sunk to the floor as if anticipating harsh words and physical punishment. My hand slid to his head and then with both hands I lifted his face and began crooning softly to him.

I persisted gently, calmly. At last his head went heavy in my hands and this huge hulk of a dog climbed onto the couch. Yet even then, he cringed into a ball next to me, trying not to touch me or look at me.

The incredible thing about animals is that they never lie. They don't rely on words like we limited humans do. I didn't try to talk reason into him or spew promises that he would never be harmed again. What works with animals is behaviors. They believe what they see. They sense what is real by actions, not words. So as I spoke my heart in kind words, I knew the way to reassure him was in my touch. No matter what he had experienced, he needed to know that from this moment on, life was going to be different.

I reached out and began to stroke him as he cowered beside me. My hands told him a new story. They told him he was wanted, he was accepted, and he was to be a part of my home and my life. They told him he was not going to get beaten or slapped or dragged on a chain ever again. They told him he was not going to be abandoned, forlorn and lonely, outside without attention or shelter.

My hands never stopped stroking him as he lay on that couch. My tiredness vanished. It didn't matter that it was 3:00 a.m.

This dog had to know that two-leggeds could bring comfort instead of pain. He had to feel the love of a person instead of her wrath.

In time, I could feel his muscles relax as he found comfort in my touch. Eventually, he laid his head on my lap. Soon I was covered with drool, but it didn't matter. Joey was letting go of the old rules and beginning to learn the new ones. I kept sliding my hands over him, joining our hearts into the rise of the sun.

When I went to bed that morning, he followed me and lay down next to me on the floor. From that morning on, Joey understood that life was different, that I was his Missus, and that I would love him and care for him forever. From that morning on, when Joey needed comfort, he went to his couch. It became his sanctuary, his place of love and happiness. In one of my most beloved photos of him he is sleeping on the couch, the soft winter sunlight of the window warming him.

Joey grew to love everyone. He grew to trust everyone. When people came to the farm to look at our foals he would follow them around as though he were the farm's ambassador. I suppose he actually was! Wherever we went, children poured on him like syrup on pancakes. He would stand there, in his hugeness, and let them wrap their arms around his neck and crawl under his belly and pick up his ears and spread out his lips and count his toes and wiggle his huge jowls, and he accepted all this curiosity with his huge Newfy smile.

My friends called Joey the Buddha Dog because they thought he imparted such peace and wisdom. When I took him to the hospital to visit a friend, a staff member asked if I would mind taking him to visit some additional patients. We ended up going to other departments and other floors. Joey visited patients for three hours, and he gave every one of them his big, happy smile.

Some days I would catch Joey lying outside the broodmare paddock watching the fouls kick and squeal and race around enjoying the new world they had been born into. I often thought this was his version of television.

Joey and I spent five beautiful years together. He enjoyed a good life at the farm. With time, his weight increased from 90 to 220 pounds. Yet his early neglect remained evident in some areas. His coat never became rich and full, and his body aged fast. He developed congestive heart failure and spinal arthritis. He walked funny, like a crocodile, legs splaying out with a curved sway. But Joey never stopped smiling.

I was Joey's more than he was mine. He was never far from my legs and if my hands were down, it was his pleasure to nudge his head under one of them. I felt he trusted me and believed in me and would do anything I asked of him. He became a happy, playful dog, and loved the running, bouncing, barking games we engaged in together. But he also stood by me during periods of hardship, and in the five years we spent together I experienced several painful events. Each time my world felt as though it were folding, Joey would come and lay his huge head in my lap. He would look up at me with those soulful jack-o'-lantern eyes and that sweet Newfy smile and tell me in his silent way, "You always have me, my Missus."

When it became clear that his heart failure and his arthritis were causing him serious complications, I so wanted to be selfish and keep him longer. But as every responsible pet owner knows, our companion animals rely on us to do what is right when the time is right.

On the day I took him to the vet to release his spirit from a body that was in too much pain, I was overwhelmed by his trust. We had a talk in the car before we got to the office. He stopped me as I was gasping out layers of love and told me not to bother, that he was ready, that he would do this. And he smiled at me.

He walked into the vet's office on his own, and on his way to the back he walked over to the cages and touched the noses of all the dogs that were locked inside. We watched as he spoke to each of them. I didn't listen. The exchange was between him and them. He had something important to tell them and I wanted him to have his last sacred spiritual moment between those of his own kind.

My tears could not be contained as I knelt beside him while the vet shaved his leg. Joey never licked anyone. I had taught him to touch noses to kiss us. He reached up and touched my nose with his to say goodbye. Soon he was gone. Gently and without trauma or fear he slipped to the other side.

I spent many, many days and nights weeping for his loss, but eventually the tears subsided and all that was left was the love. I smile now when I think of my boy, my Joey. Yes, the tears still come, as they do now while I write his story. But they are good tears, tears from a heart that was loved by an incredible dog.

Love doesn't stop because of death. Life gives us the chance to love, but death does not destroy it. Death is simply a pause ... until we meet again at that rainbow bridge.

*****

Not everyone wants to adopt an older dog. Older dogs are often left in shelters and with rescue organizations because people fear the sorrow of losing them too quickly. They feel their hearts are going to be won by these elders and the few years of love they receive from them will not outweigh the price of a broken heart. Joey taught me to accept and appreciate whatever time we have together and to retain that amazing ability to love after our time together is done. The older Newfies might have limited days to offer, but through their quiet dignity they impart a peace and tranquility that can rarely be equaled in a younger animal. Since my experience with Joey, I will only adopt older Newfies. And I'll do it again. And again. And again. Until we are all over the bridge together.

Teah Crew
New Middletown, Ohio, USA

Chapter 2

Holy Cow - Murphy & Bailey

Bailey was our first rescue Newf. He came to us from a big city SPCA, and had spent the first four years of his life sheltered in an upstairs apartment. Since our home is in a rural area, coming to live with us created a major change in his life. The scale of this change did not become evident until we went for our first stroll on a country lane.

When a dog owner takes his dog for a walk on leash, this can be a meaningful bonding experience for both human and dog. There are few things more pleasant than a peaceful walk along a country road with a couple of Newfs on leash. However, when those two Newfs each weigh 150 to 160 pounds, are healthy and strong, and one of them has never seen a cow, that walk can become an experience one never forgets.

This walk took place in our early Newf years during the first two weeks of Bailey's arrival. It did not occur to us that Bailey had never experienced the things we who live far from the bustling crowds take for granted. I put our five-year-old Murphy and our new boy, Bailey, each on a leash and we began our casual stroll along a quiet country road. As we meandered along in the bucolic setting we passed by a field where the farmer was keeping 10 or 15 young calves.

Murphy, who had been a country dog all of his life, never took notice of these little creatures; however, the moment Bailey caught a glimpse of them he lost control and began charging off the road towards the fenced area for a closer look. Murphy, upon seeing this, figured that he had better panic, as well. Within a split second he joined Bailey's mad dash toward these unsuspecting calves.

As luck would have it, this road was bordered by a steep, eight-foot gully on each side. Anyone can imagine that one 180-pound human is no match for 300 pounds of Newfoundland dogs, both bent on getting somewhere quickly. I was dragged on my stomach down one side of this gully and up the other by these two obsessed steam engines.

In retrospect, I guess the smart thing would have been to have let go of the leashes and calmly gone and collected these fellows at the fence. However, being a relatively new Newf owner and now experiencing the power of Newfs for the first time, my hands seemed to be one with the leash handles—instinctively gripping as tightly as possible. I like to think also that, subconsciously, I was trying to be the protector of those innocent young calves just across the gully, but I will never know if that was the case.

This incident was taking place amidst loud barking from the dogs and frantic yelling from me as I attempted to get them to stop. Our frenzied, confusing scene came to an abrupt end when we reached the fence on the far side of the gully. As suddenly as they had begun, the dogs stopped their wild stampede and began sniffing nonchalantly around the base of the fence. They were now completely disinterested in the calves and scarcely gave them a glance. The young bovines, unaware of the drama which had just unfolded in front of them, had not moved from their original positions.

This cow-induced drama took place in less than 30 seconds, but it seemed like a lifetime to me, and now, here the two dogs were, calmly sniffing the grass as if dragging a shrieking human through a deep gully was a normal daily occurrence. My heart seemed to be beating through my chest and I could not believe what had just happened. Yet once the confusion had settled, it was a simple task to lead the dogs back down the gully and up the other side.

Once back on the road, I took stock of my condition. I had grass and pebbles in my hair, a very nice abrasion on my face, the front of my once white t-shirt was now a mixture of brown mud and green grass stains, and a rip in my jeans was exposing a lovely red welt covering my left knee. But I was relieved to note that the dogs were fine, the calves remained oblivious, and I was still ambulatory. Choosing to persevere, I took a deep breath and we proceeded with our walk.

About 50 feet down the road at a railway crossing, sitting in his truck, was a railway worker. He had apparently been watching the whole incident. As I walked by, looking like a survivor from a war battle, he gave me a friendly wave which I returned. But neither of us spoke about what had just transpired. This lack of acknowledgement from both of us was just fine with me. I really don't know what I could have said that would have made the situation any less embarrassing than it already was.

As my dogs and I continued our walk I began imagining the fine tale the railroad worker would have for his wife and kids that evening. I even suspected that he would entertain every one of his friends for days at my expense.

Needless to say, this walk in the country, which resulted in my being catapulted through a roadside gully by two strong, exuberant Newfs, was powerful motivation to begin serious leash training and "cow socialization" with Bailey, the former city dog. His instruction began the very next day.

William Ball
Lancaster, Ontario, Canada
This story originally appeared in Life Among the Giants, by William Ball
www.lifeamongthegiants.com

Chapter 3

Blackie Trackie - Blackie

Blackie has always been *my* dog. When he was a baby, he spent long hours curled up with me on the ottoman of my big, comfy chair, keeping my feet warm as I studied for the CPA exam. My only study breaks were to take him for obedience classes. Not surprisingly, the first title he earned was his CD, Companion Dog. To earn the CD, a dog and handler have to score a minimum of 170 of 200 possible points from three different judges. The test consists of six exercises involving heeling and coming when called. Following the six exercises there is a one-minute sit/stay and a three-minute down/stay. Both stays are done by all the dogs together in a group.

Through the 7½ years we've been together, Blackie has stayed close by my side. Even when we can't see each other, he seems to know where I am, and often I can close my eyes and sense exactly where he is. Although he is sociable and friendly, he makes it clear to everyone that his mission in life is to take care of me and be *my* dog.

In September 2007, I tore ligaments in my left wrist. Two months later, Blackie tore ligaments in his left wrist. Following our respective surgeries we recuperated together, right down to matching casts. Before his injury, Rally Obedience was Blackie's favorite hobby. This is a relatively new dog activity that looks like a cross between agility and obedience. The dog and handler navigate a course that includes 10-20 stations, depending on the level. A sign at each station tells the handler what to have the dog do—sit, down, or heel in specific patterns. At the higher levels, there are a few jumps on the course, as well. Unfortunately, the injury to his wrist effectively ended Blackie's Rally career. I no longer felt comfortable asking him to make the required jumps.

Yet even though he could no longer compete in Rally, six-year-old Blackie was nowhere near ready to retire. He is an extrovert who has always loved going to trials and shows. He always seems convinced that everyone is there specifically to watch and cheer for him.

Since the old hobby was now off limits, I needed to find a new diversion for him, and fast. I remembered years of telling him "no sniff" all through his CD training, *and* in the show ring, *and* out with his cart for draft. Obviously, sniffing was something he really enjoyed, so what better than a Tracking course to serve as his physical therapy following the long months of post-surgical confinement.

Tracking seems to be an exciting and entertaining activity for all dogs, and Blackie was no exception. He took to it like a Newf takes to water! When training a dog for this activity the handler creates a path by walking and leaving treats and other objects for the dog to find. The dog then follows the path by sniffing the ground and indicating to the handler when he has found the objects by sitting, lying down, or some other trained reaction. From the first day of training, Tracking became Blackie's much loved, most desired, largely preferred, most favorite activity, and the two of us have spent many pleasant hours involved in it.

This year, I entered Blackie in Veteran's Obedience at our local Regional Specialty. I was serving as the Obedience Trial chair, and I wanted to be able to have Blackie with me during the two long exhausting days since he gives me strength and comfort. On the morning of the trial, I needed to find the show secretary and pick up my paperwork. My mother volunteered to hold Blackie for me while I took care of this business, so off I went, leaving the two of them sitting near the ring.

My search for the show secretary ended up taking me to another building. On my return, I was greeted with a surprise. I opened the door to the building where I had left my mother and my dog and there, right in front of me, was a very concerned Blackie with my stunned mother clinging to the end of his leash. When I asked her what had happened, she told this story:

"You were gone for longer than we expected. After awhile, Blackie whined, became restless, and finally got up. Then he put his nose to the ground and began dragging me all around the building. He was pawing at the door and trying to convince me to open it for him right before you came back. It was all quite amazing. He looked just like one of those dogs you see on TV—the ones that find the lost people."

Apparently, Blackie had gotten worried and decided to track me down. Or perhaps he simply imagined we were taking part in an unusual training session. Whatever his reasoning, he had enlisted the aid of my mother, whether she had planned to participate in a tracking activity or not! As my mother then said, "You'll never need to worry about getting lost—at least not as long as you have Blackie around!"

More recently, Blackie showed me in another way his concern for my well-being. He does not normally give kisses, but one exception is that he gives me gentle butterfly kisses on my arthritic wrists. That's why I was surprised a few weeks ago when he began dispensing his kisses to my chest. Although his kisses were gentle, as always, they were persistent, and Blackie seemed more nervous about me than usual.

I had been having chest colds off and on all year, never getting rid of them altogether. Because Blackie seemed to have become so troubled about my chest, I finally gave in and went to the doctor.

After three visits to my general practitioner, two different antibiotics, and a trip to a pulmonologist, I learned that I had blood clots in my lungs. After more procedures, more medications, and a four-day stay in the hospital, I felt better than I had in months and my family and colleagues at work told me that my "spark" was back. Left undetected and uncorrected, this lung disorder could have become life threatening. Without Blackie's butterfly kisses to my chest I would not have gone for medical help when I did. This unusual incident just gave me one more reason to love my big boy and to pay closer attention to his attempts to communicate with me. But then, as I explained earlier, he makes it clear to everyone that his mission in life is to take care of me. He has always been *my* dog.

Melissa Tabor
Lake Villa, Illinois, USA
North Central Newfoundland Club
Newfoundland Club of America

Chapter 4

Landseer Horror Show - Ophie

It was December, 1986, and my husband and I were getting ready to attend the Newfoundland Club of Southern California Annual Awards Banquet. With jackets and car keys in hand, we were walking toward the back door. That's when Ophie stepped into the room and blocked our exit. Immediate panic and horror washed over us. Our Landseer's front leg was totally covered in blood and more blood was dripping from her mouth.

What could she possibly have done to herself? We hadn't heard any noise, so it was unlikely that there had been a fight with either Gennie, our young Komondor, or Garfield, our sassy cat. And we knew our older Newf, Josephine, would never, ever, have participated in a fray.

Before rushing her to the car for a speedy trip to the local vet ER, we hoisted her into the tub and began hosing her leg to see if we could determine where all that blood was coming from.

We rinsed and rinsed and rinsed, and still the water ran red. Yet Ophie did not seem distressed, rather she acted as though she were enjoying this extra attention. Most certainly she was enjoying the extra encounter with water. Water was her passion. She was one of the best working dogs we had ever seen. We were preparing her for her Water Dog test and she was relishing every minute of the training. Yes, Ophie delighted in all activities that involved water.

Although the water continued to run red, we could find no sign of a wound on her leg, let alone one that would result in that much blood. Was the blood originating from her mouth? We refocused our attention.

Then we saw something strange. Hanging slightly outside her mouth, stuck to her upper lip, was a small piece of plastic. It looked suspiciously like a screw cap. But how could this slightly chewed piece of plastic be sharp enough to cause a gash that would produce so much blood? We attempted to wash her mouth, and although the water ran red, we could not locate a wound.

We turned our attention once more to her leg, this time working gentle fingers from her shoulder to her ankle. Finally, in the tangle of long, wet, formerly white hair on the back of her leg, we felt something hard, twisted, metallic. More probing and we were able to extract the remains of a tube. It was curled, bent, and punctured with holes. The tube had contained Burnt Sienna watercolor paint. The watercolor paint that comes in tubes is super-concentrated, allowing it to produce gallons and gallons of "blood."

The tube was a mess, and we were a mess. But our relief was palatable. There would be no need for an emergency transfusion that night, after all. We sprayed the tub clean, moved the rest of the watercolor tubes to a higher shelf, changed our clothes, and proceeded with our original plan for the evening.

But it took the whole forty-five minute trip to the awards banquet before my breathing returned to normal.

If only Ophie had chosen some other color—a nice cerulean blue, an emerald green, even a deep royal purple—she could have saved us several heart attacks. But no, this girl had chosen the one color guaranteed to make our hearts pound. But then Ophie, Shipwheel's Two If By Sea, CD, WD, Ophelia, always did have a flare for the dramatic.

Judi Randall
Chatsworth, Georgia, USA
Cru Newfoundlands
Newfoundland Club of America

Chapter 5

Interstate Interlude - Scooter

It was a hot Texas August in 1993 or '94, and we were showing Scooter, our six-year-old "special," in the River City Cluster in San Antonio. For the four days of shows, we would be commuting the 75 miles from our home in Austin to the convention center across from the famous River Walk in the heart of San Antonio.

In order to assure that we would have enough space and access to electricity for the dryer, Judi drove down in our big van the day the grooming area opened, and organized our set-up. I had packed the van for her with everything we'd need for the four days: crates, grooming tools, grooming table, dryer, extension cords, towel box, folding chairs, coolers for our food and drinks, and coolers for dog treats and bait. Since we only had one dog showing, we had decided to save money on gas by driving our little '89 Chevy Geo Metro (40 mpg) back and forth for the first three days. Then we'd drive the van on the last day and pack up all our stuff.

A friend from north of Houston and her Komondor had spent the night with us and was going to follow us to San Antonio. We were driving separately since her van, like that of most dog people, had the passenger seats removed to make room for her girl and her crates and equipment.

Even though Judi and I are tall enough to require pushing the front seats as far back as possible in the Geo, there was still ample room in the back seat for Scooter. He stretched himself out and before we had reached the busy Interstate, fell into a comfortable Newfy sleep, happily snoring away.

About 30 miles into the trip, Judi glanced into the back seat. Then she did a double-take. The back seat was empty. Instead of seeing the big black mound of Newfy she was expecting, she saw the bottoms of four huge paws. The paws were attached to the legs of the big black mound of Newfy wedged tightly into the space between the back and the front seats of the car. With all four legs sticking up in the air, Scooter looked to Judi like some gigantic water beetle marooned on its back in a stagnant, sticky pond.

This science fiction insect image caused my wife to explode with laughter. Before I could determine what was going on, she was shrieking, gasping for breath, and gesturing frantically toward the floor behind us. Tears were streaming down her face. This was way too much drama to deal with while flying down a crowded Interstate.

As soon as I was able to determine what had happen (with no help from Judi since her laughing attack prevented any verbal communication), I decided to get off the highway at the next exit. Scooter was suspended in the gap between the seats. He was stuck and the only way to get him unstuck was to stop the car, get out, move the front seats forward, and help the boy right himself.

This was back in the day before everyone had a cell phone, so we couldn't call to let the gal behind us know why we were pulling off the road. She followed us and was alarmed when we pulled over and she saw Judi leap out of the car with tears streaming down her face. Being a long-time Komondor breeder/owner, she feared something horrible had happened. Bloat came immediately to her mind.

Judi was still laughing and crying so hard she was unable to speak or be of much help in rescuing Scooter. Apparently he had rolled over in his sleep, thus trapping himself in the small gap between the seats. I moved the front seats and got Scooter out of the car. Once he was right-side up he was happy to climb back onto the seat again.

Some dogs might not have wanted to get back into the car after an experience like that, but unusual occurrences didn't faze Scooter. He was always a mellow, relaxed guy. However, we did notice that he spent the rest of the trip to San Antonio (and the whole trip back home, later in the day), sitting up on the seat with his front legs "locked" in place. He didn't want to risk lying down, perchance to fall asleep again and roll over into that worrisome abyss.

Although Scooter almost learned to sleep sitting up, for the rest of the time we owned that little Geo Metro he never again lay down in the back seat.

It seems one entrapment, and Judi's hysterical reaction to it, was enough for him.

Pat Randall
Chatsworth, Georgia, USA
Cru Newfoundlands
Newfoundland Club of America

Chapter 6

The Christmas Dolly - Yogi & Noah

Yogi, our first Newfoundland, was an "only" dog and the center of our universe. He was sweet, calm, gentle, even-tempered, huge, beautiful, and filled with a curious, fun-loving, playful spirit. He accompanied us on all our travels, greeted everyone he met with a cheerful, "roo, roo, roo," and brought us unspeakable joy.

Shortly after his fifth birthday, our lives were shattered when we learned Yogi had developed bone cancer. We began doing all we could to ease his pain and make him comfortable, but our sorrow and heartbreak was almost unbearable. After six months and much soul-searching, we decided to bring another Newfy into our home. We hoped a puppy might brighten Yogi's spirit, and ours, as we coped with his bitter illness.

Noah, a happy, inquisitive boy, joined our little family the week of Thanksgiving. To him the world was new and wonderful and he ran around the house looking for adventures. (I fondly remember nicknaming him "Blasto" because of his puppy energy.) He made a few attempts to annoy his big brother, but we made it clear to him that he was not to bother Yogi. Noah seemed to understand the seriousness of our message, and after that first week he never approached Yogi in anything but a gentle manner. Although they never became great friends, they formed somewhat of a bond, a respectful tolerance of one another, and we knew we had done the right thing by bringing young Noah home when we witnessed the two boys play biting and mouthing one another outside after the huge snowstorm we had that December, 1998.

The Christmas holidays arrived and with them all the excitement of the season. Cookie baking on Christmas Eve with both boys snuggling at my feet was a delight, followed by the doggie antics brought on by the thrill of wrapping-paper tubes. Yogi, noble Newfy that he was, lay calmly with the roll placed between his front paws and chewed it delicately. Noah, younger, healthier, and much more energetic, ran bouncing up and down the hallway with his cardboard tube before stopping to chew it into oblivion.

Papa's homecoming was always a special time for us. The boys "WOOFED" in unison because Rick's arrival meant that our pack was complete and all was right with the world. That evening my husband and I went out to visit family and exchange presents, leaving the boys behind to sleep and dream all the things dogs dream about. We would celebrate doggie Christmas when we returned.

Yogi truly loved getting presents. From the day he came to live with us he enjoyed unwrapping his gifts in order to uncover hidden treasures. He especially loved stuffed animals and would prance around the house singing a loud, "roo, roo, roo," before settling down to love his "baby." He would lie for long periods hugging the new toy with his big Newfy paws, gently gumming it and looking as content as a baby with a pacifier.

Following our Christmas visits with our human family, we celebrated Christmas with our Newfies. After a romp in the huge mounds of snow outside and a few special treats, both Yogi and Noah were excited and ready to begin the paper tearing that would reveal their new toys.

While they seemed pleased with all the new treasures, there was one toy that piqued the interests of both dogs. It was a latex Dalmatian squeaky toy addressed to young Noah, his very first Christmas present. After all the gifts had been opened, Noah took the Dalmatian, his Christmas dolly, and carried it proudly around the house. When he finally became distracted and dropped it, Yogi seized the opportunity to grab it. Off he trotted to the bedroom and hopped on the bed, placing the dolly beside him. He lay on the bed looking extremely proud and regal.

Noah soon realized his dolly was missing, so we retrieved it from Yogi for him. Yet it was not long until he dropped it again. Yogi, who had been eyeing Noah closely, snatched up the treasure and proceeded to the bedroom again. This scene was repeated several times. Each time Noah dropped the dolly, Yogi claimed it and carried it off to the bedroom. We finally realized that the ailing Yogi was letting Noah know that he was still King of the Castle and wasn't about to abdicate the throne (or his placement within our pack) to a young pup. For that night and for a few days afterward, Noah's dolly belonged to Yogi. Only when Yogi tired of it did Noah finally get to claim his prize.

A few weeks after Christmas, I hid the dolly away as a memento of that special time. Some three years later I came upon it and presented it to Noah. Ever so gently he nuzzled and licked it. No sooner had I put it up again for safe keeping than Noah cried and whined in a way I had never heard before. This was completely unlike his typical behavior. Once more I gave him the dolly. He responded as though he were a mother with a new-born pup. He lay with it between his paws, quietly licking, cleaning, nuzzling and loving it.

Noah had several replacement dollies (duplicates) and they were always his favorite toys, but he had never before reacted to any of them in this way. I believe this one elicited a special memory for him as it always will for us. The Christmas dolly represents a very special time—Noah's first Christmas and dear Yogi's last. This will always be a poignant memory in our lives, so sweet and simple, yet one we'll never forget and will always treasure.

We still have that special Christmas dolly which was shared between two very special Newfies. Yogi and Noah will be loved by us until the end of time.

Donna Mazzenga
Lake Orion, Michigan, USA
www.newfielove.com

Chapter 7

Beary, Beary Scary - Truffles

It is a brisk autumn afternoon and we are both thrilled to be at our special mile-high place in the Sierra Nevada mountains. I am galloping ahead of her, like I always do. She is calling to me to wait for her, but I'm only an eleven-month-old puppy, and, well, it's fun to run ahead when I'm off leash. Besides, what could possibly hurt me? I'm a big brave Newfy girl. I've dashed down this dirt road ahead of her many times. There are no cars here. Our 20 acres are bordered on three sides by a National Forest.

If I keep running ahead of her I might see a snow goose or a wild turkey. I could even see a deer. When these creatures see me, they always run and I love that. Even though I know she'll take the fun out of it. She'll say, "Truffles! No chase!" and she'll give me a time out. Still ... I love doing it.

Whoa! What's that smell? What's that *stench*? I've smelled it before, but it's never been this strong. She's still following me. She seems oblivious. Doesn't she smell it? This can't be good!

That does it! I'm stopping right here. I'm raising the fur on the nape of my neck. I'm raising the fur on the ridge of my back. Doesn't she even notice my warning? How am I going to alert her? Suddenly she gives me a command to go to the right. Ha! I'll go to the left. Yep! That got her attention, but listen to her. She has started talking about obedience! I'm sensing we are in mortal danger here, and she doesn't have a clue.

Now I can *feel* it. Through the pads on my paws I can feel its vibrations. Something heavy is running up from the river. Something heavy that *reeks*! Whoa! What is *that?* Never have I seen anything on four legs as big as that huge, stinky beast! And she's just standing there! An enormous, stinky, black monster is running right up behind her and she's *still talking about obedience*!

I need to think *fast*. The creature is much bigger than I, but I cannot let it near her. Okay, here goes! I'll trot to the right this time so she'll turn and watch me. I'll turn and "point" in her direction just like a hunting dog. I've got to make her to turn around. That *brute* is coming fast!

"Truffles, STOP! STOP! Truffles, BARK! TRUFFLES! BARK! BARK!"

She noticed! A huge, black, smelly monster is charging straight at her and she finally noticed! Quickly she raises her arms above her head so she'll look bigger and she's still shouting for me to bark. But ... she has been teaching me *not* to bark. She always says something about bothering the neighbors and she tells me to muffle it.

"TRUFFLES! BARK! BARK! BARK!"

The stinky, humongous creature has almost reached her. She's yelling for me to bark. This is confusing. What about bothering the neighbors? Okay, I'm going to do it. I'll just bark twice.

Whoa! The creature didn't like that! It plunged its huge claws onto the ground just inches from her work boots. And it stopped.

In the next instant the monster swishes right past her and comes straight toward me! Okay, we're a team. I learned that in Obedience Class. I'll bark again. I'll go up on my hind legs. I'll raise my arms up like she's doing. I'm over six feet tall when I stand on my hind legs.

Ha! That did it! The creature slides to a halt right in front of me. In another second it is high tailing it down toward the creek, across the road, into the trees. There! I can be big and scary, too! Maybe I should chase it. Maybe I should just be sure it's really gone.

She doesn't let me. She calls me to come to her, "Now!" She's always taking the fun out of things.

But wait, what's up with her? She seems frozen in place. Her arms are still up in the air, she's yelling louder than ever, and she's staring straight ahead toward a nearby mountain called Grizzly Peak. Calmly I creep through the bear grass and trot up to where she's standing on Grizzly Bar Road. What in the world is a *grizzly*, anyway?

I circle her on her right, then around to her left leg, and sit a hard sit. I do it just the way she taught me. I look up for her approval. She is still staring, her body is still rigid, but her left hand comes down to pat my head.

Her voice is very soft, "Truffles, you did good. Good girl."

Finally her head moves. She looks down into my brown eyes.

In a whisper she says, "Let's go find Daddy. Truffles, heel. Walk slowly."

I am not sure what else I could do. She's got a firm grip on the fur at the back of my neck. She's got her fingernails dug in.

We get half way to our sleeping shed in the woods and she tells me to, "Stop. Sit."

Then she wraps her arms around my neck and I break her fall as she sinks to the ground. Now I know we are a team. She starts shaking and tears are rolling down her face. I wait for her to give me some direction. We are still in the forest in the middle of the dirt road and I am not sure where the monster is. We need to keep moving.

"Oh, Truffie, when you stood up I could see your soft pink tummy. I was so afraid you were going to get clawed and bitten and thrown up into the air. Truffie, I love you so much! You saved us from the bear."

Her voice is shaky. I begin licking the salty droplets from her cheeks. Then I lose it and lick her nose, her eyes, her mouth. I lick her whole face.

Finally she takes some deep breaths and says, "Let's focus. We've got to find Daddy. We've got to get to the sleeping shed."

She braces herself against me and gets to her feet. We begin walking. We reach the sleeping shed. We find Daddy. We are safe. Susan and Truffie. We are a team.

Susan Liley
Napa, California, USA
Newfoundland Club of Northern California
newfpaws@att.net

Chapter 8

A Tale of Two Tails - Nana & Rosie

After having only cats for about 20 years I decided I wanted a dog. Not just any dog, I wanted a big, special dog. A friend had once asked if I would be interested in having a Newfoundland puppy. That got me thinking. A Newfoundland would be big. A Newfoundland would be special. And, a Newfoundland would love cats.

As is only natural for a teacher, I did my homework. I read many books and Internet articles, and I watched all the videos, movies, documentaries, and YouTube clips I could find.

After contacting several breeders I was disappointed that none of them were planning litters in the near future. However, when I learned that Dr. Emmy Bruno lived near my parents' seaside home, I contacted her. Dr. Bruno is a renowned breeder with a degree in Veterinarian Sciences and the *grand dame* of the Italian Newfoundland breeders. I had read her book *The Newfoundland* so I was familiar with her kennel, *Degli Angeli Neri* (Of the Black Angels).

Although Emmy wasn't planning a litter, I was delighted when she invited my mom and me for a visit. Hers would not be the first Newfoundlands I had ever seen, but they would be the first ones with whom I could interact.

The first Newf we saw on our arrival was Amabel, a very big, black female with a deep, husky voice. She welcomed us at the gate, while at the same time signaling that she was on duty there, and that we were to wait for Emmy.

Margot and Rosie, the two younger females, accompanied Emmy to the gate. While we chatted and Emmy unobtrusively checked me out as a prospective mom for one of her pups, Rosie took a shine to me and did not leave my side. To make it crystal clear that she had accepted me, she kept giving me her big, warm paw, and still today she follows me everywhere when I visit Emmy.

Since Rosie had given her approval of me, Emmy agreed I could have one of her precious puppies, and she contacted me several months later when Rosie became pregnant. While waiting for the puppies to be born I visited the *Degli Angeli Neri* kennel many times and Emmy and I became good friends.

Soon after Rosie's three puppies were born my mom and I went to see them. This was an R litter and I had chosen to name my puppy Rosalinde, from Shakespeare's *As You Like It*, and use Nana for her call name.

As we approached the whelping box we realized that Emmy was very emotional. When we saw the puppies, we knew why: the biggest and most beautiful female had been born with a miniature front paw.

With tears in her eyes Emmy said, "I've been advised to put her down because no one will want to care for her."

It was clear, though, that she would never do such a thing.

Mom and I looked at each other and cried in unison, "We'll take her, too!"

And that is how a cat person ended up with not one, but two, big, black Newfoundlands, Nana, and her sister with the miniature paw, Rosie. *Rosalinde* and *Rosabelle degli Angeli Neri.*

My decision was an emotional one. As a first-time dog mom, little did I realize what an enormous effort it would take to bring up two puppies at the same time, especially when one of them was handicapped. As she grew, Rosie's miniature paw was reabsorbed into the wrist, leaving a roundish stump. Emmy and I tried every possible contraption to help Rosie walk properly, but to no avail. If Rosie agreed to try our contraptions, Nana would take them away or destroy them.

Although my house has a big garden, the greatest obstacle when I took the puppies home was that I lived on the first floor (which is called the second floor in some countries). After carrying ever-growing Newfs up and down 18 steps several times a day, I was very happy when Nana eased my burden by learning to climb up and down alone. Before Rosie became too heavy to be carried she learned to climb up the stairs and Emmy taught me to walk down the steps in front of Rosie, helping her along by grabbing her by the side of her lion-like mane and guiding her downstairs.

Yet even after we perfected this method for climbing stairs, caring for Rosie was a formidable undertaking. For the first two months she had problems getting up and was not able to stand up quickly enough when she needed to pee. This lead to many incidents, many worries, and much discouragement on my side. There were times when I thought I would have to return her to Emmy, but my mom told me I needed to carry out and finish what I had started.

By then I had joined a Newfoundland group on Yahoo and later joined Newf-L. Many were the times I cried on the shoulders of these online friends when I became overwhelmed and felt I just couldn't manage my arduous task.

But then, overnight, everything changed. Rosie stopped peeing inside the house and learned to stand and to climb the stairs by herself. With time, she got so quick that I had to run after her when she went upstairs. She also started hopping around on three legs, swinging her stump for balance, though she preferred to lie down on her raised platform in the front yard. Notwithstanding the constant worry and effort associated with house training and Rosie's problem, it was a never ending joy to see my two girls grow and become more independent. For the next three years we bonded and I enjoyed their individual personalities.

Nana always wanted to be the center of attention. If anyone should look at Rosie or pet her, Nana would barge in and shoulder Rosie away. Yet, it was probably because of how Nana behaved that Rosie learned to stand up quickly, to play, to run around on three legs, and to hold her ground with Nana. She was never left behind. She would not have accepted it. Wherever Nana and I went, Rosie was with us.

Because Emmy had petted and pampered Rosie when she was a puppy, she always thought of herself as a lapdog. She would hop to where I was sitting, sit down on her hind legs with her front legs in my lap, hug me with her left paw and, while laying her big head on my chest and sighing contentedly, gently tap my shoulder with her stump. She was only perfectly happy when she could put her head on my chest, sigh, and get her dose of *coccole* (cuddles).

Nana was always a little more independent than Rosie, but as guard dogs go, she is all smoke and no fire. She barks and runs forward ferociously only to retreat once she gets close to the danger. If a man or boy comes into the yard she runs to and fro without letting herself be touched. Yet, last year when a man tried to climb over our fence, she ran barking to him and jumped trying to catch him. I think that in case of actual danger she will overcome her fears and protect me.

Rosie, on the other hand, would have fought to the death to prevent anyone from hurting me. With her deep voice she announced that she was very protective of the house and of me. She never left my side. Whenever I looked up, there she was looking at me, staring into my eyes with a solemn, serious look. Now it seems to me a little sad, as if she knew we would not be together for long.

When Rosie was not yet four she was diagnosed with severe kidney problems. I was devastated and could not think of losing her without bursting into tears. Her vets began treating her and notwithstanding the blood tests, which became increasingly difficult, she carried on like a little soldier. She responded to the treatment and recovered well enough so that throughout that summer and fall we had many happy days together.

However, shortly after the New Year, her health deteriorated rapidly and I knew it was time for my beautiful, brave girl to cross the Bridge.

Rosie was a perfect, extraordinary lady and not a day passes without me shedding a tear at her memory. Nana continues to share my life, and now, Maggie, another *Degli Angeli Neri* puppy, has joined us. I love these two girls, but Rosie lives in my heart as my first Newfy-love. Rosie was special.

Laura Ciandrini
Mortara, Italy
macfahy@hotmail.com

Chapter 9

Remembering Ruggles, the ... Gentleman? - Ruggles

The time was January, 2016, when Sydney University's Vet Clinic reopened following the break over the Christmas period. Julie, the vet nurse who gave Ruggles his weekly physio massages, made a most pleasing comment as we chatted while she massaged and kneaded His Lordship's muscles. Julie mentioned that over the Christmas break, one of the vets had spent a couple of days helping out down at the Uni's main campus at Camperdown in Sydney which remains open over the holidays. While there, the vet saw two different Newfoundlands, and despite their people's obvious pride and love for their dogs, neither of them were anywhere near as clean or well-groomed or *gentlemanly* as Ruggles. This remark made me, Ruggles' aging dad, feel very proud, but reminded my cynical self that when the client is told something he wants to hear, then naturally he always believes it.

The vet also made reference that neither of the Newfoundlands' people came equipped with a drool towel as do I, and each of the Newfoundlands maintained a flow of long "straws" from their flews which they regularly shook. This resulted in their abundant slime being flicked onto walls, windows, cupboards, and the vet herself.

The ever-present drool towel which I carry had gained a heightened level of appreciation with this vet. However, as for Ruggles being "gentlemanly," that reputation may have copped a bruising as we left the treatment room to return to the reception area.

I didn't have hold of Ruggles' short lead because I was supporting his rear end via the boy's "Help 'em Up" harness handle over the little fellow's hips. Julie was walking just ahead of the boy with her head turned back watching His Lordship walk. We turned into the corridor and further along against one wall there were two female vet techs deep in serious conversation. They were standing facing each other and, as we walked past them, Ruggles' wandering nose "goosed" the nearer tech BIG TIME!

The startled female turned facing me. The raging vengeance in her eyes honed in on my expression of helplessness and apology. It was clear that I was about to be on the receiving end of a totally undeserved slap when Julie rescued me by loudly calling out, "Ruggles! Don't do that or you'll get your dad an injury!"

The rightfully incensed girl look quickly at Ruggles, then at the innocent me, unsure then which of us was responsible for her indignity. Julie had already grabbed Ruggles' lead and kept my mischievous boy walking, which in turn, kept me walking. Thankfully we were quickly out of range of the young lady who appeared still unsure of events. The vet tech she had been talking to was speechless trying none too successfully to stifle an out-and-out belly laugh. Hopefully, when able to give voice, she enlightened her justifiably indignant companion as to which "boy" was responsible for the affront.

Thoughtfully, Julie made no further mention of the incident. In the world of gentlemanly Newfoundlands, some things are better left unsaid.

Arthur Witten
Sydney, New South Wales, Australia

Chapter 10

A Catholic Newf - Mariah

Now, everyone has a grandmother who will often give you words of wisdom whether you want them or not. My grandmother was one who rarely spoke her mind, but when she did, you always remembered what she said.

I was eight years old when I asked the famous question that all grandchildren ask, "Which of your nine children is your favorite, Grandma?"

Fully expecting her to say it was my own father, I was surprised when she smiled and answered, "The sickest ... until they are well."

I could still hear those words ringing from heaven when I had my four-legged family of five Newfoundlands and one little brown dog who thought he was a Newf.

When Shannollet Like the Wind Mariah (Ma-rye-ah) was born, all seemed well until she was about five weeks of age and began walking. Both my husband and I noticed that her tail was quite crooked and that her back legs began to twist to the right. Her spine began to roach and her mother began to shove her away as all canine mothers do when there is something wrong with the pup.

Her X-rays showed no hip dysplasia. Instead they revealed a fusion of the spine from lumbar 1 through 5 with the right hip pelvis rotated clockwise. This made both back legs twist to the right. The diagnosis was spondylolisthesis. I had to re-evaluate and learn how to exercise her without causing more damage to her legs and spine.

As Mariah grew she began to develop greasy seborrhea with constant otitis media and dermatitis and yeast infections all over her body. The diagnosis was food allergies to corn, beef, rye, and wheat. I had to special order kangaroo meat from Australia so she could have nourishment.

Throughout this whole time, my goofy Newfy was determine to win hearts with her personality and charm. She loved and greeted everyone who came to the house with her drooly kisses and head hugs. She trained and showed at the Berrien County Youth Fair with her 4-H handler who, like Mariah, was also disabled because of a crooked spine. Once her 4-H handler said to me as she watched Mariah walk up the low impact A-Frame, "If My-My's spine is crooked and she still can walk, then I can do it, too."

Mariah was the first to give the alarm when intruders approached, the first at the food table, and the first to go to bed every night. But what she became most famous for was her instigation of free-for-alls among her siblings. When the romping got into full swing she would come stand innocently behind me as if to say to her cavorting siblings, "Ohhhhh, you're going to get it now!" while I put an end to their raucous fun.

Mariah lived each day with joy in what she could explore, discover and just love. She was serenely stoic, giving very little indication of the pain she was really in. Yet she was determined to beat the odds when it came to her health issues. And with a little help and guidance from God ... she did just that.

When Mariah was two years old my friend told me that the local Catholic Church was celebrating the "Blessing of the Animals" on St. Francis of Assisi Day. Knowing that my dear, crippled Mariah needed all the blessing she could get, I bathed, groomed, and got her and our little brown dog all gussied up for the event and set out for the church.

It was a hot, bright evening with the sun setting over Lake Michigan. This made poor Mariah drool even more than usual. Thankfully I had taken four drool towels with me.

Before the event began Father Brown introduced himself and petted the animals. Naturally, when he came to Mariah she slimed his black robe in her eagerness to be petted and hugged. I apologized as I handed him a drool towel.

He just laughed and said, "That's a Newfoundland for you."

When the ceremony was finished, Father came around again blessing the animals with the normal, "God bless you in the Name of the Father, the Son, and the Holy Ghost," and sprinkled Holy Water over them.

But when he came upon my cripple Newf, his blessing for her was, "I baptize thee, as you have baptized me, in the Name of the Father, the Son, and the Holy Ghost."

I honestly believe that my Newf, my Mariah, is the only Newf that has ever been baptized in the Catholic Church. And I truly believe that God was behind Mariah's baptism because soon afterwards her health began to improve. She lived a full, happy and productive life until God called her to her heavenly home at nine years of age.

Linda Shannon-Chaillet
Shannollet Kennel
Benton Harbor, Michigan, USA
www.bf4hclub.com

Chapter 11

Mariah's Loveliest Song

by Charles W. Chaillet, Jr.
May 30, 2006

The gentlest soul,
God did grant,
A daily strength
Silently
unmatched.
The power of love
Drove her on.
Determination to
beat all odds was
Mariah's Loveliest
Song.

Chapter 12

Monsters in the Morning - Seamus

Twenty years ago we lived in a rural farmland area in Pennsylvania. In order to get to work on time I had to walk Seamus by 5:30 a.m. However, we enjoyed these peaceful predawn mornings because we had the whole countryside to ourselves.

Across the street from our home was a tiny preschool with a small parking lot. There was no exterior illumination around the school beyond the immediate entrance, so it was always pitch black when we began our walks. Because the area was rural and perceived safe, Seamus was allowed off leash to wander through the mowed fields, high grass meadows, and a several hundred acre woods that surrounded the preschool.

Although he was born with a big white patch on his chest, once Seamus grew into a 155-pound Newf, his white patch had shrunk to the size of my fist, thus providing little to identify "Himself" once he began his morning free range activities into the darkness. A black Newf in a black environment creates a near-perfect camouflage.

I wasn't one to be frightened for my safety, but being a policeman's daughter, I knew to be aware of my surroundings at O'Dark Thirty even in the country. One cold fall morning Seamus and I began our walk, as usual. I wandered behind him as my big black Newf entered the high grass meadow. I could track his whereabouts only by the rustling sound of his lumbering gait through the dry brush.

After about twenty minutes I felt an immediate sense of alarm when I heard something rustle a short distance behind Seamus' footsteps. Instantly, I called his name, and the tone of my voice got his attention. He was very obedient and trotted several steps in my direction.

I had been standing about twenty yards from the "sound of him" and, to my alarm, the noise I heard behind Seamus moved along with him in my direction. I was afraid it was a hunter who had come out of the woods in pursuit of a big black "bear," or someone else wishing to do us harm.

I started scurrying toward home calling, "Seamus, *come!*"

Obediently, he followed. I had no idea who or what was out there in the dark, but as we hurried along I sensed that the noise now seemed to be low to the ground. I jumped to the conclusion that only a rabid wild animal would keep following us with me calling out.

I increased my speed yelling, "*RUN,* Seamus, *RUN!*"

I could hear the wild creature still in pursuit behind us through the deep, dry clumps of grass and weeds.

I ran faster and called out again, "*RUN,* Seamus!"

To my absolute *horror* I could hear that the rabid beast was still behind my Newf.

Periodically Seamus would start to turn back toward the terrifying creature that was chasing us.

Each time he did this I would frantically call out again, "NO! Seamus, *RUN!*"

As we approached the preschool parking lot I knew we were going to have to take a left turn to get home. I thought about what we should do when we had to scale the steps up the deck to make it safely into the house. I knew the rabid wild beast was going to make up time on both of us.

Seamus was right on my heels. I didn't have anything to defend us with and I was terrified that in some heroic attempt to defend me Seamus would get into a blood bath with the rabid creature.

I had seen *Out of Africa* that weekend. I visualized Meryl Streep and that whip she wielded to protect her cows from the lion attack. Holding that image and gripping Seamus' leash tightly in my hand, I spun around. With the heavy metal clasp end of the leash I whipped the ground behind Seamus trying to impede the devil beast that was after us.

By now we were closer to the dim light over the door of the preschool and I could see that the look on Seamus' face was one of complete shock and total confusion.

Why was I yelling at him to run? Why was I wielding his leash in this manner?

I shouted, "*GO HOME!*" to him, so I could keep after the beast.

This time, instead of obeying my frantic command, Seamus stopped. He looked up at me, then calmly turned around to view the creature behind him. Startled by his behavior I paused long enough to take my first real look at the beast that was about to attack us.

That's when I realized that we were not being chased by a rabid fox or raccoon at all. That's when I realized that I had been savagely beating a very long briar that had attached itself to the end of Seamus' tail.

As Seamus had moseyed along through the brush, a collection of dry grass and weeds had become attached to the briar. As the collection of dry grass and weeds grew bigger, it created threatening noises.

It *could* have been an evil hunter with bad intentions. It *could* have been a rabid, deadly, ground-dwelling beast.

Although Seamus and I took many more predawn walks in this rural farmland, my poor boy never looked at me the same way again. To him I was forever his raving mad momma. He never understood why I panicked and refused to cooperate when all he wanted to do was get a worrisome briar off his tail.

Elizabeth McCully
Fallston, Maryland, USA

Chapter 13

Finger Licking Good - Abra & Shiloh

One summer morning I took Abra, my four-year-old brown Newfy, and her two-year-old nephew, Shiloh, my sweet black boy, out for a long walk/run on a friend's farm. This is the dogs' favorite place to go—360 acres of fields, forest, and wetlands. The stream which runs through the property is crossed by three bridges. These bridges provide a great place to stop and refresh between bouts of running through fields, greeting cows, exploring the woods, and chasing the wetland birds.

After more than two hours of exercise it was time to go home. We climbed back into my station wagon which I had converted into a Newf mobile by folding the back seats down and covering them with blankets. We headed home with the windows mostly rolled down to let in the cooling breeze.

Since it was nearing noon, lunchtime for me, I decided to visit a KFC drive-thru and pick up a quick snack to eat when we got home. By this point in the ride both Abra and Shiloh were peacefully zonked out in their part of the vehicle. However, once I slowed down and turned into the drive-thru, they immediately became alert to the change of scenery and, without doubt, the change of scents wafting through the air. Immediately they were wide awake, sitting at attention, ready to take in whatever new experience might present itself.

Without any fanfare I gave my order and drove up to the pick-up window. I paid for my order and was waiting for delivery when the teenaged attendant at the window noticed the dog heads sticking out the back window. She asked me if she could feed them some chicken strips.

I said, "Sure," and moved the car a bit forward so the back window was even with the drive-thru window.

Almost immediately the young lady was joined by a couple of other young people at the window. The fun the teenagers were having interacting with the dogs and feeding them chicken strips paled in comparison with the joy Abra and Shiloh were experiencing. The dogs were thrilled with this unprecedented food-related transaction.

I was watching the fun through my side-view mirror when I saw Abra starting to climb out of the back window. Apparently she decided she could gain a competitive edge over Shiloh if she moved closer to the kids. I watched in frozen shock as she climbed into the drive-thru window. Before I could react, there she was—her hind legs in the car, her middle section resting on the ledge of the drive-thru window, and her whole front end inside the KFC with her front legs dangling down over the window frame.

The kids inside were alternately screaming and laughing. This was a unique development for which they had not been trained and they clearly did not know what to do.

I reached over the back seat trying to pull Abra back into the car, but I could not get enough leverage. I couldn't open the door on the driver side because I was too close to the building. The screaming and laughing from inside the KFC building continued as I crawled over the gear box and out the passenger door.

Even though I was rushing to open the rear door of the station wagon to get to the dogs, I glanced back and saw the people in the cars in line behind me. They were watching this dramatic Newfy production with mixed expressions—amusement, astonishment, horror.

I climbed into the back of the car, pushed poor, bewildered Shiloh out of the way, and managed to drag a very reluctant Abra back into the car. I rolled up the window, then reversed the process I had used for getting into the back seat in order to get back to the driver's seat.

By that time my order was ready, the kids had regained their composure, and the dogs had accepted the fact that any additional treats would now come from the front seat. I took my order, quickly apologized, and drove off—watching out the rear-view mirror as the young teenager washed the window ledge before attending to the next customer.

Even though I had learned a valuable lesson about Newfy drive-thru protocol, this was the first and last time I ever went to KFC with dogs in the car. With some Newfy experiences, once is enough.

Jeanne Ward
Lacey, Washington, USA
Harmony House Newfoundlands
www.harmonyhousenewfoundlands.com
Newfoundland Club of Seattle
Pacific Northwest Newfoundland Club
Newfoundland Club of America

Chapter 14

The Dreaded Sucking Machine - Annie & Seven-of-Nine & Rowdy & Molly

We have had many Gentle Giants in our twenty-plus years of owning Newfs, and all were special beasts. Each had their own personality which endeared them to us in their own different way. Throughout this time we have enjoyed the mischievous puppy years only twice. We have, instead, been appreciating the mature, more calm personality of Newfs who have come to us at the age of four or older. The reason for this is that we have been re-homing Champion Newfs from a breeder friend of ours, Nina Cote of Marcarpents Kennels. Because of this arrangement, our family has often included four or more adult Newfs that have been retired from breeding and showing. Nina passed away recently, but the legacy of her dogs will stay with us forever.

Although every now and then, mostly when talking with someone who is experiencing the joy of picking up a Newf pup from a breeder, we wish we could once again feel the soft breath of a puppy or walk in the fields and enjoy a puppy running exuberant circles around us, adopting a mature Newf has advantages: no house training, very little obedience training, less tendency to destroy family treasures, more appreciation for quality relaxing time.

Our present gaggle of Newfs, Molly and Annie at 10 years old, and Rowdy and Seven-of-Nine at 12½, are truly a sedate lot. When we walk in the fields it certainly is not a walk for human exercise. It is more of a dawdle, a slow stroll, or sometimes even a stand-around-and-wait while the dogs finish the twenty minute sniff of a particular clump of grass.

Because of their age, our dogs' hearing and eyesight are diminished and they are prone to senior moments when they don't quite seem to know where they are or what they are supposed to do. All of them have become very dependent on the humans in their lives and somehow this has made us cherish them even more.

Molly, our premier twice-yearly coat blower, has reluctantly taken over as leader of the pack since our old boy Rimshot left us. The other three, Annie, once known as Full Speed Annie because of her boundless energy; sweet, gentle Rowdy, the formerly agile, rambunctious guy who loved to run; and our tranquil, relaxed girl Seven, definitely do not want to be anyone's boss. These three struggle to occupy the bottom rung of the "in charge" ladder. Ours is, indeed, an exceptionally calm pack of Newfs.

However, this all changes when we vacuum the house, which, of course, is a daily or sometimes twice daily activity. Molly,

Annie, and Rowdy show no difference in their regular laid-back demeanour. They will either plop down in front of the machine and have to be physically pushed out of the way, or they will stroll outside to the deck and lie down there just to maintain the peace and quiet in their lives.

Surprisingly, Seven-of-Nine, who just happens to be the oldest of the bunch and the second oldest Newf we have ever had, is the exception. When the vacuum comes out Seven comes alive. The moment we plug the hose into the wall receptacle she appears and begins charging around looking for a toy to carry in her mouth. Clearly, the word "charging" for Seven means something completely different than it does for others. Her "charge" is more like a fast walk. But regardless of the speed, her determination and excitement are very much in evidence. Her eyes are suddenly aglow, her tongue is hanging out of her mouth, and her head is held high.

The attack is on! Despite competing for last place on the dominance scale, Seven seems to think she is the only one around who is capable of protecting her pack from this dangerous, marauding, sucking monster.

Seven's full court press makes it difficult to accomplish our task but we persevere, dodging our courageous Newf and vacuuming around the other three who usually seem to be in the way. Throughout the cleaning event Seven storms the power head and harasses the sweeper tube. She is relentless in her heroic efforts to rid the area of the threat.

Once the job is done and the hose unplugged, Seven's mission is complete. She relaxes and immediately reverts to her slow moving, meandering self, fitting quite nicely once again into the senior Newf mold.

Nevertheless, it is reassuring to know that the next time the carpets develop that black and white fuzzy look and we bring out the vacuum, Seven-of-Nine will once again transform from her impression of a bear rug to a vicious "pack protector." Our brave, gallant old girl will again quell the beast and save us all from horrifying, unthinkable harm.

Ingrid Ball
Lancaster, Ontario, Canada

Chapter 15

Living and Laughing With Lulu - Lulu

When I googled "Why does home renovation stress marriages?" I got "Tips to Protect Your Marriage During a Home Remodel," "How to Remodel and Keep Your Marriage Together, " "How to Survive Home Renovation Without Killing Your Spouse," and over eight million similar results in just 37 seconds.

While I didn't read all eight million articles, I was disappointed that the articles I did scan didn't mention the exceptionally effective way we found to survive a home renovation project.

Our foolproof way is this: engage the help of a lively, fun-loving, resourceful Newf like our Lulu in the renovation proposal. With all of our energy focused on responding to her prolific and ingenious capers, we had no time to fixate on setbacks and frustrations. Lulu provided constant distractions from any remodeling worries and woes that could have occurred.

From the moment she joined us at 10 weeks old, Lulu has been way too smart. She kept us, our seven-year-old Newf, and our eleven-year-old mixed breed rescue constantly on guard.

When she was still very young I found her staring up at a bag of dog goodies I'd stashed on top of the china cabinet. She would look at the bag, then at the chair next to the china cabinet, then back at the bag. I knew then that this was an indication of things to come.

Thus, it was no great surprise when a few years later Lulu responded with obvious delight to our first-floor renovation project. Clearly, she interpreted the whole enterprise as a problem-solving challenge created especially for her entertainment. There was no end to the things she got into.

Lulu was quick to prove that the "do as I do" training method works. She perfected two new tricks that she apparently learned from watching me. First, while the new kitchen cabinets were being installed we confined the dogs to the living/dining room area during the day. That secure confinement ended when Lulu took advantage of the workers' failure to close the front door.

She let herself outside by hopping over an end table and pushing a credenza aside just as she had seen me do. At least now I know she's firmly attached to me since all she did was dash around to the back yard where I was talking to the contractor.

For a second new trick Lulu aced feeding herself. Each dogs' food was stored in a bin locked with clips. We moved the bins into a spare bedroom for the renovation and closed the door.

Somehow Lulu managed to open that door and drag the bin of another dog's food off the top of her bin. Once she uncovered her bin she opened it and helped herself. We kept blaming each other for leaving the door and the bin open. But finally we caught her in the act and on that morning there was no doubt about who was doing what. All the bins were immediately moved to the basement.

As the renovation continued, Lulu's mind never stopped. Her creative energy ran high and she continued astonishing us with her tricks. Late one night I heard rustling and the tap-tap of Newf toenails downstairs. Knowing something was amiss, I went down the back stairs only to see Lulu waddling up the front stairs. Knowing she's almost always up to no good, I followed her to her open crate.

There she sat with sad eyes, a big white face, and white feet. The only problem is that she's an all-black Newf. What was this white madness? I closed the crate and headed back downstairs.

On the family room floor I found a tangle of moving quilts highlighted with pools of white paint, an upturned paint tray, snarls of cling wrap, and an assortment of mostly eaten human food.

Unfortunately, the workers had wrapped their lunch leftovers in a swaddle of moving quilts, along with a tray of paint covered with cling wrap. (Why would workers cover a paint tray with cling wrap?) While searching for their very fragrant lunch leftovers, Lulu managed to smear white paint all over her face and feet. There were white footprints everywhere. What a night!

Despite Lulu's indulgences in high jinks and shenanigans, she provides a beautiful balance by being incredibly loving, especially to those in need. And she's remarkably perceptive at picking out those who are most in need. She always manages to find the person who will benefit most from a gentle, affectionate hug and bestows one freely and completely.

The joy Lulu gives to others is tangible and sometimes even brings tears to my eyes. Once on a visit to our garden center she snuggled up to a burn victim and gave him every bit of her heart for thirty minutes. On another occasion Lulu slammed to the floor in response to a five-year-old's oral "Down" command, along with the appropriate hand gesture I had taught her to use. The child had been diagnosed with autism and "Down" was her very first word ever.

EVER! I have learned never to underestimate canine power, Newfoundland power, Lulu power.

Kathy, Mike, & Lulu
Fairfax, Virginia, USA
Colonial Newfoundland Club
Newfoundland Club of America

Chapter 16

First Responder - Shandy

One spring, the owner of the training school my Landseer Newf, Shandy, and I attended held an informal gathering for everyone who had participated in classes during the previous year. The event took place in the rural area of the school and consisted of a walk followed by a pot-luck lunch.

On the morning of the walk, the people and their dogs gathered at the training barn on the property. Then we began a leisurely stroll down a gentle hill, across a field, and into a little wood. Most of the dogs were off leash and joyfully running together ahead of us with just an occasional "cut it out" from the trainer to keep them in order.

We people walked in groups, chatting away and stopping for a group photo en route. After a brief time in the woods we began retracing our steps back across the field and back up the hill toward the barn area where we were to have lunch. Again, most of the dogs were running ahead of us.

I was in the last group to reach the barn and I suddenly realized I couldn't see Shandy playing about with the other dogs. Puzzled, I looked back and saw her some distance down the hill. She was walking beside a petite lady with two small Schnauzers. I noticed that the lady was using a walking cane. Happy to see that Shandy had found new friends, I turned back and continued chatting with the other people.

It was not too long before Shandy joined me at the barn, but I didn't see the lady again as she wasn't staying for lunch. It was not until some weeks later, when I signed up for a tracking seminar, that I learned why Shandy had been escorting the lady up the hill.

I did not recognize the instructor for the tracking seminar, but she turned out to be the petite lady with the two Schnauzers that Shandy had befriended on the day of the training school gathering. Although she did not recognize me either, she recognized Shandy immediately and greeted her warmly. Then, with her hand still stroking Shandy, she introduced herself as "Christa" and told me the following story.

As I had noticed on the day of the gathering, Christa had been quite a way behind the rest of the group. She was only in the middle of the field when the rest of us had almost reached the barn. Distracted with socializing and anticipating the lunch preparations, we did not notice when she stumbled and fell to the ground way behind us. She struggled, but she could not get up, and her dogs were too small to help her. She saw how far away the rest of us were and knew her voice wouldn't reach us. But before she had time to panic, she saw that a white and black Newfoundland dog had left the group and was trotting straight back down the hill toward her, tail wagging.

When the dog reached them, it sniffed her and the Schnauzers, then turned, and, facing the barn, stood right beside her, squarely and still, as if extending an invitation. Christa was able to put her arms over Shandy's back and pull herself to her feet. Then Shandy walked right at her side across the field and up the hill until they reached her car. Once Christa and the Schnauzers were safely inside the car Shandy left them and rejoined me.

I was so pleased to hear Christa's explanation of how she and Shandy came to be walking together. I was very proud of my Newf for providing help when and where it was needed.

We enjoyed the tracking seminar that Christa gave, and I became and remain friends with her. Shandy is gone now and Christa is in her nineties. But Christa has never forgotten Shandy and has always been grateful for the help she gave so freely.

Ena Fulton
Alliston, Ontario, Canada

Chapter 17

Stick to the Script - Mandy

Seeking adventure, in 2002 I accepted a teaching position in tiny San Vicente Elementary School in Big Bend National Park, Texas. The school in this remote park is about the nearest thing we have to a one-room school in the twenty-first century. John not only graciously went along with my plan, he also volunteered as my full-time paraprofessional, making teaching fourteen children, ages four through eight, simultaneously, *almost* possible.

Our black Newfy, Mandy, was about seven months old when we arrived in the park. With her outgoing, exuberant personality she immediately became popular with the children and our walks through the resident neighborhood where all of us lived often included stops so she could be petted, hugged, and generally loved.

During our time at San Vicente the entire school, students and staff, celebrated the Bicentennial of the Lewis and Clark Expedition in a two-year extravaganza of projects, field trips, and "let's pretend."

As history would have it, a Newfoundland dog accompanied the adventurers on this expedition, the amazing Seaman. While the students and teachers all took roles of people who participated in the expedition, Mandy enthusiastically stepped in as Seaman.

As the two-year project drew to a close, we set out to present The San Vicente Corps of Discovery II Lewis and Clark Perspectives: Past and Present, and filled our gym with the artifacts of our studies. In addition to inviting parents and park personnel, we sent invitations to the students and staffs of other schools in the district. Everyone accepted.

With all these guests coming to call, Mandy, aka Seaman, needed to be in top form physically and mentally. I spent most of the weekend before the big event preparing her for guests. The bath, the trimming, the ear cleaning, and the brush-out went well. She was a glossy, gleaming, black beauty. Next we walked over to the school gym to review the three tricks she had performed on several occasions in her role as Seaman.

The tricks were a "down-stay," a "speak" in a loud voice to alert us when friendly visitors might be approaching, and a "whisper" in a quiet voice to alert us when unfriendly or dangerous visitors might be in the area.

The Lewis and Clark keelboat, which a student and his dad had built from an old canoe, had been housed in the gym ever since it had been used in the Christmas play. The keelboat jumped right out at me the minute I opened the gym door.

"Mandy! Let's do your tricks in the keelboat! How dramatic is that?"

Mandy and I practiced the whole routine a couple of times: walking into the gym, hopping into the keelboat, "down-staying," "speaking," and "whispering."

Because it was oral and quiet, rather than visual and showy, I asked Mandy to perform her whispering trick twice, just in case the audience had not heard her the first time. After the second whisper we would hop out of the boat, sashay off stage, and exit through the gym door.

The day of the Perspectives arrived and our visitors appeared. After everyone had strolled around the gym examining the exhibits, listening to the presentations, and partaking of the refreshments, the enactments began.

In one scene the two boys who had played Lewis and Clark in the Christmas play discussed their purchase of Seaman, the Newfoundland dog that was to accompany them on the journey. On cue, Mandy and I appeared and hopped into the keelboat. I would explain the advantage of a trick to the audience, then Mandy would execute the trick.

Since few of the visitors in this wild, isolated part of Texas had ever seen a Newfy, her size alone impressed them, but they were astonished upon discovering that she was also brilliant. Her first two tricks, "down-stay" and "speak," bought hearty rounds of applause.

Then it was time for her whisper. And it was the whisper that brought down the house. Gasps of surprise and delight followed her first whisper. Her second whisper set off peals of laughter and shouts of glee.

Oh, my! This trick is a winner. We'd better do it one more time.

"Mandy, whisper!"

"Are you kidding me, Mom? My contract calls for two whispers and two whispers only. That's what you requested. That's what we practiced. That's what I did. Now, I'm outta here!"

And with that, she hopped out of the keelboat and pranced to the exit, stage right. Performance over! That's all folks! Nothing more to see here!

Mere mortals can neither understand nor alter the enigma that is artistic temperament. Mandy was happy to take it again from the top, but there were to be only two whispers per performance. Period. Dot. I was left to chuckle, acquiesce, and yes, ultimately accept the whims of my prima donna. Mandy, aka Seaman, held firm to her contract.

Pat Seawell
San Antonio, Texas, USA
Newfoundland Club of America

Chapter 18

Conversing With Hoomans - Heffalump

Dear Global Newf Pack,

My Person showed me I could ring the bell tied to the back door when I want to go out. I taught her that when I ring the bell, I either want to go out OR I want her to pay attention while I tell her what I really want. Yesterday, I needed to convey to her a highly complicated series of instructions that required THREE sentences:

1. I rang the bell, and My Person obligingly opened the back door. I refused to go out, indicating that the bell was just a sign of Important Communication to Come. My Person got this! She closed the door and looked expectantly at me, awaiting further orders, so ...
2. I pointed my nose at my food bin. I had previously taught My Person that THIS means I want to be fed, so, like the Good Person she (usually) is, she scooped out a cup of my

normal food and put it in my bowl. But that was NOT the food I wanted this time. So I ignored the food in my bowl and ...

3. I pointed my nose at the yummy, deliciously drool-inducing, greasy-smelling sandwich on the counter ...

Well, it started out auspiciously. My Person looked at me! She looked where my nose was pointing! She looked back at me with Comprehension Dawning! She walked over to my sandwich and picked it up! But then, then, then (oh, this is so painful I can hardly bear to say it), then she put my sandwich in the ... Treasure Chest! (Inexplicably, My Person calls this magical trove something utterly unrelated to its intrinsic identity. I think the misnomer she uses is "ice box.") What? I mean I was SO clear! I was SO close!

I expressed my feelings on her Poor Product Placement with a Moose Bay of Deep Despair, but even THEN, she didn't get it.

Clearly, My Person needs more training. But I fear the real problem is one of intelligence. Maybe she just isn't CAPABLE of following three sentences in a row. Next time, if I skip the bell and the bin and just point immediately and definitively at the sandwich, maybe ...

I NEVER, well, don't USUALLY, well, SOMETIMES, don't complain about My Person. I mean they are only hooman, so we can't judge them by Newf Standards, but I need guidance. This is, after all, a genuine YTAE (Yummy Treat Accessibility Emergency), and I know I can rely on you, the World Newf Genius Reserve, for advice.

Woof,

Heffalump

*****

Dear Global Newf Pack,

Yesterday I wrote to y'all from the Depths of My Despair about my Tragic Sandwich Loss. Happily, over the course of the night the emails came pouring back. I watch My Person's face as she read one after the other this morning. At first she looked amused, but then she started to look increasingly uncomfortable and, finally, guilty! She sighed in resignation, got up from her chair and said that our pack had made it VERY clear I deserved some of that sandwich. So down we flew (well, I flew, she sort of trudged). She opened the Treasure Chest, unveiled the Precious Prize, cut off a tiny piece, paused as she studied my glowing, expectant, deserving face, cut off a larger piece, paused as she looked up to where the computer lives, shook her head sadly, and then...then...then...GAVE ME THE WHOLE SANDWICH!

My life is now complete; and I owe it all to you, the best pack a Newf could have!

Woof,

Heffalump

P.S. And a special thanks to Jackson who pointed out that the next time My Person accidentally leaves my treat on the counter, I can push a chair over to help myself. At dog park there is a small pack of Bad Dogs (no Newfs, of course) who hang out together at the back corner and snigger about something they smugly refer to as "counter surfing." But if I push a chair like Jackson recommended, then, even though a chair is logistically unnecessary, given my size, I'm not counter surfing, I'm just "eating at the Breakfast Bar" like the Hoomans do!

Heffalump & Marisol Ravicz
Silver Spring, Maryland, USA

Chapter 19

Newf Sitting 101 - Jack & Cree

Jack and Cree were my very first Newfoundlands. In January, 1994, Charles and I had to go to Florida on family business. We could not take the dogs with us so we had Jeff, the handsome, twenty-something son of Jan Wach, a fellow Berrien Kennel Club (all-breeds) member, come and stay at the house with the dogs while we were gone. Jan came to visit almost daily bringing her Collie, Sunny, to play with Jack and Cree.

Jeff loved burgers from a local burger stand called Roxy's, so going there for burgers became part of the daily lunch routine. Jeff, Jack, and Cree would get into the car and head for burgers at Roxy's. Then they would drive around visiting Jeff's friends until it was time to come home for dinner.

After Charles and I returned home we discovered exactly what kind of "dog parent" Jeff was. His parenting skills included dogs sleeping on our bed with him, begging for food and treats, and eating "*cookies, candy, cakes galore.*" Of course all of this was a BIG NO-NO with Charles and me, but Jack and Cree got away with it with Jeff.

Jan was a wonderful hobby author and she wrote the following poem from Jack's point of view. I had the poem framed and it is still hanging on my wall. Since Jan and Jeff died a few years back, I thought including her poem would be a lovely tribute to the two of them, and to Jack and Cree.

Linda Shannon-Chaillet
Benton Harbor, Michigan, USA
www.bf4hclub.com

****

Welcome Home, Dear Mom and Dad

By Jan Wach
January 20, 1994

Dear Mom and Dad, we missed you so,
Both Cree and I thought you should know.
But if again you go away,
Then dear Jeff with us must stay.
Your set of rules we just threw out.
And new ones made, you'll hear about,
Don't you worry, don't you fret,
They're not so hard, you'll learn them yet.
Couches are meant to watch TV,
And this includes dear Cree and me.
Beds are nice on which to rest,
And Mom and Dad, you've got the best!
Cookies, candy, cakes galore,
All this we ate and even more.

Dear Jeff said, "Don't tell Mom and Dad,
'Cause they will say we've all been bad."
McDonald's burgers are still O.K.
But Roxy's are better, all the way.
Pickles, mustard, onions, too,
You surely won't say they're taboo.
Ice cream cone? Ummm, lick your lip,
'Specially when you get a triple dip!
Play time lasts throughout the day,
And nighttime, too, if we have our way.
When Jeffrey has a snack or two,
To share with us is right to do.
We sit and watch, wait for a bite
And when we win, it's quite all right.
In the car we ride and go many places,
Just to see looks on his friends' faces.
He says, "Look in the car, but beware,
I'm hauling a dog and a big, black bear."
We've learned to master the old "sad eyes."
If this won't work, we start to cry.
Jeffery says, "Don't cry. O.K.
We'll do what you want, whatever you say."
Aunt Jan came to see us once or twice
But compared to Jeff, she's not so nice.
She says to us, "You have to mind,
Or there'll be trouble, you will find."
We've really not been spoiled you see,
It's just that folks *love* dear Cree and me.
We're happy you're home, sweet Mom and Dad,
From your little girl, and your bigger lad.
Love,
Brackenshire Juno Jack and Hickory Ridge White Tip Cree.

Chapter 20

A Perfect Name - Bear

Hayley was stroking a Newfoundland puppy. He was just six weeks old and was looking at her with big dark eyes. He was so soft to stroke, even better than her favourite teddy.

The puppy was completely black, but was wearing a red collar. He soon started to wriggle, as he wanted to go back and play with his brother and three sisters.

"Put him down gently," said Mum.

It was only yesterday that Mum and Dad had told Hayley they were going to see some puppies. When they arrived at the house the owner, Jackie, talked to Mum and Dad as Hayley listened. Jackie then brought the puppies' mother and father, Bessie and Bert, in to meet the visitors.

The dogs bounced into the room and Hayley looked up to see Bert's huge, black head gazing down at her. He leaned forward and looked closely as Hayley held her breath. Then his giant tongue slipped out and licked the side of her face.

"Oh," squeaked Hayley in surprise. Then she reached forward and scratched Bert behind the ears.

Jackie was watching Hayley carefully to see if she were scared of such a large dog, but her smile told Mum and Dad that she was happy with Hayley's reaction.

Jackie invited them into a different room to see the puppies. There, inside a playpen to keep them safe, lay five little black balls of fluff. Bessie climbed into the pen while Bert went back to his kennel.

Jackie showed Hayley how to hold the puppies. Bessie watched Hayley carefully and licked each puppy as it was put back into the pen after being held. Hayley asked why the puppies all had different coloured collars and Jackie told her it was to help her recognise each one.

It had been a long drive, but it was worth it just to hold those little bundles of fur for a few minutes. When they got home, Dad told Hayley that in a few weeks he and Mum would go again and bring the puppy with the red collar home with them.

In those few weeks Dad checked for holes in the garden fence where a puppy might escape, and he and Hayley bought a bed, toys, and the food Jackie had told them would be appropriate for a puppy.

Then one evening Dad told Hayley there was a problem. She slumped in her seat fearing the worst news possible, fearing that they could not have a puppy.

"We have to decide on a name for the puppy," said Dad.

"Phew," thought Hayley, "that's not a problem!"

Dad added, "Our puppy is a boy so we need a name that he can recognise and that we can call him by when he's outside. Remember that the puppy will grow to be as big as his father so the name has to be good for a puppy and good for an older, dignified dog. Something like Fluffy Bottom may not be the best name. We need to think carefully. Tomorrow teatime we will each suggest a name, then choose the best one."

That night Hayley thought of all the boy names she could: boys at school, cousins, TV stars. But she was not doing very well. By the time tea was ready next day she did not like any of her names.

Mum said the best she had thought of was "Oscar."

Dad said he had thought about how strong and important Newfoundlands looked and thought "Hugo" would be a good name. They talked about shouting, "Hugo!" to call him back when he was running free in the field. Mum agreed that Hugo was a good name.

Dad said, "Well, that seems to be sorted. 'Hugo' it is."

Mum looked at Hayley, "We have not asked you, Hayley, what do you think? Do you like Hugo for a name?"

Hayley swallowed, "When I first saw the puppies I thought they looked like small bears with fluffy, friendly faces and huge paws. So I thought we might call him 'Bear.'"

She looked up to see Mum and Dad staring at her, mouths open.

"Well," said Dad. "That, Hayley, is a fantastic name!"

"Yes," agreed Mum. "That's a great name!"

That night in bed Hayley had the biggest smile you could ever imagine. Her puppy would be called "Bear." She had chosen the *perfect* name and that's all that mattered.

Within weeks the house was filled with mud, hair, and slobber, but mainly laughter, as Hayley and Bear became inseparable. By attending classes and practising every day at home Hayley taught Bear walking to heal, sit, and down. Working together, day after day, their love and trust for each other became ever stronger.

Bear enjoyed the attention of humans when he was out walking with Hayley and they always stopped to have his ears tickled. Everyone they ever met agreed that this big, black Newfy reminded them of a bear. Yes, Hayley had chosen the *perfect* name.

In later years when Hayley was at school, Bear would sometimes walk with Dad. Although Bear would do anything for Hayley, Dad always said he preferred to make his own decisions when interacting with the rest of the family. But that was acceptable to Dad and Mum. They understood that in growing up together Hayley and Bear had developed a warm, enduring bond. They understood that few things are sweeter than the love between a Newfoundland and his special human.

Alan Brown
Uttoxeter, England, UK

Chapter 21

A Newfy Open Door Policy - Molly

Our very first Newfy, Molly, was one of the largest we ever owned. She was loving, gentle, and, due to her size, somewhat scary looking to all those not familiar with the breed. She never understood people's hesitancy to get to know her, but ultimately she won everyone over with her friendly exuberance and sweetness.

She especially loved our next-door neighbor, Steve. As the years passed, it became a habit of Molly's to slip through our screen door around six o'clock in the evening and head over to Steve's house for a wrestle session and a hug after his hard day of work and her hard day of sleep. Both of them loved this ritual.

After about four years in this neighborhood, we needed more bedrooms (baby on the way!), and had to move from our "starter home" to a new home in another town. We sold our old place very quickly and unfortunately, because of that, we had to rent a temporary house until we could move to our new one.

[Side note: I would not recommend this. What a pain to move *twice* in less than three months!]

One evening soon after our move my husband and I were working in the backyard of the rental and came inside to an empty house. No Molly.

Not an easy breed to hide, we searched our yard, our block, and even considered that she had tried to walk back to our old place in her confusion about our move. With keys in hand, we headed to our car for the search when we heard an unearthly shriek coming from the house to our left.

We rushed to the aid of the screamer only to find that Molly was the cause of the terror. She had somehow opened the neighbor's screen door, made her way into the living room, and sat herself down in front of the couch, face-to-face with the neighbor who was napping. There, patiently and politely, Molly had waited for the neighbor to wake up and give her a cuddle.

Imagine that woman's shock when she woke up from her comfy nap on the couch and saw a huge black "bear" staring at her from very close quarters!

Thankfully, it all ended with laughter (and maybe some soiled clothing), but I think there were no hearts broken nor tears shed by our frightened neighbor when we left that house a month later.

And yes, in view of Molly's abundant love and enthusiasm for sharing it with neighbors, we introduced her to the family next door *ahead of time* at our new home.

They cherished her as much as Steve had. And Molly's steadfast love affair with our neighbors continued throughout her lifetime.

Peggy Daulton
Hillsborough, California, USA

Chapter 22

A Bird in the Mouth Is Worth Two in the Bush - Kahlua

As a newly married couple back in the 80's, my wife and I knew that a house, a dog, and a child would be in our future, in that order. After checking off the first item on our bucket list shortly after our "I do's," we started our research in order to fulfill our second family requirement.

Buying a large encyclopedia-type book on dog breeds and their attributes, we began our canine investigation. In the beginning, we only knew that my wife preferred a dog that was easy to hug and cuddle, and I wanted a large dog. Of course we both agreed that a breed that was great with kids was a must to support our bucket list goal number three. An added bonus of a terrific disposition around strangers would be welcome, as well.

When we reached the N's in our book, we knew we had found our match. Big, cuddly, gentle, and loyal. We decided that if a Newfoundland was good enough for the Darling Family to use as a nanny in the famous Peter Pan books, a Newfoundland would be a wonderful dog for our own children. We were...Hooked.

We welcomed our first puppy into our home in 1983, and since that time, our family has always included one, sometimes two, gentle giants. We are now the happy parents of our fifth Newfy and we see no end in sight.

Our third Newfy, Kahlua, joined our family in July of 2003 at the age of ten weeks. Even more so than our first two girls, Kahlua was a lover of all creatures big and small.

I took sweet, kind-hearted Kahlua out into the yard one spring afternoon when she was a little less than a year old. She was still bursting with the exuberance of a young pup and still very mischievous.

I watched her examine bees too closely and eat flowers with great gusto. I laughed as she focused on a bird jumping close to her while thinking to myself, "She will never be a bird dog!"

Suddenly, in the next split second, my laughter turned to shouts of horror as Kahlua jumped in unison with the bird and, just as it launched into mid-flight, caught the entire creature in her mouth.

Kahlua ran around the yard with that darn bird completely engulfed in her jowls. She was probably freaking out at all the noise I was making. I was shouting, "Drop it! Drop it! Drop it!" non-stop at the top of my lungs. (Trust me. The whole neighborhood heard my shouts.)

Finally, after about two minutes, which seemed like twenty, Kahlua calmly laid down on the grass, leisurely opened her mouth, and watched the bird hop out. Not a broken wing. Not a misplaced feather. Not a single scratch. The bird shook off the slobber, bobbed its tail, regained its bearings, then nonchalantly flew away. It never realized that its fate that afternoon had been in the jaws of a giant. Surely this was the first known "automatic bird bath" in history.

The next day we bought a real birdbath for the yard. Newfy washing machines are probably a bit unsettling, even when operating on the gentle cycle.

Russ Daulton
Hillsborough, California, USA

Chapter 23

Losing Osa - Osa

When I was in college, I read *With Love from Karen* by Marie Killilea. It is the touching story of the author's daughter who was born prematurely in 1940. In those times, treatments for premature babies were limited, and the family was advised to commit the child to an asylum and forget about her. Instead, they began the daunting challenge of caring for Karen at home.

One of the things they did to involve Karen was to find a dog that she could show. Karen was adamant that she wanted a large dog that she could reach to pet, one that she could look at eye-to-eye. It was a Newfoundland that grabbed her heart, and from that time on, it was a Newfoundland that grabbed my heart, as well.

"*Someday*," I thought, "I want a Newfoundland!"

Earl and I were thrilled when we were given a lovely Golden Retriever puppy as a wedding gift, but that was the first time I proclaimed to him, "*Someday*, I want a Newfoundland!" With each successive dog that came into our lives, and there were several, I would repeat my mantra, "*Someday,* I want a Newfoundland!"

Finally, one evening after 31 years of marriage, successful careers and retirements, four children grown and flown from the nest, Earl mentioned something about a Newfoundland.

My instant response was the usual, "*Someday,* I want a Newfoundland!"

To my delight he asked, "Why don't you look into it?"

Within weeks Osa became our precious puppy. But before long we realized that she wasn't the Newfoundland described in the breed standard, nor the Newfoundland that I had fallen in love with from the book I'd read in college. Although she was a love with people once she got to know them, she was terrified of strangers. As she grew, her fear of strangers increased and she could seem menacing with her lunging and barking at people she did not know.

However, we learned to manage Osa's fears and were careful to muzzle her whenever we anticipated meeting strangers. And always, as soon as she knew that she could trust a new person, she became the epitome of sweetness.

But it was Osa's fear aggression that made losing her so terrifying. Thoughts of that day still give me nightmares.

It was my job during the winter months to turn on the heat in the early morning in our cherished Covenant Presbyterian Church, located next to the Copper Queen Hotel in the heart of the historic district of Old Bisbee, Arizona. I often took Osa along for the ride and she would wander around, exploring the 100-year-old church while I turned on the heat and sound system, filled the candles with liquid wax, put the hymn numbers on the number board, and otherwise got the sanctuary ready for the service later in the morning.

The morning I lost Osa, I went about my usual routine, going from the sanctuary to the different rooms to complete my tasks. Within twenty minutes I finished the various jobs and returned to the sanctuary to collect Osa only to find that she was not there. A quick search along the aisles and between the pews revealed not a trace.

I had left the door between the sanctuary and the church parlor open so I went to check that room. Not only did I not find Osa, I was even more alarmed when I found the outside door of the parlor open. Evidently, it had not closed behind us when we entered the church.

My heart went to my throat with the realization that Osa had probably found the open door and wandered outside. This immediately added to my panic because of her fear aggression toward strangers. I ran outside in hopes of seeing her in the church yard. She was not in the yard nor in view on the narrow street. Then I heard the door shut behind me and realized that my church keys were locked inside.

Fortunately, I had my car keys in my pocket so I started driving around the nearby streets stopping to ask the few people up at that hour if they had seen a large black dog in the area. They hadn't. Feeling more and more panicked, I started wondering if maybe I had missed Osa back in the church.

By then it was almost 6:30, and I tried to think of someone who might also have church keys whom I could bother at that early hour. I remembered one church member who lived nearby, so I drove to her house and was encouraged when I saw that her lights were on.

Much to my relief, Mary Alice responded to my frantic knock. When I explained my predicament, she handed me her church keys.

Back at the church I opened the parlor door in hopes of seeing Osa. But there was no Osa. The church was perfectly quiet. Calling for her, I again checked the sanctuary, and then began checking the rooms where I had been earlier.

Much to my utter relief, when I opened the door to the sound system room, I found Osa waiting patiently on the other side. She looked up at me with question marks in her eyes, obviously wondering why I had closed the door and left her there.

Apparently, as I went from room to room relying only on my small flashlight to see where I was going and closing each door behind me, Osa had been following me. Not realizing that my big black Newfy was melding into the darkness behind me, I had closed the door to one room too quickly.

Never had I been so happy to see my sweet girl, and she was clearly happy to see me. But even though she had had to wait alone in the dark sound system room, I could see the trust in those eyes. Her eyes told me that she knew I wouldn't forget her. Her eyes told me that she knew I would come back, sooner or later, to find her and bring her home.

Osa was our first Newfoundland, Emma is our second, and most recently, Yogi has become our third. *Someday* finally arrived.

Judy Pike
Bisbee, Arizona, USA

Chapter 24

Mamut's Camping Capers - Mamut

For several years Pete and I have spent much of our travel time camping in the many state and national parks that grace our country. We enjoy exploring these lovely places and our three-year-old black Newfy, Mamut, delights in these trips as much as we do.

Mamut gets suspicious about a week ahead of the trip when we begin packing. His excitement builds daily as he watches us go back and forth loading the camper. He becomes exceptionally keyed up when we begin loading *his stuff*.

On "camping day" he goes from frenzied pacing by the door of the house to crazed pacing by the door of the truck. By the time we lock the house he is emitting a high-pitched squeak and is just about jumping out of his skin. Yes, Mamut does love the adventures he knows await him in the parks throughout our nation.

Mamut is especially fond of camping places that involve water, be it a lake, a river, or an ocean. However, on these occasions he always has a conflict between the water and the neighbor campers who want to lavish attention on him. In these situations he tends to go back and forth between the strangers and the inviting water.

Although he was fascinated with all the aromas of the ocean at Cape Hatteras, North Carolina, he was even more interested in the people, especially the kids, who were wanting to say "hello" and take pictures with him. Mamut was particularly vigilant when the children played in the water. We wondered if he was keeping tabs on them in case they wandered out to the deep water.

On the coast of Maine Mamut did a lot of sniffing on the mud flats as the tide went out, and collected many stinky beach treasures in which to roll. But all his sniffing and rolling was secondary to making sure the grandkids were safe. Once again, he seemed to be keeping tabs on the children. We thought he was demonstrating his water rescue heritage.

One summer when we traveled through Arkansas there was no lake at our campsite and it was pretty hot there for a Newfy. So I filled his 18" x 24" six-inch-deep plastic drinking bin with cool water from the pump. The next time I looked at the water bin Mamut had finished drinking and decided to sit in it, all 160 pounds of him. Aside from his tail hanging over the edge, he sat in the water bin like a proud king on a throne. A sultry Arkansas park with no lake is not a problem for a Newfy with good problem-solving skills.

Occasionally, Mamut-inspired camping dilemmas involve his eating habits. When we stayed at a beautiful campground by a lake near Glacier National Park in Montana for several days, Mamut's appetite seemed to be excellent, and he sure enjoyed swimming each day. But we were puzzled when we began noticing that his bowl was always empty, yet he was beginning to look a bit thin.

The morning came for us to break camp, and Pete opened the hood of the truck to check the engine belts. There, sitting on the top of the air filter, was a giant pile of dog kibble. All of us had been duped by some diligent chipmunks laying in a cache of vittles for the winter.

At Rocky Mountain National Park in Colorado they have some very specific rules regarding food in the campsites. Visitors are even warned against leaving a water dish outside because it attracts wildlife. We understood and we sincerely tried to follow the rules. But one day I accidentally left the food dish in Mamut's exercise pen next to our camper. It was mostly kibble with a tin of sardines for flavoring. Normally he eats everything so, thinking the bowl was empty, we packed up the truck and left for a day of sightseeing and photography.

Upon our return there was a bright-colored notice on our camper informing us that we hadn't paid attention to the rules, that the food bowl had been confiscated, and that it could be retrieved at the ranger office.

We were very apologetic when we walked into the office, deserving a lecture about our carelessness. However, there was no lecture. After determining which campsite was ours, the rangers exclaimed, "It's the *stinky* bowl!" and immediately handed it to us without delay.

Evidently, the rangers had been suffering with the fishy aroma for hours because all confiscated bowls were kept in the front office. Of course Mamut thought the additional "ripening" time had made his breakfast even more appealing, and immediately chowed down to finish it.

Mamut adds an extra dimension to our camping trips. His friendly, outgoing personality brings an added measure of fun to fellow campers. We are always proud of our big boy and the big smiles he leaves on his new friends' faces.

Louise Jandacek
Los Alamos, New Mexico, USA
www.jandacek.com

Chapter 25

Celebrating Susy - Susy

The journey of how Susy came to be a part of my life began in March, 2007. During a horrible snowstorm, I began to hear a roaring in my head. The roaring became worse and worse. Eventually, I realized that the hearing in my left ear was gone. Since I had lost the hearing in my right ear six years earlier, I was now completely deaf.

I went to bed terrified that night. After a restless sleep I awoke before dawn and lay in bed trying to imagine how my life would change.

I got a shower and was standing in the bathroom with my hands on the vanity. What was I going to do? Suddenly I felt a vibration on the counter. Boom! Boom! Boom! Then another boom, boom, boom.

I realized the vibration was caused by my Sheltie, Taylor, and my Newfy, Joey, barking downstairs. My boys! I grew calmer. My boys were with me. I would be okay. I was encouraged by how quickly my other senses seemed to be taking over.

The ENT doctor confirmed that I was completely deaf, probably from a viral infection in the inner ear. Writing on a tablet he told me about a new procedure that was showing some success. It required steroid injections in the inner ear.

After six weeks of weekly injections I was in the shower one morning when I thought I could hear water running. I was overjoyed! I immediately texted my mom and shared the news. Gradually, over the next two weeks, the hearing in my left ear came back to about 70%. Now I wear a hearing aid in my left ear and communicate pretty well, but I am still deaf in the right ear.

So, you might ask, how did this experience lead to Susy? The loss of my hearing was a life-altering event. It caused me to take stock of my future and contemplate the things I still wanted to accomplish. For me, an important aspect of moving forward included owning a show dog.

After regaining my partial hearing, adjusting to my hearing aid, and recovering emotionally from the ordeal, I was ready for my show dog. I wanted a male Newfoundland.

The puppies were born on February 29, 2008, almost a year after the terrible night I lost my hearing. In May I went to visit. While I was looking at the males, a little female kept coming over to lean against my leg.

I'd say, "Oh, you are so sweet. Who are you?"

It was Green Girl. I'd give her a little pat, then look back at the boys. But throughout the visit, Green Girl persisted in attaching herself to me.

I told the breeder I would call with my decision that evening, and began my four-hour drive home. But I just couldn't stop thinking about Green Girl.

Halfway home I called and said, "I want Green Girl!"

Susy came home with me two weeks later. Along the way we took a little break at a rest stop. As we sat on the ground under a tree I told Susy that she was my first show dog and that we would have great adventures. And did we ever!

I started showing Susy in September, 2008, when she was six months old. She won her first show and that was just the beginning. She went on to become my first for everything: Champion, Grand Champion, many Best of Breed, and Rally Obedience. Susy was an incredible girl and we were having a blast in the show ring.

In the summer of 2011, Susy and I began training for water work. Soon she could do everything except beach the boat. She would tow the boat to the shore, but the minute she felt the drag on the shore she would drop the line. The day before the test was the first time she actually beached the boat.

The next day, as Hurricane Irene was bearing down on the test site, Susy was successfully completing every exercise. When it came time for towing the boat she took the line and towed the boat to the shore. Lo and behold, for the second time ever, she beached the boat. We successfully completed the swim with handler and Susy earned her Water Dog title. She had added another first for me.

Susy was a fun show dog. Her warm-hearted spirit and exciting winnings helped me through the early years of my hearing loss. But she was also a wonderful family dog, and Spike, my sweet Maine Coon cat, was part of our family. In May, 2010, she showed how much she cared for him.

We had just returned from the Newfoundland National where Susy had gotten fourth place in Open. It was a beautiful spring day, and when I came home from work I took Taylor, Joey, and Susy for a walk. Afterward, I fed the dogs, and began making dinner for myself.

I began to hear barking. At first I wasn't sure where it was coming from or who was barking. Then I saw Susy barking at the top of the stairs. I made her come down, but she kept going back up and barking.

When I finally went upstairs to check, Susy was looking into the bedroom and barking. There I found Spike in obvious distress. He was lying on his side panting heavily. I rushed him to the vet, telling him all the way how much I loved him and what a great cat he was.

But suddenly, I could feel him pass. My beloved Spike was no longer with me. The vet said he probably suffered a heart attack.

I will never forget how Susy tried with all her heart to save her buddy. Her barking was purposeful and demanding. Her effort to alert me to Spike's emergency made her even more special to me.

Thank you, my Susy. Thank you for everything.

Kathy Havran
Mechanicsburg, Pennsylvania, USA
New-Pen-Del Newfoundland Club
Newfoundland Club of America

Chapter 26

Twice Blessed - Harley Bean & Coda

One year ago today, we drove two hours north to Flagstaff to pick up a five-year-old brown female Newfy who had been surrendered to a local shelter under mysterious circumstances—abuse? neglect? puppy mill situation? all of the above? When we saw her eyes in the picture that was posted, all we knew for sure was that she was coming home with us.

We arrived to discover that she had been shaved from her chest to the tip of her tail because she was so filthy and matted. She struggled to get up and down and hobbled with a gait the vet suggested was consistent with having been confined to a small area for a long time. A tumor the size of a golf ball hung from her chest and she constantly tried to scratch at it with her rear feet. She was a bit of a mess, but we fell hopelessly in love. We named her Harley Bean.

Waiting for us at home was our ten-year-old female Newf, Coda, whom we had adopted five years previously from a breeder who was retiring her. She came to us well cared for and well loved, and she saw me through a particularly rough period in my life. She was, and still is, my heart and soul. Because of that, we had wrestled for more than a year with whether to invite a second dog into our family.

We've always had pairs of dogs and love that dynamic, but we constantly asked ourselves, "Why would we want to mess with a perfect situation?"

We did agree, however, that if we learned of a dog in our area who was in need, we would take a chance. Harley Bean was the chance we took.

When we arrived home with Harley, she roo-roo'd enthusiastically at Coda, who wagged her tail in response. Then we went for a stroll around the backyard.

When it seemed that Coda was comfortable with the idea of another dog entering her house, we went inside. Harley glanced around shyly, took one look at the enormous dog bed in the living room (which Coda had ignored from the day it first arrived), plopped down on it, and slept for four hours straight.

Harley got up that evening long enough to eat some dinner and go outside to the bathroom, and then slept through the rest of the night. I don't believe she had slept that soundly in years.

Harley blended almost seamlessly into our family—no surprise for a dog who has received little attention or affection in her life. We lavished it on her, and she soaked it up like a sponge. She fell instantly in love with Coda and followed her everywhere.

Coda appeared to enjoy the company. Then, on day three, as I was handing them their afternoon treats, Coda snarled at Harley and snatched the treat away from her. Harley yelped and cowered, and I was between them in an instant. Fortunately, it was over as quickly as it started and no one was physically the worse for wear. There's no doubt, though, that in that moment, Coda let Harley know, now and forever, who is in charge. And Harley got the message loud and clear. It took her a day to get up enough courage to start following Coda again, and at first she did so timidly. But soon enough, they settled into a special companionship that has grown with each and every day.

After a month of good nourishment and joint supplements, Harley was able to get up a little easier, and though she'll probably never run or be able to navigate stairs, she has perfected what we call the Harley Hustle—it's not always pretty, but it gets the job done and she's the first one to the door when she hears the jingle of the leashes.

It took six months for Harley's coat to grow back in, and because she was shaved, it's wiry and nappy and different from the fur on her front end. But we think both ends of her are beautiful. We decided to wait to have the tumor removed until after she had settled in a bit, but to our amazement, it started to shrink within a month, and two months later, it was gone. *Gone.* I've never seen anything like that in all my years with dogs.

Today, our two sweet girls are the best of friends and we cannot remember what our lives were like without them.

Thank you, Harley Bean, for your quiet grace, your soaring spirit, and your endless joy in the little things—a belly rub, a slice of cold apple. And thank you for reminding us that love is powerful, that it can change everything, and that it's the only thing that really matters. Love is the only thing. We are blessed.

Marilyn Burnett
Scottsdale, Arizona, USA

Chapter 27

Contagious Love - Gummy Bear

My Newf story starts 38 years ago. At age twelve I wanted a *dog*. My fourteen-year-old brother helped me harass our parents for a dog. We would not stop! We begged, cried, and we would ask, ask, and ask! Our parents didn't like dogs being that they had had negative experiences related to dogs.

One day my mom lost her patience and said, "You want a dog! Okay, but it will need to stay out 365 days a year, 24/24!"

Dog shopping started at that exact moment.

Why do I have a Newf? At the age of twelve my only option was to look into the dictionary under "dog." When I did this, I saw a big black dog that looked like a bear. It was called a Newfoundland. Perfect! That was the dog I wanted.

After a few dozen long distance calls to talk with different Newfoundland breeders, my brother and I found one who had puppies. We tricked Dad to go look at the puppies by combining his annual father-son fishing trip with a stop at the kennel.

When Dad saw the puppies, and saw how gentle their parents were with the breeder's three kids, he knew he had no more reason to say "no" to a dog, and Mom had to hold her deal. So nine weeks later we went as a family to pick up our puppy.

Before leaving, the breeder told my parents, "Once you go Newf, you will never go back."

I didn't understand what she meant but I didn't care. I had a dog!

After all their reluctance to get a dog, our parents fell in love with our puppy. Dad came to every walk after supper with me, and the puppy learned just where to stand to get a cookie from Mom when the two of them were alone together during the day. Then, as soon as the first snowflake fell from the sky, Mom asked me to bring the dog inside.

That first Newf was called Channelle, and I kept her twelve years. I grew from a little girl to a woman with Channelle by my side. Having to bring her to the vet so that she would stop suffering was the hardest thing I ever had to do.

A few months after came Chanoux, then over the years, Huggy Bear, and Snuggle. My father developed a special bond with Snuggle. For several years he walked her and cared for her while I was at work. During this time he began to develop memory problems, and with time, it was cleared that he had Alzheimer's. It became necessary for him and Mom to move to an elderly home.

I noticed the good care Snuggle gave to my dad. When he came to my house she would always lie beside him and would make sure to follow him. She was his bodyguard. When I saw the good her presence did for him, I knew my next Newf could help me, not only with my dad, but also with other elderly people.

During the next three years my parents were both going in and out of hospitals for different reasons. It was during this busy time that we also had to say good-bye to Snuggle. Two more years passed, but I still couldn't stop dreaming of owning another Newf.

My parents' health stabilized and they were able to live together again at the elderly home. I visited them every day, and I got on a waiting list for a puppy. I promised them I would bring my puppy for visits as often as I could.

Finally came Gummy Bear! She is simply perfect! I call her my little Smiley Baby Gummy. I brought her to see my parents as soon as I got her. I sat her near my mom who wasn't too sure, but one little lick from Gummy Bear and Mama was in love! With his memory problems Dad was more nervous in front of this little fur ball.

But even my twin sister, who has always been nervous around big dogs, knows that Newfs are gentle and loving. She has proudly accepted the position as Gummy Bear's godmother. She always cuddles with Gummy Bear during her weekly visits and will even accept a few little licks.

On one of Gummy Bear's first visits to the elderly home we met a women with Alzheimer's in the hallway. I never heard that lady talk.

As soon as she saw Gummy Bear, she began clapping and saying, "*Beau chien! Beau chien!* " ("Beautiful dog! Beautiful dog!")

On that day I decided Gummy Bear would become a certified therapy dog, but I knew she would need more training.

Gummy Bear did her preschool courses followed by her Primary One. We took other classes so she would get use to being petted and would not be too curious about the walkers some of the elderly use. She needed to learn to walk calmly with a harness and most importantly, not to jump on people.

Now she is practicing. She is able to do all of her basic commands with me just doing a sign with my hands. In the spring she will be ready for Primary Two and from that point we will register for every course she needs to become a certified therapy dog.

But already Gummy Bear is bringing happiness to many of the residents. When we walk through the hallways and public areas on our way to my parents' apartment, the other residents smile and stop to pet her. Gummy Bear loves to walk slowly, and proudly shows them the stuffie she is carrying in her mouth.

The staff also loves Gummy Bear's visits. I notice they take longer breaks when they sit on the floor with her. Everyone benefits from her visits. With time, I hope she becomes the mascot of the center.

Newfoundlands are what I call walking fluffy hearts. They have no mean bone. They are happy to simply be part of our lives and only ask for love and cuddles in return.

I will forever be truly thankful towards my parents for allowing our first Newf into my life.

Nathalie Brault
St. Bruno, Quebec, Canada
Canadian Kennel Club
This story is dedicated with love to my dad, Jean-Paul Brault
April 11, 1931—December 27, 2019
RIP, Pop, xoxo
Facebook: GummyBearThe Newf

Chapter 28

An Indoor Pool and A Bank Job - River & Malcolm

As I watch our Newfies sleep, I'm reminded of the moments of peace and delight they've brought our household. I recall the extra snuggles when I was sick, the patient way my large male Newfy walked beside a toddler who was gripping his fur to stand upright, and the exuberant romps in freshly fallen snow.

But the memories that bring a smile to my face are the heart-stopping antics that added grey hairs and deepened my laugh lines. Raising a Newfoundland dog is not for the faint of heart.

River was our first Newfoundland and a challenging dog. We made a million mistakes before eventually hiring a behaviorist. One of this Newfy's most outlandish performances occurred one morning as I got ready for work. Over the spray of the shower, I could hear thumping and scraping. I was immediately alarmed as it was just River and me at home.

River was two years old and finally growing out of the sassy, mouthy, stubborn adolescent phase. Except for the barking. They'll tell you Newfoundlands don't bark, but River was the exception. She barked to play, she barked for attention, she barked for food, she barked for water, she barked to hear the sound of her own bark, and she barked until we gave in and left the back door open day and night so she could go in and out as she pleased.

Our house was a mess, mostly because of the kiddie pool in the backyard. River insisted on being able to take a dip at her leisure. She'd tear through the house, down the deck stairs, leap into the pool and wallow around like a hippopotamus before racing back into the house flinging water in all directions.

I stood under the hot water trying to calculate how much trouble she could possibly get into in the next few moments. *CRASH!* The sound was of one large object colliding with another large object. I leapt out of the shower, wrapped a towel around myself, and ran to the living room.

That headstrong dog was pulling the rigid, plastic kiddie pool that had been full of water in the backyard through the narrow doorway between the kitchen and living room.

I was too astonished to react. I just watched as the wiry, 95-pound dog wrestled the pool into the living room, flipped it over, and climbed on top.

She lay on her crumpled, upside down pool, right in the middle of my living room, and looked at me as if to say, "There! Now I don't need to go outside. You can just fill up the pool right here."

I sat down right there in the living room, wrapped in the towel, and laughed until I cried.

We had fifteen steep deck stairs between the kitchen and the backyard. How she had dumped out the water, pulled the pool up those stairs, through the sliding glass doors, and around into the living room remains a mystery to this day.

Yes, River was a scamp as a youngster, but now, at 11 years old, she's an angel. A barking angel.

Although he has never been as outrageous as River, Malcolm, our second Newfy, has had his moments. One of his unnerving escapades unfolded as I was returning home from a business trip.

When my flight landed mid-morning in the Twin Cities, I turned on my phone and checked my messages.

I was surprised to see a voicemail from a local number. "This is Officer XXX, Oakdale Police Department. We have your big brown dog."

The panic hit like a wave of cold water. My "big brown dog" was 175-pound, seven-year-old, Malcolm. Although he was blessed with an abundance of love, he had a real lack of street smarts. I immediately called the officer.

"Your dog was wandering around the bank parking lot. We think we found where he was getting out of the fence and put him back in."

I couldn't understand. "My dog was out? They're *house* dogs!"

The officer was cold as he informed me that he *could* have taken him in and that it was *irresponsible* of me to have an unsecured fence and no collars on my dogs.

I was in shock and just kept repeating, "But they're *house* dogs!"

Finally I remembered to ask about River, Malcolm's conspirator in crime.

"We didn't see a black dog. Like I said, we put him back in the fence."

I could not get off that plane fast enough. I called my husband at work and grilled him about what happened. He remembered both dogs inside when he left early that morning and had no explanation for a wandering Malcolm.

The thirty minute ride home was agony as I kept picturing worst-case scenarios. We had about two acres fenced in the back and there was a very busy road at the end of our long driveway. The driveway ran along the bank property where apparently Malcolm had been off adventuring earlier.

When the taxi pulled up the drive I threw my bags out and ran to the back screaming Malcolm's name. There was no lumbering brown bear to greet me, but fortunately there was a frantically barking black dog in the house. I checked on River who was agitated, but fine. The house was closed up—no open-door escape routes. I ran around the house again, but there was no sign of Malcolm anywhere. On my third lap around the house, I noticed a note on the front door.

Hello neighbors!

Your dog has gotten out of the fence a couple times this morning and has come to visit us. We did try knocking on the door for you, but I'm guessing you are not home.

We didn't want him running around the parking lot and busy street, so we brought him into the bank.

When you get back home please come over to get him.

Thank you,

Your neighbors at XXXX Bank

I paused for a moment to laugh and then raced over to the bank. The parking lot was full as men and women in suits went about their business. I went to the front door and there, in the middle of the floor, was a sprawled-out Newfoundland dog. He seemed as content with strangers stepping over him in the unfamiliar bank lobby as he was when relaxing in his own living room. He was so still he looked like an extra fluffy bear rug.

When the bank employees saw my frantic face, they laughed and ran over. Malcolm stood slowly and wandered over to join us.

"He's the most wonderful dog! We love him!"

I apologized over and over and thanked them for keeping him rather than letting the police take him in.

"We could tell he was nice, and we didn't want him just wandering around," the bank manager explained. "Honestly, our customers loved him. He can be an honorary bank employee any time."

I tried not to notice all the dried slobber streaks on the suit pants gathered around us.

The next morning, when Malcolm and I walked over with donuts and a thank you card, Malcolm plopped down in the middle of the lobby like he belonged there.

As I'm writing this, Malcolm is snoring like an outboard motor at my feet. He and River have enjoyed taking advantage of any opportunity for an adventure that comes along, and I wouldn't have it any other way.

Jackie Madison
St. Paul, Minnesota, USA

Chapter 29

Alaskan Life Savers - Cassiopeia

It had been two years since our Newf, Georgie Girl, had gone to the Rainbow Bridge, and Winky, our little American Eskimo, was still depressed. We decided to get another Newf, and after an extensive search we located Cassiopeia, a five-year-old rescue in California.

On a hot, late August afternoon, Cassie arrived in Juneau via Alaska Airlines. I opened the dog kennel and peered into the inky blackness within. I was holding a small offering—a little wish in the palm of my outstretched hand.

Cassie stepped toward me, and when my eyes met hers, electricity shot between us. She gently leaned forward and accepted my offer. Before I knew it, we were outside walking together toward the car on fresh-cut grass.

We had no idea if she had been exposed to small dogs so we were wary of this first introduction to Winky. But he threw caution to the wind and leapt out of the car window before we could stop him. He threw himself into Cassie's face with a little whining cry in the back of his throat. It was like he recognized in her whatever it was he loved in the Newfoundland girl who had passed away. Cassie, with great dignity and gentleness, laid her head over him and stood there hugging him while he quivered and cried. It was a poignant moment. Never had I realized just how much a dog can grieve for another.

During the summer we lived aboard our 50' Trimaran and explored Alaskan coastal areas, but every October we went to a remote bay on an island in Southeast Alaska to take care of a wilderness lodge for eight months. We were quite isolated there as the few people who lived in that area were across the bay from the lodge.

A large family of river otters lived across the bay, but they often came to the docks at the lodge to look for mussels and fish residue to snack on. Their presence drove Cassie and Winky crazy. The dogs would run around on the docks barking in a frenzy while the otters stayed under the docks hissing and chirping, teasing the dogs relentlessly. Little Winky, especially, loved to bark at them and he was fearless.

We loved to watch the river otters but there was one little thing about them that was not so nice. They would gang up on a dog caught in the water, grab it, and maul it while dragging it down into the deep.

One afternoon, shortly after we had arrived for the winter, I was in our sailboat packing things to move to the lodge. I had left Cassie and Winky outside on the docks. I heard a ruckus start and figured the otters had arrived, but I did not worry overmuch. I was busy and ignored the barking. Randy, meanwhile, was all the way up at the lodge. He was running the carpet cleaner so he did not hear anything at all.

Suddenly Cassie appeared in the doorway of the boat, barking frantically. When I turned and looked at her she immediately ran back off the boat. I thought she was just having fun so I went back to work. She continued her deep barking, but when she went silent I realized, all at once, that I did not hear Winky barking at all.

We had three docks at the lodge that rocked independently with the movement of the ocean. There was an eighteen-inch gap between two of the docks which was treacherous to cross if you were not watching your footing.

I pictured the dangerous gap and knew instantly that Winky was in the water. I rushed out of the boat to see Cassie with her head and shoulders completely underwater in the gap between the two heaving, unsteady docks. She came up with a mouthful of white hair, but no Winky!

I flung myself onto the dock and stuck my own head and shoulders into the gap. I could hardly see Winky. Evidently he had fallen into the water and the otters had dragged him under the dock. He was stuck, but he had his little nose crammed into a crack and had air. He was barely holding his own, and I knew he was going to tire and sink if the otters didn't get him first. They were biting at his belly right in front of me. I raised my head from the water and started screaming for Randy.

To my complete surprise, Cassie rushed to the lodge and barked frantically at Randy. When he stepped outside he heard me screaming. Cassie raced back to the dock with Randy at a dead run behind her.

When Cassie reached me, I was trying to grab Winky with my hand and was crying with frustration because I could not find him. Suddenly, Cassie again stuck her head completely under water to her shoulders. I grabbed her to keep her from falling in and was able to follow with my finger down her nose and grab my little dog. Together we pulled him to safety. When he was on the dock Cassie fussed over him like a puppy. He was soaked, cold, scared, and bitten. But he wasn't hurt badly, and he was alive!

Although much of the pleasure of living at the wilderness lodge was that it gave us opportunities to enjoy the wildlife, this encounter with the otters was frightening. Little did we know that another unnerving wildlife encounter was yet to come.

A brown bear had begun hanging around the lodge that fall. After all the other people left, it became quite bold. It began attempting to tear open the smoker and the freezers after its natural food source of fish in the creek went away. We tried everything to drive it off, including rubber slugs and loud noises, but nothing worked.

The bear continued to grow more brazen. One morning it appeared on our front deck and sauntered down the boardwalk to the docks. Randy chased it but it just ambled away nonchalantly. That was not a good sign. Now we were becoming seriously concerned. The bear was becoming a danger.

We contacted the wildlife control but we were out of their jurisdiction and they would not come and live trap the bear to remove it. They said we could kill it since it was a threat to our home and animals, but we did not want it to come to that.

Two evenings later the situation came to a head. It was storming and the wind was blowing hard so Randy decided to walk down to the dock and check the boat and lines. It was twilight, not quite dark yet.

When Randy got about halfway to the dock the bear jumped out of the woods onto the boardwalk between him and the lodge. Randy yelled and waved his arms, but this time the bear did not go away. This time it charged! Just before it reached him Randy dodged onto a side trail off the boardwalk.

I had been watching Randy from the doorway and I did the only thing I could. While breathing a prayer to please keep them all safe, I let the dogs out of the house and ran for the rifle.

Cassie literally *roared* her challenge to this intruder that was invading our home. Without a thought for her own safety she raced to Randy's protection with a fierceness that was frightening. She flung herself between the bear and my husband, giving him the chance he needed to escape. I came running with the gun, then Randy and I turned to try and save Cassie from certain death.

The bear had risen up on its hind legs, and Cassie was leaping at it and snarling with rage. Suddenly, a streak of white shot right past Cassie and the bear, and latched viciously onto the bear's behind. The bear whirled around in the middle of the boardwalk with that little, twenty-pound Winky, swinging like a fat, white tick stuck to its rear.

At that point Winky's teeth must have connected because the next thing we heard was the bear roaring in pain. Then it turned and bolted away with Cassie and Winky literally on its tail. They drove it off the boardwalk and into the woods before they returned to us.

We were stunned. Randy had survived because of a big black dog who loved him. Cassie had survived because of a little white dog who owed her a life debt.

For the next month we never went anywhere without the rife, but that bear had had enough. It never returned.

I don't know why things work out the way they do, but we do know that there are no words that fit how we feel about Cassie. I am so grateful that she was allowed to come to us. Protecting us was the job she chose, and we were reassured by her very great presence. I felt safer that year than I ever had before. Cassie was always by our side, looking out for us in that wilderness where we had chosen to live alone for most of the year.

Our sweet Cassiopeia, the universe aptly named her, for her personality unfolded like stars and constellations almost too beautiful to behold—she takes our breath away.

Jeanne Alford
Juneau, Alaska, USA

Chapter 30

Jeter's Journey - Jeter

The distance from my home in California to the test site in Colorado was absurd, and I'd never trained a dog or seen a water test. But I trusted the friend who suggested that I train Jeter for this water test, I trusted Jeter, and the prospect sounded like fun.

At that time Jeter was almost three and had been with me since he was 11 weeks old. Shortly after he had joined me, I'd sat in a dark hospital room with my precious puppy whose inert body reminded me of a beautiful stuffed animal from FAO Schwartz. During these surreal visits I feared losing him; and I certainly could not have predicted our future journey.

I began preparing for our first water test by reading Judi Adler's compendium on Newfoundland water training and attending two water seminars. Soon Jeter and I began making the weekly 400-mile round trips to train with regional club members, in addition to practicing alone at our local lake.

Jeter amazed me with his response to water training. He approached the task with relaxed purposefulness. He was focused, driven, stimulated to be doing his job, and patient as the two of us connected in a growing partnership.

Some of this response is innate in a working dog; however, through Jeter's training progression I developed respect for his individual assets of physical ability, drive, intelligence, confidence, attitude, and relationship with me. These are attributes which cannot be taught through drills, books, and seminars.

During our water training Jeter showed his initiative on many occasions including his gallant and successful effort in retrieving a boat cushion that was quickly being blown out to sea, and his calm and confident swim with handler during a challenging group training that had to be aborted due to vicious winds and waves.

At our first water test Jeter earned both his Water Dog and Water Rescue Dog titles, a rare feat. I smiled throughout the 1200-mile trip home. I was still energized from this unprecedented partnership with an animal when, three months later, my friend encouraged me to train Jeter for draft.

"What's draft?" I asked.

She explained that this involved a dog pulling a cart in harness and executing various maneuvers.

I chuckled, and declined. Immediately following the phone call, I ordered a cart.

After a month of draft training Jeter earned his first draft title. Four months later he easily earned his second draft title with virtually no additional practice. Team Jeter sought a greater challenge, advanced draft. Our training at this level further deepened our partnership as we learned together to navigate a test which requires stamina, precision, and shared trust.

Training at the highest levels of draft and water work developed intimacy in our partnership. I shall be forever grateful to Jeter for introducing me to both the world of the working Newfoundland and to the intimacy achievable in the training partnership.

Jeter retired from working events with eight advanced draft titles to accompany his two junior draft titles and his nine water titles. As we currently navigate the ladder in scent work trials, he is demonstrating the same spirit, intelligence, focus, willingness, and confidence that he exhibited in water and draft work.

Jeter personifies the spirit of the Newfoundland—doing his job calmly, with focus, and with intimate connection to his human. His consistency in doing this has been all the more remarkable and endearing in light of his medical history. If state of the art veterinary care had not been available, Jeter would have died as a young puppy. If specialized surgical intervention had not been available, he would have had to be euthanized before he reached his second birthday.

Despite every precaution to protect a puppy whose immunity is not yet established, Jeter contracted Parvo as a very young puppy. This virus is highly contagious and causes a potentially fatal gastrointestinal illness. My new puppy was gravely ill; but after four days of hospitalization, undergoing IV's and transfusions, his energy rebounded. Staff credited his recovery to state of the art veterinary care, my visits with him in the hospital, and his invincible spirit.

From the age of six months to 21 months Jeter struggled with several serious orthopedic issues: bilateral elbow dysplasia, bilateral patellar luxation, and bilateral cruciate ligament tears. He underwent surgeries on all four legs, for a total of six surgeries. I believe that our rehabilitation regimens strengthened our bond of partnership, evident in his success in water, draft, and scent work tests and trials.

Today, at nearly nine years old, Jeter is arthritic yet he continues to swim effortlessly, negotiate draft exercises with precision, and locate odor with confidence. He and I have learned together, and my other Newfoundlands are the beneficiaries of our journey. Jeter's spirit has enabled our journey. It has been a glorious honor to have been able to help him, to grow with him, and to know that both of us have done the very best we could do throughout his odyssey.

We continue to go on endurance swims together at dawn. I feel his awareness of me by his side with our every stroke. The only sounds are our breathing, jumping fish, and birds. The bond is indescribable.

Randy Robinson
Fresno, California, USA
Northern California Newfoundland Club

Chapter 31

First Day At Doggie School - Taz

Jeanne decided that since I was stronger than she was, I should be the one to take Taz , our brown and white six-month-old Newf, to doggie school. Finally I relented, and Taz and I joined a class with 10 other puppies of various breeds.

The only downside about this class was the size of the trainers. Perry was a little guy, diminutive, and I could tell he was intimidated by Taz and her size. I could see it in his eyes. Although Janine didn't seem intimidated, she was petite, a little woman.

It didn't help that I had to explain to a dozen folks that Taz was wearing a Gentle Leader, not a muzzle. I even tried to switch to a leash but Taz instantly began a pulling contest that I could never have won, so I gave up and went back to the Gentle Leader. A few people continued to look at us warily.

Small though they were, both Perry and Janine knew their stuff, and in a short period I learned ways to coax Taz to leave my side, and then willingly come back without pulling on the leash.

We were put through a course of obstacles that included poles to weave around, crackly plastic to walk over, hoops to leap through, and a pool of water to swim across. The very last of the obstacles was an agility tunnel, five feet long and 26 inches in diameter, with a wet towel lying on the floor at the exit. The puppies were to walk through the tunnel and over the wet towel.

Taz looked at me through the tunnel, woofed, then, crouching in order to fit, began squeezing through. I was feeling proud. We had done exceptionally well on the rest of the course, positively excelling at the swim across the pool. Taz loves water and wet things. I knew the wet towel at the exit of the tunnel would not be a problem.

But just as she reached the end of the tunnel, Taz stopped. She glared at the wet towel. Suddenly, without warning, the evil Tazilla twin appeared. Taz started barking at the towel and wouldn't *budge* across it!

I tried everything short of dragging her out of the tunnel. At first she just continued barking at the towel. But then she suddenly bunched up her body and, making a rocket of herself, she leapt over the towel and landed on the floor in front of it. Then she turned on a dime, snatched up the big, wet towel, and began racing around the room shaking and flinging it all over the place, scattering dogs and owners like confetti!

Taz would not return to call. She continued playing keep-away with her prize. In the midst of the chaos, Perry suggested he deal with her. Getting all firm and no-nonsense, he called her to come.

Taz screeched to a stop, then joyfully rushed up to Perry. However, just as he reached for her she spotted the parachute-type rope cords dangling from his sleeve.

I never learned whether securing long sleeves with paracord was some sort of dog trainer safety measure or just a fashion statement, but Taz interpreted the dangling cords as, uh-oh! Puppy lures!

Taz had always found dangling objects irresistible—lines on our boat, shoe laces, towels wrapped around us as we headed for the hot tub. Jeanne and I called these dangling objects "puppy lures."

And now Perry was reaching for her. And he was offering her *puppy lures!* Taz dropped the towel and grabbed the paracords dangling from his sleeve. Game on!

Taz began hopping backwards, jerking Perry off his feet after her. His free arm was flailing, his legs flipping in all directions, his head snapping in whiplash with Taz's every hop.

Around the room they went, Taz in reverse with that mischievous light in her eyes, anticipating Perry's every move and trick. She had seen it all before.

Perry's face held a fixed snarl or grin, I'm not sure which, but he kept saying, "No, no, don't step in! I will stop her!"

The other trainer was laughing so hard she was crying. She was trying to video this spectacle.

Several minutes later, and as a last resort, Perry just went limp and fell to the floor thinking Taz could not drag his 110 pounds around.

Taz never slowed down, she just pulled harder and Perry went with her, arm stretched out and body dragging. Now he had no way to struggle to his feet. Having been reduced to this embarrassing position he finally shouted at me.

"DO something!"

I had tried to tell them from the beginning that Taz was the *debil* dog, and I had brought along my secret weapon, just in case.

I dug into my pack and grabbed the secret weapon. I readied myself, hunkering down into a crouch, tensing my muscles so I could leap straight up at the right moment.

I whipped out the clothespin. CLICK-CLICK!

Taz dropped Perry and was onto me so fast I was almost toppled. Leaping up from the crouch, I managed to stuff the clothespin into my pocket before she could get it. Then I grabbed her leash and commanded her to "sit," all before I regained my balance.

Taz sat like a perfect lady, eyes boring into mine as Perry straggled over to us. He was now covered in dirty floor muck, dog hair, and drool.

I was feeling self-conscious, rattled. I was also nervous that he was going to give us our walking papers. At least Taz didn't bite him. That was never her intention, at all.

"Was that a clothespin I just saw?" he asked.

"Yup," I said, "she loves them, loves to be tortured with them. And, by the way, she likes to grab things and play tug of war. We've been trying to break her of this, but ... I guess she lost control."

Perry gave a big sigh, then patted Taz on the head.

"You need to work on the release command," he instructed me, quietly.

So the first day of doggie school passed, and we weren't expelled. Instead, we were given homework. We have a choice. We can teach our pups to walk backward on command, or we can teach them to leap into our arms when called. Maybe Jeanne will help me decide which skill Taz and I should practice.

Randy Alford
Juneau, Alaska, USA

Chapter 32

Who Do You Call? - Wendell & Shadow

It's Labor Day, 2009. One a.m. A Newf barks. All three Newfs are sleeping in our bedroom. Someone must need a potty break. Each girl is in her crate and Wendell is sleeping in the doorway on the bathroom floor. My decision to let Shadow and Wendell go out to the back yard to pee was the right choice.

Shadow and Wendell bolt out the screen door and begin running back and forth. Evidently, nobody needed the potty. It is now obvious that they are hot on the trail of something else, something as yet unidentified.

Both dogs disappear. In a small back yard. With a security light. Where could two dogs who each weigh over 100 pounds hide?

Now I realize that two bushes very close to the house are concealing a battle. I see flashes of the spirited skirmish that's in progress. Shadow is barking and Wendell is tending to business.

It's the armadillo! The dogs had heard the pesky creature that has been plaguing our garden for weeks. They are now making it understand that it is not welcome.

I run inside to tell Ted the situation and return to see Wendell appear from behind the bushes with a *large* armadillo in his mouth. Also, protruding from his mouth, is a generous-sized limb from one of the bushes.

Now Wendell is not sure what to do. ("Dad has been complaining about this thing. Now I have it! What next?")

Safety of the dogs is my priority. I encourage Shadow to go inside, as she has done her part in this escapade. Once she is inside, I can hear her frantically ringing the bell non-stop, begging to come back out. She wants to continue participating in the chaos with Wendell and the armadillo. I ignore her request to rejoin the fight.

Wendell is walking around with the armadillo in his mouth. I tell him "don't let go" and my brilliant dog knows exactly what I'm saying. He holds on to the 'dillo.

Ted arrives on the scene wearing nothing but a pair of Birkenstocks and a look of amazement. Wendell wants to bring his prize into the house. I'm thinking, *bad idea*!

Ted and I are wondering what to do next. We have Wendell go into the outdoor kennel, a 10' x 20' room with a wooden floor. We close him in with the 'dillo. I wait while Ted decides the next step. The 'dillo is still in Wendell's mouth but it isn't moving. However, I doubt it is dead. Armadillo shells are very hard and Newfs are very gentle.

While Ted is collecting gloves and a flashlight, as well as more appropriate attire, I pick up a shovel to use as a weapon in case the armadillo becomes my responsibility.

At that point, while still in the kennel, Wendell puts the 'dillo down. It is still very much alive. Wendell quickly gets the critter safely back into his powerful jaws. Meanwhile, the humans are discussing what's to be done next. Wendell has done his part, and now he's waiting for us to complete the process. Whatever that is.

Ted brings out a plastic box that is just about the right size to hold an armadillo and we encourage Wendell to let the 'dillo down. We'll take over from here. Reluctantly, he drops the armadillo and Ted places the plastic box over the frightened, somewhat injured animal.

Why Wendell lets the 'dillo go for a few small dog biscuits, I'll never know. He must be the best dog ever. I put Wendell in the garage with a large bowl of water. He's hot and thirsty after his mighty efforts.

Shadow's still inside the house, ringing the bell. Tiny's still in the bedroom, snoozing in her crate.

We get a large board and slide it under the plastic box and then, after stuffing the 'dillo's tail into the box with him, we tie the box and the board together. We have become aware that armadillos, especially frightened armadillos, really, really stink.

In less than 45 minutes the armadillo is confined, and some of the smell and 'dillo blood is cleaned off the kennel floor. Shadow is back in her crate, trying to sleep. Tiny, at almost 12 years old, is thankful she was allowed to sit this one out. Ted has returned to bed. And Wendell is lying next to me as I type this account of our early morning caper.

The armadillo didn't look to be in good shape as we put him in the box. I doubt his situation will improve come morning. He picked the wrong Newf with whom to tussle. Ted's been trying to get that thing for weeks. Wendell is our hero.

*****

Next morning we talk with the neighbors who have been having armadillo problems, too. Their concerns lay with their horses and the large holes left in the paddock after the 'dillo has been searching for food. We are all hoping this is the one, the armadillo that has been ravaging the neighborhood.

There is no talk of relocating the armadillo. It did not survive. Disposition of the contents of the box is the discussion, and whether the box needs to be saved.

Ted loads the "packaged" armadillo into our old pickup truck and drives down the neighbor's lane. The next step is to bury the entire mess and be done with it.

We all believe this armadillo was a lone wolf. The next few days will tell the tale. However, if new holes appear in our garden or lawn, or in the neighbor's horse paddock, we know who to call: Wendell, the 'dillo buster!

Melanie Peck
Galena, Missouri, USA

Chapter 33

Life Changer - Gabriel

"He's going to change your life," the breeder told me as I loaded my new baby Landseer boy into my SUV.

Change it? Hardly! I have had many dogs during the last 25 years, both first-home pups and equally beloved rescues. Each one has enhanced and enriched my life beyond measure, but not *changed* my life.

I named my new puppy Gabriel, after the archangel, for even as a baby he seemed wise, calm, and caring beyond his years. I had been fostering dogs for years and Gabriel became an integral part of my fostering activity. He put every new dog at ease with his calm, patient, loving demeanor.

I once was fostering a new dog who was going through heartworm treatment. I was keeping him on our very quiet, peaceful back porch. As I was walking there to feed him for the first time, Gabriel pushed past me, rushing to the porch. Why?

I soon found out. Gabriel simply wanted to be with our foster, and the foster was obviously calmed by Gabriel's presence. He ate his dinner happily. The two dogs slept together on the porch every night until the treatment was over and the foster could join the rest of the gang on a full-time basis.

A few weeks later, Gabriel again showed his concern for other animals. That morning he and my Boxer, Hank, were in the yard when I heard Hank barking. Hank only barked when there was a reason to do so.

I ran outside to see Hank at the fence, barking at the road. I did not see anything on the road or near it. More importantly, where was Gabe? You would think it would be hard to lose a 135-pound black and white dog in a two-acre fenced yard, but he was not there. I looked at the gate to make certain it was locked. It was. Where was my boy?

I started scanning neighboring areas and spotted Gabe in the field to the right of our house. How? Why? I did not call him for fear he would go into the road and risk getting hit. Instead, I got Hank in the house, grabbed a leash, then ran over to the field.

Gabe had his face down to the ground and seemed to be trying to move something with his muzzle. When I got closer, it all became clear. There on the ground was a young doe. Her back legs had been crushed. She must have been hit by a speeding car. She was either thrown or had dragged herself to this spot.

Gabriel came over to me. I leashed him and he led me back to the doe. He looked at me as if he expected me to help her. Then she lifted her head and looked at me. Now both Gabriel and the doe were looking to me for help. I will have this picture in my head for the rest of my life.

At this point I was crying. I buried my sobbing face into my incredible boy's ruff and told him there was nothing either of us could do. We sadly walked home, and I called animal control.

When I got home that afternoon, our neighbor told me that animal control never came. She had flagged down a police officer, and he had put the long-suffering doe out of her misery with a bullet.

As soon as Gabe got out of the house he wanted to go check on the deer. We walked over and he sniffed her and seemed to understand that she was dead. But he insisted on checking on her during every walk until her carcass was finally removed, days later. He had never before, nor has he since, jumped our fence. But that morning he had seen a being in need, and he went to do whatever he could.

Gabriel blossomed into a magnificent looking Newf. His breeders wanted him shown. I had never entered a show ring in my life, but I agreed to try. When another breeder volunteered to show him, I was thrilled that an expert was willing to help. When we got to the first show, she asked to practice with Gabe.

I left them to rehearse but soon she came over to me and said, "You are going to have to show him. He refuses to move for me."

"What? I have no clue how to do this!"

She gave me a few quick pointers, then we had to hurry into the ring. It was an outdoor show and I was wearing a long skirt with boots. Not exactly ring attire.

Somehow, we plodded through the show. Gabriel placed and I was elated. I can do this! Gabe and I began practicing and, the more we worked together, the stronger our bond grew.

After watching us in the ring, the breeder said, "He does not like to be shown. He is only doing this because he loves you so much."

I knew that, and my heart swelled ever more over this incredible boy.

Gabe's breeders thought I was taking too long getting his championship so they asked to help. They also wanted to breed him. Thus, for about two months, they took him. I cried before he left and for many days after.

One day his breeder called. He was laughing when I answered the phone.

"He is bullheaded, isn't he?"

"You think?" I replied.

He proceeded to tell me that Gabe had broken a show lead, as he had refused to move in the ring.

At our last show, when Gabe got out of our SUV and realized we were at a show he turned around and jumped back to our vehicle. I convinced him to let me show him *one last time*, since we were already there.

"Then you can enjoy the rest of your days just as you want," I promised.

Gabriel did obtain his Championship and he *did* change my life. Over the past 12 years, I have learned the magic of this magnificent breed. I will never be without a Newfoundland.

Lisa Lathrop
Warwick, Maryland, USA
Colonial Newfoundland Club
New-Pen-Del Newfoundland Club
Newfoundland Club of America

Chapter 34

A Newfy and His Pig - Gus

It was a dark, frigid, rainy night in late fall and my husband, son, and I were outside with our Newfoundland, Gus, feeding our farm animals. As we neared the area where our four pigs are housed, Gus began alerting us that something wasn't quite right. He was visibly agitated. His eyes darted from left to right and he carried his head much higher than usual. It was then that we heard the weak, plaintive cry of a newborn piglet. The realization washed over me that our sow, Lola, had given birth.

Quickly we gathered flashlights, entered the pigs' enclosure, and began searching for the source of the cries. Gus stood guard at the gate, watching us intently and giving an occasional whine of concern. We soon discovered that Lola, a first-time mother, had chosen to birth her four piglets just outside the entrance to the pig hut. On the ground in the cold mud we found three of the piglets already chilled and lifeless. But one small pink piglet was still crying, fighting to stay alive. I scooped up the tiny piglet, placed him inside my shirt directly against my skin to warm him, and immediately headed for the house with Gus hot on my heels.

Once inside, I lowered myself into a chair in the kitchen, still holding the piglet to my chest. It was apparent that Gus was deeply concerned for this little creature, as he incessantly nudged the bulge in my shirt with his nose, while whimpering softly. As I removed the shivering piglet from inside my shirt and placed him in my lap, Gus immediately began licking him feverishly while glancing at me for reassurance. Soon, the piglet stopped shivering, calmed, and snuggled down into my lap.

"Good boy, Gus. He's going to be okay," I said, as I gave our attentive Newf an approving pat on his head.

I gently scooped the sleeping piglet from my lap and headed to the closet to gather towels and a heating pad. Gus stuck to my side, refusing to let the piglet out of his sight. He watched as I wrapped the piglet in a warm towel and then followed me to the living room. I placed the bundle on the floor, then hurried to the garage to retrieve the dog crate Gus had used as a puppy.

I returned moments later to find Gus lying with the towel-wrapped piglet between his front legs. He was wearing a proud, content look on his face. While I prepared the crate and warmed a bottle of milk, Gus continued to tend to his small, vulnerable charge. It was apparent that our little piglet was in very good hands ... or should I say, paws.

I bottle fed our new little friend as Gus sat quietly next to me, watching intently and giving the piglet an occasional sniff and a gentle lick.

"Gus, your piggy needs a name," I said to him. "How about Banjo?"

Gus quickly responded with a slight stomp of his paw and a look that could only be described as a smile. So "Banjo" it was.

That night Gus slept at the door of Banjo's crate, and he did not hesitate to wake me when his piglet was hungry and ready for his next bottle.

When we awoke the next morning I filled Gus's food bowl with his breakfast as usual, but he refused to budge from his post in front of Banjo's crate. After several failed attempts to coax him away, I delivered his bowl to him where he lay, and he happily ate while he watched Banjo sleeping soundly. So began the friendship between a Newfoundland and his pig.

Banjo lived in the house with us for several weeks while he grew stronger. During that time Gus and Banjo were rarely apart. They ate their meals together, enjoyed chasing each other around the yard, followed one another around the house, and Gus continued to sleep at the door of Banjo's crate every night. Banjo grew strong and confident under Gus's watchful eye and, eventually, the time came for Banjo to rejoin his mother and our other pigs.

Late one afternoon, Gus accompanied Banjo and me out to the pig hut that would now become Banjo's new home. He was greeted by his mother and the other pigs as I walked with him through the gate into their enclosure. Once Banjo was safely inside, I stepped back out the gate and stood next to Gus, stroking his head gently. We watched quietly as Banjo became acquainted with his pig family and explored his new surroundings. Now a strong, confident young pig, he easily adapted to his new situation and was accepted by the other pigs.

I frequently take Gus out to visit his friend, Banjo. I like to think that Banjo looks forward to our visits because he runs excitedly to the fence to greet us as soon as he sees us heading in his direction. Once we reach the fence, Gus gives him an affectionate lick on the nose while Banjo grunts in approval. Gus then settles himself down in the grass and contently observes his friend until it is time for us to return to the house. Their lasting bond is a testament to the Newfoundland's love, sense of duty, and intuitive ability to nurture those in need.

Megan Myers
Worthington, Indiana, USA
Hickory Creek Newfoundlands

Chapter 35

A True Easter Bunny Tale - Brandy, Mercedes & Maverick

Last night about 10:00 I heard a bark come from outside the back door. My three pups had just gone out for their last potty break of the evening.

I walked out to see what was happening. It was so dark it was hard to see anything at all, but I heard a little squeal come from the mouth of four-year-old Brandy, my sweetest, most gentle girl. It sounded like a squeaky toy. But I was sure there were no squeaky toys in the yard. Something was up.

I brought Brandy inside and asked her what she had. Whatever it was, was so small it was completely concealed within those big jowls. On my request to "drop it" Brandy opened her mouth and gently laid a baby bunny at my feet.

Then she looked up at me as if to say, "Can you help it, Mom?"

Thankfully, rather than a tiny pink, hairless, helpless bunny, this one was well covered with thick silky fur, so I knew it was at least a couple of weeks old. I picked it up, wrapped it in a towel, and handed it to my husband to hold. Then I returned to the yard. I knew this little bunny probably wasn't the only one whose explorations had been interrupted.

Sure enough, here came my other two pups, seventeen-month-old Maverick and three-year-old Mercedes, both bringing me a gift of a bunny. At that point I kept the pups inside and went out with a flash light. It didn't take me long to find two more little bunnies.

I suspected the bunny nest must not have been in our yard or my pups would have found it days earlier. But in exercising their new-found independence, the little bunnies had hopped into the wrong yard. Since there was no chance of re-nesting them with my mothering furries around, I decided to take care of them overnight.

I've raised babies like this before and it is a huge, 24/7 job; one I'm just not prepared for. So I chose to turn the job over to a professional. I contacted Wild Rescue, Inc. where a very special woman instructed me on exactly what to do and where to deliver the babies the next day. The bunnies spent the rest of the night cuddled in a comfortable towel nest with a heating pad, and all five were doing well when I dropped them off the next morning. I will remember this as the Easter we were blessed with a visit from five sweet little Easter bunnies. I hope they all survive and are released back into the wild from which they came.

I will also remember the image of those three huge dogs walking in, opening their mouths, and placing baby bunnies on the floor for me. Although they were a bit damp with drool, the bunnies were completely unharmed. It is amazing how gentle the pups were with these little creatures, and certainly a true testament to the Newfoundland temperament. My pups had shown, once again, that they were true gentle giants, and I was reminded, once again, why I had chosen to share my home with Newfs.

While I had acquired Brandy and Mercedes from breeders in the usual way after extensive research and planning, Maverick's arrival was totally unconventional and unexpected. Late one evening I received a phone call from a frantic-sounding man who told me he was searching for a Newfoundland rescue group. Since I have helped with rescue transport through our regional Newf club, the key word "rescue" had pulled up my website. He told me his beloved Newf pup had chewed someone's shoes in the home where he was living temporarily, and the homeowners were threatening to take the dog to the pound the next day after he left for work. He was desperate to find someone to take him, as he knew keeping him was not an option in his current situation.

Without hesitation I jumped in the car and made the eight-hour round trip to retrieve this pup. No, I had not planned on adding another giant to the family, but I am so glad I did! Over the past 12 years Maverick has created his own special space in my heart. Now he and my husband are inseparable and both old guys still get excited about their long daily walks. And be assured, Mav can still sniff out bunnies ... he just can't catch them anymore.

I will be forever grateful for the opportunities I've had to associate with Newfoundlands. I first learned about this breed when I had to choose a book for a book report in middle school. I wasn't particularly fond of reading, but I was very fond of animals, especially dogs. So I chose a book with a big, black dog on the front cover. I can't remember the title of the book, but the big, black dog was, indeed, a Newfoundland, and my interest was sparked.

I continued to think about, read about, and ask about Newfoundlands into my adulthood. I knew I wanted to own one of these beauties some day. After all my human kiddos were grown, I finally made that dream come true. I have owned and bred Newfoundlands for almost 17 years now.

Sometimes I think maybe angels come without wings, without announcement, wearing fur coats. I feel so fortunate to have these big, gentle angels in my life.

Tracy
Flower Mound, Texas, USA
Rio Nova Newfoundlands
Old West Newfoundland Club
Newfoundland Club Of America

Chapter 36

Henry the Therapy Dog - Henry

It was 2009 and I was at Pymatuning State Park in Pennsylvania for the Penn-Ohio Newfoundland Club's water test with my two Newfies. This water test is well attended and very popular for spectators. Among the spectators was a group of special needs young teens with their counselors.

It was an exciting day for me, as both of my Newfies had passed their Water Rescue Dog (WRD) tests. While I was walking Glory, my seven-year-old black Newfy, one of the counselors approached and asked if I could bring Glory over to visit with the kids. Glory was a very sweet Newfy, but visiting with a group of kids was way outside her comfort zone. I explained this to the counselor and said I would bring my other Newfy over.

Henry, my three-year-old Landseer, was a very confident Newf who loved attention and loved kids. He was delighted to meet the kids. He was a big hit with them and provided a great photo opportunity for them.

While we were visiting, I noticed one teen hanging back away from the group. Some of the counselors tried to encourage him to come over to Henry and get his picture taken. He adamantly refused. One could see he was terrified of Henry. He was left alone, and the rest of the kids gave hugs and pets to Henry while the adults took pictures.

After a while, the boy came up to one of the counselors and said, "Okay, I will have my picture taken with that dog, but I don't want him looking at me."

The counselor looked at me. I nodded and said, "We can do that."

I put Henry in a "sit" and we had the boy sit down at Henry's back so Henry was facing away from him. One could see the tension in this young man, but he was brave and let the counselors take pictures.

Henry sat perfectly still with his back to the boy. After a few minutes, the boy slowly raised one of his hands and very tentatively started petting Henry on the back. Henry continued sitting perfectly still. He never moved nor looked at the boy. It was as if he knew any movement, any acknowledgement of that touch, would trigger the boy to run away. We were all in awe at what we were witnessing.

Henry was my "once in a lifetime" dog. He excelled at everything we did. He easily obtained his championship in the show ring. He did well in obedience and rally. He was an outstanding water dog and was quickly learning draft work at that time. But when I saw how he intuitively knew how to act with this child who was terrified of dogs, I knew at that moment his true calling. Henry was born for therapy work.

That summer we worked on getting Henry certified with a Therapy Dog Program. He became our local elementary school's reading dog and participated in the library's "Read to the Dog" program. A friend of mine told the local hospital about us, and we were invited to interview for a position with the Hospital Therapy Dog Program. This is a very popular program with lots of applicants, but few admissions. The requirements are very strict for obvious reasons.

Henry passed the hospital therapy dog test with flying colors and we were assigned to work with the pediatric rehab center. Henry worked with the babies who needed stretching exercises. These exercises could be painful, so Henry was a great distraction for the babies while they were being manipulated. He did not mind if there was some crying.

Henry helped encourage young children to exercise their legs by either walking next to them or having them ride their special bikes alongside of him. He always matched his pace with that of the young charge next to him.

Chew therapy was Henry's favorite therapy work. Sometimes young children experience the difficulty of gagging on food after being intubated during surgery. When this happens, they work with a therapist and practice eating foods with different textures. Henry served as an inspiration to try the different foods. He would sit next to the highchair and the therapist would give him the food item. He would gently take it from her fingers and chew it. The therapist would then give the same item to the youngster and the child would mimic Henry. He provided the encouragement the children needed and was credited with helping lots of toddlers who experienced this gagging problem. Henry's favorite foods were slices of kiwis, bananas, apples, and cheese.

There were many other instances when Henry intuitively knew what the child needed and would proceed to do it without any training. Once he backed up between two balance bars while facing the child and maintaining eye contact with her so she would follow him through the balance bars. There were many different types of equipment that he worked around, but he never showed fear from any of it.

Henry was nominated by the staff at the rehab center for the President's Award of Excellence. It was the first time a volunteer was nominated, let alone a volunteer who was a dog! Henry was invited to the ceremony in the auditorium and was given a certificate from the President of the Hospital. I accompanied Henry to the stage, and he shook hands with the president, much to the delight of the attendees. Afterwards we were invited to join everyone for refreshments in the banquet room. Try to imagine a room full of medical personal eating food around a large, drooling Newf. Henry did pretty well with the drooling, and I made sure we had an appropriate bib on hand.

Through the years, Henry and I did many more hospital visits and continued our reading programs with the schools and library. He was an excellent role model for the Newfy pups we added to our family during his lifetime. Henry retired from therapy work at 10 years of age, and enjoyed good health, lazy walks, and leisurely swims in his golden years. He peacefully passed in his sleep shortly before his 13th birthday.

Presently, I am doing therapy work with Henry's son, Spencer, who shows great promise in being as intuitive with people's needs as Henry was.

The magic of a Newfy helping people relax and feel calm continues.

Sue Putt
Paw Paw, Michigan, USA
Great Lakes Newfoundland Club
Newfoundland Club of America

Chapter 37

Happy Accidental Kona Bear - Kona

I was just supposed to be the driver taking my two best friends to a breeder in Missouri to pick up their Old English Sheepdog puppies. After all, I already had three dogs, was recently divorced and down to one income. Plus, I rescue. I don't buy puppies.

But when we arrived, over in the corner pen was one shaggy, black ball of fur, just sitting calmly in the middle of all the commotion. Curious, and recognizing the distinctive, sweet Newfy face, I asked about her.

"Last one in the litter, no one wants her."

"How much?"

"Make me an offer."

Whoops. I hastened to explain my situation and let the lady know I was just curious, not in the market for another dog.

But she pulled the little 15-week-old girl out of her pen and let her run around with the puppies my friends were getting to know. I picked her up. The pictures taken show me almost completely hidden by an enormous black ball of fur. But I'm grinning from ear to ear. What a sucker.

As I watched the Newfy puppy tumble and play with the other two puppies, the breeder and I talked about many things, and several times I was asked to make an offer. Each time I declined with my same excuses.

Imagine my surprise when, as we were packing up to leave, the breeder approached me with a folder containing the Newfy's AKC registration papers and vet records.

"... I know you will give her a great home, which is more important than the money. She's going home with you today."

How could I turn down that sweet Newfy face?

She was christened Kona on the way home to Texas.

When first meeting her new pack, they growled, and Kona peed in her crate. That was Day One. Day Two found her stealing her brothers' beds and trying to get the ancient, crotchety terrier to play with her. By Day Three she was chasing everyone in circles around the backyard, playing hockey with an empty milk jug, and starting to learn her name.

We joined the local Newfoundland club because she was my first of the breed. When we went to the first meeting she was only about four months old. Next to well-bred Newfies, it is apparent she's no show dog, but she's extremely sweet and so anxious to please. She showed her belly to everyone she met and loved all the attention.

Kona was the hardest dog I've ever tried to house train, but when she eventually got it ... she got it! Now she pokes me with her nose to get my attention so my entire wardrobe ends up with Kona slobber on it at some point. But as I tell her other slobber victims, slobber washes out.

She's not a big eater and will frequently just stare at her food. But if the terrier finishes first and starts sneaking up on Kona's bowl, suddenly that food is delicious! Or if Mommy pretends to gobble it down ... oh, Kona must have it then!

Six months ago, in an exuberant round of roughhousing with her brother, she discovered how to jump on the bed. Oh, joyous day! Now she is convinced she *must* sleep on the bed but feels she needs help to get up there. So she paces anxiously beside my bed with a toy in her mouth until I get up. Then she puts her front feet on the bed while she waits for me to lift her big, shaggy rear end up the rest of the way, and on my bed is where she stays the rest of the night.

All stuffed squeaky toys are disemboweled so she can reach the squeaky device, which she proceeds to toss and chew until I realize what she's doing. Then, as soon as I start getting up to retrieve the device, she freezes. She remains completely still, as if I can't see what she's doing if she doesn't move. She cracks me up.

She knows "feeties-feeties" means to stop and let me wipe off muddy paws, but in her case, I'm wiping off the whole muddy dog. And she loves every minute of it! She's laughing the whole time.

She also knows "brush-brush" means something that feels good, but she only wants to be brushed where *she* wants to be brushed. When that brush starts moving toward a leg or her chest, she's done.

Most of the time, Kona impersonates a rug. Apparently, that's what she does best and it's her job for life. She will always lie, without fail, in *exactly* the spot I where need to walk at that moment. Stepping over her 52 times carrying totes full of Christmas decorations was not fun last week, but for two hours as she napped on the threshold between the garage and the hallway, I managed. I've learned to look down at the floor a *lot*.

My house sitters say when I am gone, she tries to sneak up on the couch. She *never* does that when I am home, so she is using her sweet face and loving personality to manipulate these young people who are supposed to be in charge. I will need more assertive house sitters who won't fall for that Newfy face.

Now, at two years old, Kona has captured the hearts of everyone in our small town. We stop at the General Store on the square every day where the owner comes out for her Kona love, as does the girl from the insurance office next door. People stop me on the street to ask what kind of dog she is, and always ask if they can pet her. She loves them all, especially the children.

Last week a little girl was watching out the window of the General Store. When she saw us approaching she started dancing, clapping her hands, and squealing with delight. Then she ran straight out to my gentle giant who began smothering her in kisses. Kona's tail was going a mile a minute and it appeared to those of us watching there was no one else in the universe for either dog or child.

A couple of times I gathered up the dogs to continue our walk, but the little girl kept trying to run after us, so I would give in. We stayed much longer than usual so the love fest could continue. Eventually, the dogs and I started off down the sidewalk while the mom held onto the little girl's hand to keep her from following again.

That was the worst thing ever.

The little girl watched us for a moment, then suddenly and dramatically threw herself to the sidewalk, wailing at the top of her lungs, tears flowing down her little face! We were three stores away down the sidewalk and I was jerked to a stop when Kona whirled around, pulling to the end of her leash. Her ears were up, her tail was up and waving.

The owner of the General Store called out to me, "Oh, you should see Kona's face!"

So, I turned her loose.

Kona galloped back to that little girl and began licking her from head to toe. What a miracle! Those tears dried up immediately, replaced by giggles, smiles, and squeals of laughter.

This was a wonderful testament to the Newfoundland temperament ... no water in sight but the Newfy instinct to "save" a child in obvious distress showed through, regardless. Kona was "saving" her new little friend, and they both loved every minute of it.

Kona truly is my "happy accident." She brings joy to me and to everyone she encounters.

Now I cannot imagine life without this big, shaggy, slobbery, sweet, wonderful dog.

Cynthiana Jones
Pilot Point, Texas, USA
Old West Newfoundland Club

Chapter 38

Wonder Girl - Cheyenne

My four-year-old Newfy, Cheyenne, has been "in" school with me since she was 12 weeks old. The students in my health classes (most consistently, members of the football and basketball teams) helped socialize her and train her as she took the steps toward the several certifications she has earned. She has become so competent at supporting students experiencing anxiety episodes and other stress-related events that she is now an official staff member with her own ID badge and photo in the yearbook.

But it is the confident way Cheyenne takes the initiative in handling unusual situations that leaves me in awe of her. She began demonstrating this initiative several years ago when we were volunteering at a local hospital. As we approached one of the various clinics we could hear "kid noise," indicating children playing while waiting to be seen.

The volunteer accompanying us got permission from the children's parents for a therapy dog visit, then motioned for us to enter. Cheyenne and I stepped into a very large room filled with at least 25 kids of various ages.

The moment we entered the room a tiny, little, two-year-old boy screamed, "DOG!" at the top of his lungs and began running towards us with his little fists pounding the air up and down, up and down.

As the little boy started toward us, his mother turned to see her son charging toward what must have looked like a huge black bear. She also began running towards us shouting the child's name.

Everyone in the clinic froze. I'm not sure what they thought was going to happen, but the memory of all those faces filled with apprehension and fear is still embedded in my brain.

The little guy reached Cheyenne and began banging on her head with his little fists. As I reached down to gently move him away, Cheyenne lifted her paw and calmly pressed down on both of his little arms while sliding into a down position. She began licking one little arm and then the other. As the little boy was slowly pressed to his knees, Cheyenne kept licking.

This entire scenario unfolded in seconds Little boy yelling, running, pounding. Cheyenne pressing, sitting, licking. Audience gasping, fearing, dreading. Mother panicking, screaming, running.

The mom reached us just as the little boy began to sink to the floor while still mumbling "dog, dog, dog" in a quieter and quieter voice until it faded away. In what seemed like no time, his little face was resting on Cheyenne's forehead and, to my amazement, he closed his little eyes and fell sound asleep. Cheyenne kept licking, very gently now.

His mom looked at me and tears began pouring from her eyes. Then tears poured from my eyes, then from the volunteer's eyes, and finally, from the eyes of most of the moms in the waiting room. We were all just a mess!

The boy's mom said, "My son is autistic. He never sleeps. I've never seen him sleep during the day. I'm a single parent. I'm always exhausted. Where do I get a therapy dog like that?"

My heart broke for her. Meanwhile, Cheyenne kept licking. After using my sleeve to halt my pouring nose, (I'm an ugly crier), I told her I was not sure, but I'd do some research. I did not have the heart to tell her that her little guy was probably too young to get a dog from most assistance agencies.

After several minutes Cheyenne stopped licking, and the little dynamo immediately woke up and charged off. The volunteer handed me some tissues and, still crying, announced that we needed to move on to other clinics.

Cheyenne stood up, looking like it was no big deal, and we left the clinic. We did not do any more visits that day. The volunteer and I were a mess. Cheyenne and I went home and I gave her a huge piece of watermelon for being the most amazing dog I've ever had.

That was the day I learned to trust Cheyenne's ability to handle new or unusual hospital visit situations. From her perspective there are no awkward or uncomfortable moments.

Some months later, the canine volunteer teams received an email saying an elderly man who was very ill really wanted dogs to come visit. The first time we visited, I was working with another canine therapy team. We arrived on the floor and asked about the gentleman who had requested a dog visit. We were told we could try, but he probably wouldn't want to be visited as he was very grumpy and just didn't feel well.

The other team visited him first. My friend introduced herself and her dog and picked up her dog for the man to pet. He looked at the beautifully groomed Sheltie and grunted. My friend waited a second and then put her dog down.

A few minutes later, Cheyenne and I slowly entered the room. While she is enthusiastic about most aspects of hospital visits, Cheyenne *hates* visiting people in hospital beds so she was not happy when we walked into the room.

The man was lying on his side with his face resting on his hand and his eyes closed. I introduced myself and Cheyenne, but he did not acknowledge us. I told Cheyenne to say "Hi" expecting her usual "drive by" routine of a quick swing around toward the door. Instead, she walked to the bed, put her head in the man's free hand, and gently licked his face.

Everyone knows therapy dogs are not allowed to lick. Cheyenne is primarily a service dog, an anxiety alert service dog, and she will lick if someone has high choline levels due to stress. Why had Cheyenne laid her head in this man's hand and then licked his face?

Slowly he opened his eyes and looked at her. She planted a huge, slobbery kiss on him and kind of snuggled into his hand.

He said, "Hi, aren't you a sweet one."

He talked to her for about two minutes before he asked me what her name was, how old she was, and the other usual questions.

I said, "You seem to have a gift for dogs. She does not just walk up and love all over someone. She's always polite, but seldom overtly loving."

Then he told me he had trained field dogs for most of his life. He told me dogs always loved him because he loved them. He said he had had many national champions over the years. He had trained water dogs, labs, and just about any breed that did field work.

I asked him if he had a dog at home and he said he'd been sick, and in and out of the hospital for so long he had had to give his last dog away. I was close to tears. Just the thought of having to give one of my dogs away broke my heart.

He said, "I just want to die."

I said, "I imagine your family would miss you."

He replied, "Don't have any family left."

There is a reason I'm not a counselor. I did not know what to say.

Finally I said, "I imagine heaven's full of dogs waiting for you to get there."

He said, "Yeah, and it's not happening fast enough."

He asked me to pray with him that God would hurry up and take him, and I did.

Cheyenne and I visited the man two more times. On the last visit Cheyenne was standing bedside with her head in his hand when suddenly she started trying to climb into bed with him. He was so fragile and weak, I thought she'd crush him. She was pulling against the lead to get on his bed when the alarms went off.

I looked up to see the flat line on his cardiac monitor. The man had died. Stunned, I uttered a swear word, and then the nurses were rushing us out of the room. We waited at the door with Cheyenne straining to get back inside.

The physician arrived, stayed in the room for what seemed like two seconds, and then left.

The nurses came out and said, "He has passed, but go on in and let Cheyenne say goodbye."

We entered the room and I lowered the bed so Cheyenne could climb up. She lay down by her friend's side with her head on his chest for about five minutes. Then she got down by herself.

Witnessing Cheyenne give her poignant goodbye filled me with emotion. In a quiet and very private way she said farewell to a man who had *always* loved dogs.

Karen Blackwell
The Colony, Texas, USA
Old West Newfoundland Club
Newfoundland Club of America
Facebook: Cheyenne Dog

Chapter 39

My Good Boy - Angus

My love for Newfs blossomed seventeen years ago with my first, Himself Angus McDubh. We acquired him as a 12-week-old puppy, and when he was 16 months old we added his half-sister to the family. Who can stop at just one Newf?

Our two Newfs were great friends and got along well, but when Angus was a bit over two years old, thinking to give him more one-on-one time, I joined members of the Newfoundland Club of New England who were training their Newfs for water work. We trained together at a lake every Saturday in July and August. Additionally, Angus and I practiced obedience, retrieving, and commands during the week on dry land at home.

I thought we were just having fun until the day our instructor informed us there would be a test at the end of August. Panic ensued. But Angus and I dutifully registered for the event and hoped for the best.

The weekend of the test was warm, windy, and rainy, as there was a hurricane off the coast. On Saturday we began with basic obedience which Angus passed easily and then on to the water. His retrieves were easy, but he ran out of time on one exercise and was hesitant on bringing the rope out to the steward. He did everything else effortlessly.

On Sunday morning it was still stormy when Angus and I headed out once more for the completion of the test. On the way to the obedience ring he seemed upset and had some loose bowels. Then at his first command to sit he hesitated and stared at me. I persisted and he finally sat, but he was looking at me in a quizzical way.

Next we moved around the ring and, at a prescribed spot, he was required to sit again and then return to me. Once more he hesitated just a bit, but sat properly. A spectator later told me she almost laughed because Angus gave me such a glare.

Finally it was time to go back to the water for the completion of the test. Retrieves ... good. Line to handler ... fast and perfect. Pulling a boat ... born to it!

As we entered the water for next part of the test I was overjoyed because I realized it was the final exercise. When we completed this exercise, Angus would have his Water Dog title.

For the final exercise the dog and his handler must wade into the water, swim out into the lake together until the judge signals them to turn around, then swim back. On the return, the handler is to gently grasp the dog's hips and float beside him as he pulls her back to shore. It was as I entered the water that I failed my Angus. Realizing he had passed all the other exercises, I was so excited I joyfully dove into the water and splashed out into the lake without waiting for Angus to reach my side and swim out into the lake with me.

When he saw me splashing out into the lake Angus immediately determined I was drowning. His instinct to "save mom" kicked in and he valiantly swam after me, trying with all his might to grab my life jacket and save my life. He was actually doing what he was born to do. But that was not the rule here.

His gallant effort was rewarded with a mournful wail of the judge's whistle. Failed! Ah, well. The judges praised him for his steady, mature work attitude, and said that at two years old he worked like an "old soul." I have always treasured those words. They still bring tears to my eyes. And I have always treasured a comment on his score sheet, "He wants to be a good boy."

With our participation in the test over, we relaxed and cheered for our friends the rest of the day. Once home, when drying Angus I saw a hot spot on his flank, then further inspection showed another on the opposite flank. No wonder he hadn't wanted to sit. The hot spots were raw, oozing, bleeding wounds in the creases of his haunches. I trimmed his fur and treated the hot spots the best I could.

Early the next morning the vet shaved two huge swaths on his sides to let the air get at his wounds. He also determined both Angus' ears and eyes were inflamed with yeast and bacteria, likely from the pond where the trials were held.

I took our bagful of medicines and headed home with Angus resting in the back of the Wrangler. I cried all the way home. In spite of all his pain and misery he was stoic and never let on he was hurting. He performed all his water duties like the good dog he was trying so hard to be.

Because his wounds were still healing we never entered the next water test a couple of weeks later. Sadly, two months after that, my good boy died of bloat, a condition in which the stomach fills with gas, then twists, blocking blood from returning to the heart. He was two years and eight months old.

Again, he was so stoic, he never showed any signs he was in discomfort. I know now this instinct to hide pain or weakness is common in animals. Weakness indicates vulnerability and, in the wild, being vulnerable is dangerous.

Unfortunately, our pets retain this instinct. Like their ancestors, they do their utmost to hide pain. When it comes to suffering in silence, Newfies are superstars. Their signs of distress are subtle and can include behavioral changes such as restless pacing, excessive drooling, heavy panting, loose bowels, and attempts at vomiting. Being aware of these signs and this characteristic to hide pain could save a life.

Angus was the dog of my dreams and I see him in my mind's eye to this day. He never complained, never cried. He did his job as he was asked. His spirit, his loyalty, his courage touched my heart. Angus was my good boy.

Anne Atherley
New Salem, Massachusetts, USA
Newfoundland Club of New England

Chapter 40

Tourist Attractions - Duchess, Jackson Brown & Maggie Mae

What do people who visit Newfoundland expect to see? What do they need to see in order to make their holiday complete? Big, beautiful, friendly Newfoundland dogs? Yes! Big, beautiful, friendly Newfoundland dogs. Our dogs!

In 2006 I picked up my first Newfoundland. I had dreamed of owning one all my life. Sandy didn't grow into a giant, but her heart was massive and we were quite happy with our little girl. It was Sandy's father who made me want a brown Newf. He was the most handsome Newfoundland I had ever seen. My next Newf had to be a "brown."

I got on a waiting list. Three years passed. Then, well, an urgent matter arouse, I drove two hours through a snow storm, picked up a black Newf puppy, returned home, and presented her to a surprised hubby. We already had Sandy, two older rescue dogs, and three cats. Wayne was not ready for another Newfoundland.

But I told him, "Here's your Newfoundland. You can name her."

When he whispered, "Duchess," I knew he was in love.

Shortly after Duchess arrived and stole our hearts, I got the call. *The call.* A brown Newf was available. But our house was full. I had to turn it down. I was heartbroken.

Three more years flew by. We still had all the dogs and cats. But when the second call came, and the pictures of the brown puppy began arriving, there was no turning back. Jackson Brown had to be mine!

A bit later, sweet, funny Maggie Mae made her way into our hearts. In so many ways she reminds us of our dear, little Sandy. Black like Sandy, Maggie Mae always approaches us with a smile, wagging her tail, and swaying those amazing Newfy-girl hips.

We didn't exactly plan it this way, but for the past several years our gang of three has been in the business of making tourists happy. Eight-year-old Jackson is the star, as he is brown and rare to see, but our eleven-year-old Duchess and our five-year-old Maggie Mae are strong supporting actors in the attempt to provide an authentic Newfoundland/Canadian experience for visitors.

Our Newfs have greeted cruise ships, accepted cuddles at Niagara Falls, provided welcoming wags at festivals, participated in photo shoots for rally races, given hugs in front of the Parliament building, nuzzled people on our local wharf, and generally, conducted themselves as the ambassadors they were born to be. However, their big chance to shine came last September when the Newfoundland and Labrador Tourism Board decided to introduce our beautiful Burin Peninsula to the rest of the world.

I love showing off my dogs, so when auditions for a tourism video were held, I attended. The day was too hot and the lines were too long to take the dogs, but I told the casting director I had three beautiful Newfoundlands. A few days later the producers called and asked to meet my dogs.

The production crew loved the dogs and liked the idea that, all I had to do, was open the door and the dogs would run across the back yard to the beach. The director wanted a shot of the dogs jumping off our wharf. I explained I never allow them to do that, so I wasn't surprised when they politely refused to jump for him.

A couple of days later, we took the dogs to the town wharf where part of the shoot was staged. Somehow, the dogs pushed the van side-door open and all three gentle giants began running everywhere, happy to see everyone who had come to watch the shoot. I had to tell people to stay away from the edge of the wharf, as they could easily be knocked over. With help, I finally got the dogs rounded up and into the boat to take them to the wharf where the crew wanted to video them jumping into the bay.

Again, the dogs refused to jump. Even with Wayne in the water begging them to jump, freezing to death in his wet suit, they cheerfully remained on the wharf. The crew tried enticing them into the water with a drone, and although the dogs watched the drone with interest, they would not jump. Finally the crew gave up on the "Newf jumping into the water" idea, and came back to our house. This is where one of the producers had wanted to do the video, in the first place.

The video crew set up on the side of a hill to catch the dogs running to the beach, and I opened the back door. On the first take, while Jackson and Duchess raced down to the beach and splashed into the water, Maggie Mae had to go and say "hi" to the crew. So they had to do another take. Then another, another, another. Adding to the excitement, our friend's little girl, who was participating in other parts of the video, was invited to join this part, as well.

The crew was patient, but getting the dogs back from the beach is never easy. I had to set up the van and yell, "Ride in the van!" to get them to return to the starting point. I would dry them with towels, then Wayne would yell from the beach, "Come see Dad!" and back they would race to the water. The dogs were having so much fun playing this new game we couldn't get impatient with them. We just had to laugh.

Finally the crew had what they needed and our Newfs' magnificent six seconds of fame can now be viewed on a delightful YouTube video (a tangled tale, tv ad, Newfoundland and Labrador). A few weeks later our dogs continued flirting with fame when a photo of Jackson and Duchess appeared in a historical Internet article, "The Shipwrecks of Newfoundland and Labrador." Attention seems to come easily to Newfs in Newfoundland.

My dream of owning a Newfoundland has come true in gleaming black and brown. Since 2006 our house has been home to one or more Newfoundlands.

My dogs and I have lived many stories of laughter, many stories of sadness, and many stories of all the stuff that comes in between. My wish is that our house will always be home to a Newfoundland. Or two. Or three.

Bonnie & Wayne Intveld
Garnish, Newfoundland, Canada
Canadian Kennel Club

Chapter 41

To Yogi with Love - Yogi

He was the most beautiful puppy I had ever seen—a gorgeous bundle of black fluff with a little pink tongue and a white spot in the middle of his chest. We named him Yogi. He was so little, so sweet, and he was ours. I still remember him trying to walk away with one of our fingers, as if it were a new toy he had discovered. Yogi was an exceptionally easy pup to raise. He understood everything asked of him.

We lived across from a park with a creek running through it—some parts were deep enough for a swim. I introduced Yogi to the water as a wee pup and he loved it. We walked along the creek every day and I let him wade on warmer days.

Our walks would be cut short if Yogi found a stick that met his idea of "perfect," about an inch in circumference and 18 to 24 inches long. He could not pass up a stick of that size. He became obsessed, a "man on a mission." He would pick up the stick, look at us with an air of accomplishment, turn around, and head for home. "I've found my treasure. We can go home now." Over time his stick pile in our back yard grew into a thing of beauty.

Yogi was a wonderful Newfoundland ambassador. Since he was our first and only Newf we took him with us everywhere. Whether we were attempting to cross a hotel lobby in a city or ski down a hill in the countryside, we could not walk five feet without someone stopping us to meet Yogi. With a tail wag and a kiss from the flicker of his tongue, he was always happy to accommodate his many fans.

We were astonished by how tender and mother-like Yogi was toward other animals. From tiny beings like moles to larger ones like his miniature horse friend, Pokey, Yogi was consistently gentle. He had a truly magnificent temperament.

Throughout his life, Yogi suffered different maladies—hip dysplasia (and two Triple Pelvic Osteotomy surgeries in an effort to improve his hip function), allergies, and a cruciate tear. Always a good boy, he took all the medical procedures in stride. However, when Yogi started limping in the early spring of 1998 I felt the warm lump on his leg and I knew—bone cancer. He was only five years old.

I still remember the Saturday morning I stumbled upon the article in the paper about a place where people could attend camp with their dogs and participate in all sorts of activities—Dog Scout Camp in Gregory, Michigan. I knew I just *had* to take Yogi!

I called to inquire about the camp and reached Lonnie Olson—Director/Founder of Dog Scouts of America. She listened to my story about Yogi. I asked if we could attend a couple days of camp since we didn't have funds for an entire week because of the expense of Yogi's illness. Lonnie immediately deemed him a deserving recipient of a Dog Scout scholarship and offered it to us. I was elated! What better gift could I give this dog than to spend a week entirely with him with a lake right at our doorstep?

We checked in at the camp and Yogi was in Heaven. There were so many dogs to meet and friends to make. We didn't participate in many activities because of his leg, but we learned so much and enjoyed this time together. Yogi swam every day, several times a day. I was there for the whole week and Rick joined us for a three-day weekend. It could not have been more perfect.

Dog Scout Camp was organized with a series of progressive daily activities geared toward dogs earning merit badges—like Boy Scouts. Yogi earned his Canine Good Citizen certificate, his Therapy Dog title, and became a Dog Scout. But, the badge that meant the most to us was the Water Rescue badge. He worked for this badge and, with only one day of training, he earned it. Like Newfoundlands before him, the requirements for the Water Rescue badge came instinctively. Although this wasn't a Newfoundland Club of America sponsored event, Yogi accomplished all the same Water Rescue tasks required by the NCA.

In the Dog Scout Scoop newsletter, Sept - Nov 1998, Lonnie Olson, DSA Director wrote about Yogi:

> *"... He didn't try out for too many merit badges, as Donna did not want to stress him too much, but after several days of "just watching" the water rescue training classes, she decided that maybe he would be inclined to try to learn the things necessary to earn the Water Rescue merit badge. Needless to say, Yogi was a natural. All of his New-*

fie instincts came out, and with very little effort, Donna had him doing everything.

He was so remarkable. He did it with purpose. He did it as if he wrote the rules himself. And, indeed the Water Rescue Titles and training were developed by fanciers of the Newfs who wanted a test to recognize the natural life-saving instincts and water skills of this marvelous breed. Yogi made it look easy. Without any previous training, he completed the requirement in only one day of practice. I wish you could have seen the look on his face. It said, "Just doin' my job, Ma'am."

In April, 1998, we were told we'd only have Yogi for four months. But the winter came and went—he loved snow. Spring came and his tumor started to enlarge, but he was still happy. But by summer, life was becoming harder for him.

Then one day in July, my birthday, Yogi had the look that said, "I've had enough. Please let me go now."

We knew what had to be done. Yogi died in our arms, on our bed, and in his home. Yogi gave love and was always surrounded by love. After the doctors left, we went to church to say a prayer for Yogi's safe journey "home."

My beloved Yogi, Sandy Cove Bear Trax, CGC, TDI, DSA, March 8, 1993 - July 27, 1999. Your spirit is ever present in our hearts.

You will surely be a shining light in Heaven as you were an angel on earth. Your eyes always revealed a very old soul filled with great wisdom and understanding. Yogi, you were my Heaven. Until we can be together again, my precious Yogi ...

Donna Mazzenga
Lake Orion, Michigan, USA
Penn-Ohio Newfoundland Club

Chapter 42

The Nature of Norman - Norman

In the hot summer of 2017, several separate wildfires were sweeping through British Columbia, consuming everything in their path and creating chaos and confusion throughout our province. Early in July, a mandatory evacuation of two neighboring communities was declared. Our son and two of our friends, along with their three cats and a Basset Hound, evacuated to our farm, believing it to be a safe haven.

As the days passed and the danger increased, our animal population continued to grow. In addition to our own animals—Newfies Norman and Sadie, two house cats, and 38 horses—we were taking in other animals in need, including two miniature goats and three chinchillas.

By mid-July we knew it was time to evacuate the animals. With the help of kind strangers who were volunteering, we loaded the horses and goats into trucks and trailers and moved them to safer ground. The next day we evacuated with our two Newfies, two cats, three chinchillas, and two miniature horse stallions. This evacuation involved a 13-hour trip with the highways backed up, and included a ferry crossing.

These were terrifying times and most of the animals were traumatized. Yet Norman and Sadie seemed to regard the whole event as a great adventure. As far as they were concerned, the humans were organizing a giant camping trip and they were delighted to be a part of it.

After ten days, with two of the fires under control, we were able to return to our home with the Newfies, the cats, and the chinchillas. However, just a few days after we had travelled to pick up the miniature horse stallions, one of the larger fires, which had been many kilometers away, changed directions and headed our way. The sky was red, smoke and ash filled the air. A mandatory evacuation was ordered for our area, and, once more, we evacuated with the Newfies, the cats, the chinchillas, and the stallions.

It was during these trying, stressful days that I noticed an unusual behavior in the Newfies. They had always felt it their duty, and probably also their pleasure, to bark at and chase away the ravens who flew in to annoy the other animals and steal their food. Yet, for days, ravens had been arriving through the smoke-filled air with feathers fluffed and beaks open, gasping for air. Many of them looked like they had been close to the fires and were seeking safety. They were in rough shape. Although Norman and Sadie were aware of the growing crowd of distressed ravens, they did not attempt to disturb them in any way.

As we prepared to evacuate for the second time, I filled the horse troughs and extra pans with water for the ravens. We were just about to get Sadie and Norman settled into their travel compartment, the roomy tack section in the nose of the horse trailer, when Norman sat right down and wouldn't budge. He turned his head towards the gasping ravens and let out a low woof. Both Newfs gave me baleful looks. Did they think I should put food out for the ravens?

I had stocked up on large bags of dog kibble before we were in danger of fires. I was fortunate to be able to help out others in need of dog food when stores were not accessible, and I had kept back several bags for our own Newfs.

With Norman refusing to get into the travel compartment and Sadie giving me woeful looks, I ran to the barn and lugged out a 16-kilogram bag of dog kibble. I placed it on its side and ripped it open lengthwise. The pans of water were nearby.

Norman stood up, satisfied, and he and Sadie were then happy to get into the travel compartment with bones to chew on. Once we dropped the two mini-stallions off at their temporary home and settled into our own temporary home, we cleaned out the horse trailer and moved Sadie and Norman into the bigger space. This became their hotel room and they enjoyed it.

At last, 13 days later, the fires had been controlled and we were able to return to our home. The water in the horse troughs was low, the pans of water I had filled were empty, and all the kibble I had left out for the ravens was gone. We still had a couple of ravens hanging out, but they seemed subdued and didn't cause any issues.

We sadly lost Sadie in 2019 and now, at 8½-years-old, Norman spends most of his time chewing bones. When he goes outside, he likes to take his bone with him. Always, in the past, he would bring it back inside when he returned. Then one day he didn't bring his bone back in. When I checked outside, I couldn't find it. He began losing his bones more and more frequently, and I worried he was getting senile. Where was he misplacing his bones?

Recently, when feeding the horses, I started spotting Norman's bones out in the fenced paddock with Lucky, one of the mini-stallions. Often a raven was pecking at the bones. Norman could not get into this secure area. How were his bones getting into Lucky's paddock? This was puzzling.

Then I saw Norman with his fresh bone on the porch. Two ravens were on the porch with him. He seemed to be sharing his bone!

What can I say about Norman? He is very sensitive and sweet, and not too much of a guard dog. The ravens picked at his bone and he allowed them to do so. When I looked out a bit later, his bone was gone.

Norman is generous, and the ravens take advantage of him. On the other hand, by allowing the ravens to share his bones and carry them to other parts of the farm, he keeps them from bothering the other animals. In his golden years, Norman has discovered an effective but easygoing way of fulfilling his guard duty. And, yes, Norman gets a fresh bone in the house after he comes back inside after sharing.

Joanne Seabloom
Lone Butte, British Columbia, Canada
www.seabloom.ca

Chapter 43

Run Free, My Rudy, Run Free - Rudy

On a cold December morning I headed to South Dakota, not knowing that the Newfoundland puppy I was about to meet would become my universe. But the moment I walked in and saw Rudy sitting on the kitchen floor, I started to cry. I sat down beside him and held him close. Our connection was electrical. I had sent a blanket with my smells to the breeder so Rudy knew my scent. He was the perfect puppy. I couldn't believe he was my baby.

Rudy was born October 14, 2014, and waiting ten weeks to pick him up had seemed like an eternity. But I wanted all the testing done to ensure he was a healthy boy. With the exception of one quick break on the five-hour trip back to Minnesota, Rudy did not leave my arms. I held him and enjoyed smelling his fur and his puppy breath. He lay in my arms feeling my heart beat. On that trip home we became one.

Rudy was a fast learner. During the next two years he went from puppy kindergarten to Certified Canine Good Citizen to

Certified Therapy Dog. He loved people. He especially loved old people and anyone who was in crisis. He understood what people felt and his desire to make people happy was uncanny.

On our first visit to a nursing home people kept smiling and I kept hearing, "He's a real dog!" He would sit by the residences' wheelchairs or beds and wait until they were calm and relaxed.

Once, when I was talking to a resident, a lady in a wheelchair nearby said, "I wish he would come closer. I want a kiss from him."

Rudy stood up, walked to the lady, and put his head on her lap. He knew kisses weren't allowed, but he remained beside her until she was ready to move on.

Rudy and I often walked near a townhome complex for older people. If we encountered a resident, Rudy would stop and sit next to them. They would pet him and always say, "What a good boy." They would comment on what a smart and beautiful boy he was. He brought happiness to everyone he met. One elderly gentleman told me he had once seen Rudy turn suddenly and almost tip me over. He said that memory still made him laugh "to this day." Then he thanked me for bring Rudy into his life.

Rudy did have his goofy side. He developed a special interest in the geese that sometimes paddled around in a pond near our home. On one early morning walk we saw a huge flock of geese in the field near the pond. I made the mistake of letting Rudy off leash to investigate. There followed an exciting few minutes with Rudy running in all directions and geese noisily skittering and scrambling. From then on, if Rudy heard a goose and was off leash he headed straight to the pond to dive in and gleefully splash toward his feathered friends. Unfortunately, the pond was murky and stinky so I would have to hose Rudy off after these encounters. But I had triggered this behavior so I had to pay. Anyway, to Rudy the hosing off was just part of the fun.

Life throws so many challenges, and many of my challenges came during the first two years Rudy was with me. This involved moving from our home, where he had a big yard and a dog door he could use whenever he wanted, to a townhome with a small patio. When things got more complicated we had to relocate to a less desirable townhome. This second rental was not ideal, but it gave us a place to live while I looked for something more suitable.

Rudy adjusted to these ongoing disruptions faster than I did. I would arrive home from work and he would greet me with his happy smile and his eyes filled with love. He would not let me into the house until I stopped and hugged him. All the bad energy of the day would be dismissed and I would feel at peace.

Throughout this confusing time my days were difficult, but my nights were worse. My restless sleep was often interrupted by nightmares and terrors. Rudy would jump on the bed, gently paw my arm and lick my face. Once I had awakened he would put his head on my chest and I would fall sound asleep.

While we were living at the townhome, Rudy learned that chemical smells gave me migraine headaches. He could smell the chemicals before I could and would try to pull me away from certain areas. I first could not figure out why he was doing this. I thought he was just being a stubborn boy who did not want to go where I wanted him to go. When I finally inquired at the rental office, I discovered they periodically sprayed for ants on the exterior of the building. After I explained the problem they began notifying me before doing anything involving chemicals. Who knew this dog would attempt to keep me out of harm's way? He was not being willful. He was keeping me safe.

My Rudy, my Briarwoods Black Magic, developed cancer and passed away in August, 2019. He went to sleep before his fifth birthday, only four months after we got settled into the home I bought for the two of us. I am heartbroken and sad, but forever grateful to have known him. He provided love and support for many people during his lifetime, but most of all he provided love and support for me when I needed it most. He knew me inside out. He took me through trying times and kept me strong and focused. He helped me believe and move on. A few days ago I picked up the urn a friend made for him. Rudy will always be missed and loved, but I know he is watching over me. Run free, Rudy, the geese are waiting and the pond is calling. Run, my sweet boy, you are free.

Judy Brueghel
White Bear Lake, Minnesota, USA
Northstar Newfoundland Club and Rescue

Photos

Luke & Gracie-Alaska Luke

Cassie & Ashana-Alaskan - Life Savers

Boulder-Boulder Bear - Promoter Extraordinaire

Gummy Bear - Contagious Love

River - An Indoor Pool & Bank Job

Jeter - Jeter's Journey

Sage - Learning to Live for the Moment

Pirate - A Life in the Limelight

Lulu - Living & Laughing With Lulu

Taylor & Splash-Miss Mild Meets Miss Mayhem

Mojo - My Heart & Soul

Nalle - A Swedish Teddy Bear

Mamut - Mamut's Camping Capers

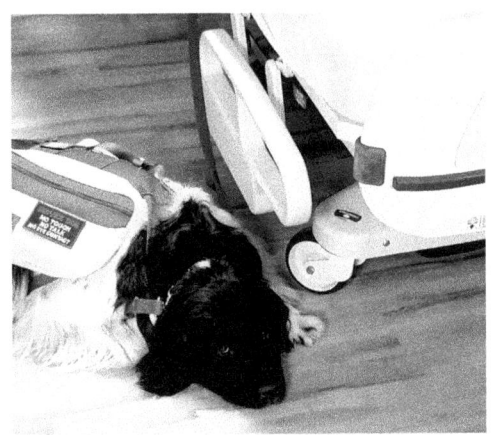

Halo - Trust - In the Midst of Chaos

Kevin, River, & Malcom - An Indoor Pool & A Bank Job

Chapter 44

Wild At Heart - Lily

We always looked forward to our annual Newfy club get-together. People from all over the state, along with their Newfoundland dogs, headed out to Camp Concordia, a summer camp near Grand Rapids, Michigan. We enjoyed getting reacquainted with friends and dogs we only saw once a year, and meeting new Newfoundland dog owners and dogs for the first time. Even folks from other Newf clubs would come. The event provided a good time for all.

Camp Concordia was a sizable camp with four large shelters and several smaller ones. The shelters were very basic—concrete floors, screens for windows and doors, and bunk beds. If you needed the washrooms at night, you had better take your flashlight. It was common to see people in the evening or the wee hours of the morning with their dogs, flashlights, and baggies.

One year we brought our two Newfs, Lily and Noah, to the get-together. Noah was a very large Newf, while Lily was small, but powerful—like a Mack truck, born for the toughest conditions and long haul challenges. Our nickname for her was "Little."

We spent the days either down by the beach, walking through the woods, or gathering at the pavilion for breakfasts of pancakes and sausage or, at noon time, delectable potluck lunches. Wandering around the camp was the perfect way to spend a hot, summer day. It was the best of times.

The annual get-together was not a typical draft or water rescue themed occasion. Instead, it was a weekend of games and educational events focused on our Newfoundland dogs. All the games were lighthearted, such as best kisser and best trick. The educational events included activities like grooming and training.

Camp Concordia had a large, lovely, shimmering lake. It was always calm and still, placid and glassy. Our club had held many water training events there and the lake held many good memories for us. But this casual weekend offered one water event I had never participated in before—a canoe race. Participants had to board a canoe with their Newf and attempt to be the first to reach a designated point in the lake. That had to be fun! I signed up for the challenge.

There was no question which of our Newfs I would choose for the ride along. It had to be Lily. She was small and compact. She weighed less than Noah. Besides, she loved the water more than life itself. There was no doubt. I was sure she would be a great passenger. A close friend decided to join us. Race time came and we climbed into the canoe. I was at one end, Chuck at the other, Lily in the middle.

We pushed off and Lily was delighted with all the water surrounding the little boat. She had never been in a canoe before. Chuck and I got our rhythm rowing. Lily sat like a little soldier taking in the sights and smells of the lake. We were off, making good time, and all was well.

However, it wasn't long before the lake started calling Lily, calling her name. The water was all around her, so close she could almost touch it with her muzzle. For a dog who loved water and loved swimming, this was just *too much temptation!* When she could no longer resist, she leaned over, way over. Then, as the canoe tipped upside down, into the water she glided. And into the water Chuck and I glided with her—wearing pants, shirts, shoes, and ultra stunned faces.

The canoe bobbled a little, then remained upside down. It seemed like it happened in slow motion, but there we were in the water, all three of us.

Chuck and I got our bearings. He held onto the canoe and I held onto the canoe and onto Lily's leash. Without hesitation, even though she had never had any water rescue training, Lily accepted her role in the situation. She pulled us! She swam and pulled us!

This little Newf swam toward shore with two fully-dressed, grown men and a canoe in tow. Miss Mighty Mite, little but fierce Lily, swam with all her strength, dragging her heavy load.

There were many people at the shore who groaned when the canoe tipped. Then people realized what was happening and suddenly started cheering Lily on. With enthusiastic well-wishers calling, "Come on Girl, you can do it! Come on Lily!" this determined Newf swam directly toward shore with strength and grace only a Newfoundland dog has. She did what she was bred to do—SWIM!

Lily swam her heart out and delivered to shore two very wet men and an overturned canoe. She swam because she loved it, she swam because it was an instinct deep within her.

Lily was our hero. That evening at dinner we won a little award for the most adventurous Newf. Lily truly deserved it. She had given us an adventure we would never forget.

Lily was aptly named—Moonfleet's Water Lily. Some years later in March, on a warm winter day, we happened to be out on a trail along a river valley. I took Lily down to that river and Lily did what Lily always did—she went in and had a fine swim. After the swim we received a message that her brother, Archie, had just passed away from a highly aggressive cancer.

Archie was a Landseer. As we headed back to the car, a white butterfly started following us—Archie. Three days later, we lost Lily to the same disease that took her brother. We lost her suddenly and without warning. She was almost 12 years old. With her death so soon after Archie's, whenever I see a white butterfly I imagine it's Lily saying "Hello" and looking in on us.

Lily lived life to the fullest. She enjoyed every day and had a wild spirit and joy about her. Beating inside her was the amazing heart of a Newf—a Newf born to swim.

Rick Mazzenga
Lake Orion, Michigan, USA

Chapter 45

The Nutburger - Lexi-Bear

Hi Peoples! It's me, Lexi-Bear. Oh mine goodness, Peoples, you're never going to believe another perfect day just happens to me ... let me tell Peoples. Mine day started off really good. Parents made us children scrambled eggs and toasts deliciousness for breakfast. Oh, we had happy tummies this morning.

Mr. Mom (whose real name is Shadow) decided him needed a nap after breakfast. Sister (whose real name is Kokoa, but I call her Big Bottoms Diva-Pants) decided to walk up to Daddy, swat him with her fancy polka-dots paw, tilt her head, and look up at him batting her eyes. Sister always does this as soon as her is done eating, 'cause her wants dessert. Daddy thinks this is sumfing adorable, but I thinks this is exactly why that Big Bottoms Diva-Pants has such a BIG bottoms.

Since Sister is hogging mine daddy, I go outside so I don't have to watch this injustices. When I getted outside in fresh air, I realize I has to have a potty break. I sniff all around searching for perfect spot. Just when I find exact spot, I feel hairs on back of mine neck tingles. I get spooky feelings like sumfing is watching me. I look all around, but parents, Mr. Mom, and Sister is all inside. Then I see it! Oh mine goodness, Peoples! It was naughty Gnome! Him just sitting there wanting a peek at mine bottoms! Oh, that rascal didn't trick me! Him can just sit right there. I found new perfect spot for potty break ... spot with sumfing called privacies.

Since today is Saturday, parents has day off with us children. Because today is hot outside, parents decided to hang out in pool. Oh, this makes me very happy. I love hanging out in pool. Mr. Mom and Big Bottoms Diva-Pants don't like to be outside when it's hot, so this means I get parents all to mineself.

As soon as parents get into pool, I zoom right in, too. Momma grabs my purple, which is sumfing that floats, looks like a donut deliciousness, but doesn't has a hole in middle. Parents take turns tossing mine purple into deep ends of pool. I is not scared one bit! I zoom through waters, grab that purple, and save it, over and over. I is an excellent Lifeguard ... much better than that fake Pam Sumfing who I see pretending to be lifeguard on mine TV.

Pretty soon I need a nap, too. I go inside and snuggle with Mr. Mom and mine stuffed horsey. Sister NEVER lets me snuggle her. If I try, Sister says, "Get away from me, Bratty-Bear!" Mr. Mom loves me though, and him always lets me snuggle up with him. I'm pretty sure he loves me most, but shh! That's our secrets. Don't tell nobody I sayed that.

After mine nap, I waked up with rumbly belly. Parents must be getting rumbly bellies too, 'cause them decide to start making suppers. Oh, we love suppers time! Mr. Mom wakes up, stretches, and comes into kitchen. Sister is watching every move parents is making, and I'm running around in a tizzy trying to hurry parents up before I starve to mine death! I don't have a big bottoms like Sister does. I is so skinny, sometimes Peoples thinks I is a boy 'cause I got no curves.

Yes! Finally! Suppers is served! Just in nick of time. Oh, we gobble our suppers up real quick. Do you know what happens as soon as we swallow last bite of suppers? Sister Big Bottoms Diva-Pants starts her shenanigans with her polka-dots paw again, asking mine daddy for dessert deliciousness. We all getted a vanilla cookie, so I forgetted to be mad at Sister.

Now we is all inside for night. Parents is watching sumfing on TV (not fake Pam Sumfing either). Mr. Mom is having his pre-bedtime nap. Sister is hogging all parents' attentions, and I is just sitting here watching her hogging mine parents' attentions, so I begin plotting a mischiefs.

At bedtime everyone goes in bedroom. Mr. Mom always sleeps in same place on floor on Daddy's side of bed. Sister always sleeps in her bed on Momma's side of bed. I don't do nuffing the same. Sometimes I sleeps in middle of parents, sometimes I sleeps on couch, sometimes I even sleeps in front of shower.

Well, tonight I is sumfing Daddy likes to call "jealous Nut" 'cause I is jealous of Sister. When I get mad, I turn into sumfing parents call "Nutburger." Well, tonight Nutburger did a cannonballs into middle of parents' bed and scared hecks out of them. When I seed parents' shocked faces, I giggled, then I snuggled right into middle between them.

Now I finally has parents' undivided attentions. I thinking I should be a Nutburger more often. Cannonballs into middle of parents' bed makes perfect end to perfect day.

I hope Peoples has a good night and sweet dreams.

Love,
Lexi-Bear, the sometimes Nutburger
Lexi-Bear LaVine & Jennifer Jill LaVine
Maricopa, Arizona, (hot desert), USA
Facebook: Lexi-Bear

Chapter 46

Our Penny from Heaven - Penny

Penobscot Bay-B, Penny, had a rough start. All nine of her littermates were larger and stronger than she was. She had to be tube fed and bottle fed. She would have seizures. The breeder feared she might have to be put down.

But Penny was a feisty little Landseer. When she went on solid food she outgrew the seizures. She persevered and showed she was a survivor, albeit a small one.

The breeder told us she couldn't sell Penny because she didn't know how long she would live, nor did she think keeping her in the kennel was the right place for her. She asked if we would take her, free of charge, and give her a good life as long as she lived.

We were never planning to have three dogs, but how could we say no to that? Penny came home to her two Bernese Mountain Dog brothers, Mr. Cooper and Freeport. They took her under their paws and, for the next seven years, taught her all she needed to know. Theirs was a perfect love triangle.

Small, at only 80 pounds, what Penny lacks in size she more than makes up for in personality. She is a social butterfly who loves everyone she meets, especially children. We learned early on she seems to become depressed if she does not have interactions with people. Because of this, we have done our best to keep her engaged and happy. By her first birthday she had joined her brothers by becoming a registered therapy dog and a R.E.A.D. dog.

One of the many places Penny demonstrated her powerful love for people was on college campuses. When we volunteered with the Humane Society of Rochester New York, one of her favorite activities was the Stress Relief Night held each semester during finals. All three of our dogs participated in these visits, but Penny was the most animated. She did everything she could to make everyone feel special. She would sit with a group of students and roll on her back to make sure everyone got the pleasure and benefit of giving her a belly rub. She gave each group her whole attention until another group started to come over, then she'd jump up, run to them, and repeat her routine. There were times when I couldn't see her due to the number of students fondling her.

Our move to Freeport, Maine, and Larry's transfer to LLBean in 2016 was a dream come true for Penny. Within days she and her brothers became the "town dogs," making friends with the LLBean employees and the customers alike. Again, Penny was the most outgoing of the three, pushing her brothers out of the way to get the most pets and "wooo-woooing" the events of her day to all her new friends.

Sadly and unexpectedly, within a two-month period in late 2017 and early 2018, we lost both Berners to cancer. Mr. Cooper was eight, Freeport twelve. The dogs' friends were sorry, Larry and I were heartbroken, Penny was devastated.

For the next six months, Penny never left my side. Her LLBean friends knew how upset she was so they began giving her extra attention. Dogs are allowed in the Outlet Store and the Home Store and when we stopped in for our visit an employee would announce that the "princess" had arrived and people would take their breaks to come pet her. She became a special favorite of the women who work at the Home Store. They insisted on a Penny visit if they spotted her anywhere in the area and Penny responded by adopting them as "her girls."

On one of the road trips we took during this time we visited a lighthouse. Penny loved the adventure and we loved the photos we took of her there. Maine has many lighthouses, 65. That's what gave us the idea of creating Penny's first calendar. Our many subsequent trips to lighthouses for photos provided many subsequent adventures for Penny.

In September 2018 we brought home a new Berner puppy, Acadia. Although Mr. Cooper and Freeport will always live in her heart, Acadia has brought some happiness back to Penny's life. Acadia has become part of the pack for trips into town. Friday afternoons have become "Puppy Love" time where her LLBean friends come and greet both Penny and the new puppy. Penny's friendships with her favorite people have deepened. She starts talking to them when she sees them coming down the hall. The employees love Acadia, but they are always drawn to Penny because of her gentle nature and sweet disposition.

We have continued the calendar project. The 2020 calendar idea stemmed from the fact that Penny has created a home for herself in the LLBean family and touched so many of the employees with her unconditional love. The calendar was dedicated to them in return for the love and kindness they have shown her. It is titled "Penny and Acadia With Their LLBean Family." The photos depict Penny and Acadia with their friends in different LLBean venues. It was well received and now hangs proudly in the Flagship Store, the Home Store, the Outlet Store, and the Bike, Boat, and Ski Store.

Penny may never do anything heroic in her life that would make headlines, but if the world has become a better place because of her, she will always be a hero in my eyes. I believe she ended up with us so she could touch as many lives as she can for as long as she can. She is nine years old now and we will continue fulfilling the breeder's request to give her a good life for as long as she lives. Our Penny girl. Our Penny from Heaven.

Larry & Regina Helfer
Freeport, Maine, USA

Chapter 47

Learning to Live for the Moment - Sage

Sage was always a foodie, so on the morning when he refused his breakfast I took notice, but I wasn't overly alarmed. We were at the Newfoundland National Specialty and the day before had been a busy and exciting one. Sage had competed and earned both his Beginner Novice Obedience and his Novice Rally titles. Additionally, he was taking antibiotics for a urinary tract infection so I assumed those medications were affecting his appetite. However, since he didn't seem to be feeling his best, I withdrew him from the two classes we had planned for the next day and we came home early.

But when Sage continued refusing his food I made an appoint with our vet. Dr. Joe found that Sage's liver enzymes were over the roof and his ultrasound looked suspicious. He felt we should seek help at the Ohio State University Veterinary Center.

On May 25, 2018, Sage was diagnosed with Hepatic Cellular Carcinoma (HCC). He was only four years old and the vets at

Ohio State said there was absolutely no treatment available because the disease was affecting all his liver cells, not just a part of the liver. They rarely see this in young dogs. Typically, only old dogs present with HCC, and when they do, they are usually euthanized right then. The vets sent us home with enough meds to keep Sage "comfortable" for two-to-four weeks, with instructions to see our vet when he was no longer comfortable.

I called our vet on the way home, God bless you, Dr. Joe, and told him I wanted to talk about cannabidiol oil (CBD) and get his thoughts and guidance for what to do.

Dr. Joe had been researching CBD, a non-intoxicating molecule found in hemp and marijuana. He had been consulting with a veterinary neurosurgeon in Canada who was using it for pain control with her patients and seeing promising results. Also, findings from Colorado State University Veterinary Teaching Hospital were showing CBD was having various positive effects including giving pain relief, calming inflammation, and lessening the frequency and intensity of seizures in dogs with epilepsy. Given Sage's diagnosis, it seemed reasonable to give CBD a try.

Thus, the journey began. Dr. Joe prescribed four drops of CBD oil twice a day and I began keeping a detailed journal.

Sage didn't want to take the meds OSU ordered, and I didn't want to force the issue. They weren't doing anything that would "save" him. He would not eat and over the next three months we tried everything, to no avail. What Sage would nibble on one day, he refused the next. It looked like a pet store in our dining room with all kinds of gimmicks and every treat imaginable to encourage him to eat.

The *only* consistent thing Sage did was ... run. Every day we took him to Sweet Arrow Reserve, 263 acres of woodlands, prairies, and meadows only five minutes from our home. We went early in the morning and, because Sage was so good about the word "wait," he was rarely leashed. Larry and I would walk the 1.4 mile Sage Brush Prairie Trail while Sage ran and ran and ran.

I asked all our friends on Facebook to please pray for Sage. They responded with love, support and prayers, cards and gifts. Their encouragement helped so much. Every Friday when I would report Sage's condition I'd say, "Well, that's one more week past the expiration date given at OSU."

I couldn't fault the expiration date OSU gave. Given the results of the tests he had had, along with his depressed appearance, it didn't seem possible Sage would live longer than the two-to-four weeks they had predicted.

Yet the days kept passing. It seemed that as long as Sage could get out to "his" prairie, his happy place, he didn't want to leave us.

But by mid-September Sage had lost 22 pounds and was turning jaundiced. Almost four months had passed since his initial diagnosis and, although we had gradually increased the CBD oil and were up to seven drops twice a day, we were still struggling to get him to eat.

Larry and I were both thinking it was probably time to let Sage go. The toxins were affecting him and the jaundice was bad.

We took Sage to Dr. Joe, but when the tears in our eyes met the tears in his eyes he said, "We've got nothing to lose. Let's bump up the CBD oil to two milliliters twice a day (approximately 40 drops). That's still within range of what he could have for his size."

We came home and I gave Sage the oil and, because he seemed hot, I offered him refrigerated water next to his tap water. After a couple of hours he walked over to his food bowl and looked at me like, "Why is my bowl empty?"

I gave him a small amount of kibble and he gobbled it up. I gave him a little more and he gobbled it up. I thought it was a fluke, but I set up a feeding schedule and he began eating an appropriate amount of food daily and begging for more. In fact, over the next few weeks he perfected his Begging 101 and began working on his master's degree in begging.

Sage gained back the 22 pounds he had lost and the jaundice disappeared. He still enjoyed our daily outing at the Reserve, and we began doing nose work, which he loved. This is a sport created to mimic professional detection-dog tasks.

When we took him back to OSU the oncologist said, "It appears as if you got your miracle."

But we didn't want a CT scan or a liver biopsy, as that required sedation. It wouldn't make any difference what the results showed. At this point Sage was definitely not feeling like dying. His enzymes were elevated, but not off the charts like before.

For the next ten months Sage got his regular meals, his oil twice a day, and his regular and refrigerated water. We rarely left him home alone, but he did fine when we had to. We saw the seasons change, celebrated holidays and birthdays, and even took him on a vacation to a cabin at Hocking Hills State Park. We planned to go to the cabin he loved most, near Lake Superior, when the weather cooled down. But no matter where we were, Sage enjoyed hiking with us. On May 25, 2019, we celebrated a milestone. One year had passed since his diagnosis.

In July, 2019, Sage began tiring more easily at the park and was on and off his feed. In August the jaundice returned.

I had promised God and Sage I would not let him suffer or struggle, so we helped him get his wings on August 6, 2019. I had documented his journey every day on FB with a new photo or video of a run in the park. Sage had many fans and friends, and many of them were as devastated as Larry and I were when we had to let him go.

Although our hearts were shattered, we had been blessed with 14 extra fun-filled months, and Sagey-boy had taught us how to live for the day, not for tomorrow, not for yesterday. To celebrate his life we have planted a dogwood tree and placed a personalized decorative stone near the prairie trail he loved so much. Thank you, dear Sage, dear Blackbay's Simple Sage, for teaching us how to live for the moment.

Sue DeBord
Kettering, Ohio, USA

Chapter 48

Wild Child and the Lamb - Juno & Miley

Juno's posting appeared on Craigslist: *Chocolate Newfoundland, 10-month-old male, free to good home.* I cringed when my cousin told me about it. When I contacted the owner he said others had already inquired. I told him I would take Juno if nobody else would, but *only* if no one else would, because I was going through personal trials with my mother who was dying.

About a month later Juno's owner contacted me. He told me a family with two small children returned Juno after three days. Now a second family, this one with no children, wanted to returned him after three days. The owner would ask them to bring Juno to us instead.

I had had two other Newfs in the past, both females, and I thought I understood Newfs. I thought, "How bad could he be? Maybe they just couldn't handle the fact that he is big."

But as soon as the second family dropped him off, I realized why the original owner wanted Juno delivered to us. The original owner wanted *never* to have to deal with Juno again.

With good reason! Juno was a pain in the neck! He barked 24/7. When Juno wasn't barking at us he was grabbing our clothing and, as soon as we got him released from one spot, he would grab us somewhere else. He was not hurting us, it was like he was begging for attention.

He chewed anything soft: sweatshirt hoods, slippers, boot tongues, and socks were his favorites. He didn't listen at all about anything. When we tried to walk him he would lie down and chew the leash. If he did decide to walk he would drag us along behind him.

Juno weighed 115 pounds, but he felt more like 150. He was as strong as a bull. I am no lightweight, but when I would try to put Juno in timeout in my laundry room he would fight me. He always won. I was working full-time and caring for my mother, so adding an oversized, unmanageable dog to my duties left me drained and defeated.

We couldn't let Juno outside alone because our electric fence was broken and couldn't be fixed till the thaw. We had two feet of snow on the ground so my husband made a path around our two acres with the snow blower. I thought I could walk Juno around the path and tire him. All that did was exhaust me and make him muddy. I had never seen behavior like his before. This eleven-month-old Newf was totally out of control.

Juno arrived on a Thursday. Friday was a nightmare. Saturday morning I scheduled an appointment with a trainer. Saturday afternoon I contacted Newf Rescue because the situation seemed hopeless. Saturday evening, after another wrestling match which ended with me penned in the laundry room crying in frustration, I contacted the trainer again. I told her I couldn't wait until our Wednesday appointment. I told her I was taking this unruly, uncooperative, undisciplined animal to Newf Rescue Monday morning.

She said, "I'll be there tomorrow!"

The next morning Sandy, the trainer, spent two hours working with Juno, my husband, our daughter, and me. She was awesome, amazing. She worked magic. She gave us hope. She made us believe we could create order from chaos.

Sandy came back for six more one-hour sessions. She helped us understand Juno. She reminded us that dogs bark at each other, bite, and grab each other's paws to play. By barking at us and pulling on us Juno was pleading with us to play with him. Grateful for this insight, I put a good year and a half into Juno's training and by the time he was two-and-a-half he had become a confident, polite, well-behaved boy.

The success I had transforming my wild and crazy Juno into a gracious gentleman gave me the courage to rescue another Newf. Seven-year-old Miley became part of our family even more suddenly than Juno had. I inquired about Miley from a Newf Rescue site on a Tuesday and she was mine by Thursday.

The story from the woman who brought Miley for the transfer was short and exceptionally sad. She had been a neighbor of Miley's former owner. In our ten-minute meeting the woman handed me a manila folder which held the only papers that would give me a clue about Miley's life and told me Miley's former owner, a 33-year-old woman, had died after being sick for three or four months.

During these three or four months, Miley had been boarded at a kennel. The woman had simply picked her up from the kennel and brought her to me. She also told me Miley had escaped from the kennel with a handful of other dogs and wandered the streets of Philadelphia for several days before being returned. Then the woman got Miley out of her SUV, handed me the leash, got back in her van, and drove away.

Miley and I stood on the sidewalk looking at each other. It was obvious she had not been well cared for during her kennel stay. Her beautiful chocolate coat was matted. I could smell the infection oozing from her ears. But she was calm, laid back, cooperative. When invited, she jumped into my car.

Because of her ear condition, I kept Miley away from Juno at first. He was curious but I insisted he keep his distance. I created a comfy bed for Miley in the laundry room. She was happy to rest there and, ever since, has considered that her special area. Evidently, she was trained to stay put because, even after being with us for almost two years, she still often asks permission with a little bark to leave the laundry room and join us in the rest of the house.

After Miley's ears improved she and Juno were allowed to interact. They were comfortable with each other from the very beginning. Now Miley so loves Juno she rarely leaves his side. When they rest she always lies as close to him as possible, often using him as a pillow.

Miley is still in training because she tends to have selective hearing and sometimes gives the "who me?" response to commands. Juno always joins us because he loves all the positive reinforcement and the treats. When Miley gets a treat, Juno does, too. Training time is a happy time for all of us.

I'm still using the magic techniques the trainer taught me years ago. The best advice ever was to hold a treat close to my nose when giving a command. Juno learned to look at my face, look at my eyes, listen to what I said, and, thus, know what I wanted him to do.

The second technique was used to stop Juno's barking, but it should work for most unacceptable behaviors. I would say, "That's enough!" Then I would step through the closest door, close it behind me, and count to 30 before stepping back into the room. If the barking continued, I would repeat the closed door routine. If I had to close the door a third time, I didn't come out for five minutes. Juno learned very, very quickly that the one thing he wanted most, which was my attention, went away when he did something I found unacceptable. I only had to use this technique about five times. Juno was a fast learner.

The third technique had to do with treats. I kept a little pouch of mini-treats with me and rewarded Juno throughout the day for each positive behavior. Eventually the treats were replaced with delighted "good boys," loving hugs, and generous recognition.

There were other techniques, but these were the main ones that turned Juno from a dog who almost broke me, into a dog like no other I have ever loved. At ten years old, Juno has my heart.

Because of these training techniques, sweet, cooperative Miley is learning to be even sweeter and more cooperative, our little lamb. Her gentle nature simply reinforces my strong commitment to Newfoundlands. I will provide them with a loving forever-home as often as I can.

I have been fortunate to have had many dogs to love throughout my life.

From them I have learned that all dogs, as with children, become, and are, what we put in.

Janis Good
Boyertown, Pennsylvania, USA

Chapter 49

Practically Perfect - Pinkerton

Everyone loves a puppy, and what is cuter than a Newfoundland puppy? Nothing comes to mind. But our family was complete. Our Newfs, Wendell and Shadow, were adults. We had no worries of potty problems in the house, no worries about chairs getting chewed. Life was good! We were not looking for a puppy.

But then a friend called. Although she had lost her "heart dog" some years earlier, it seems his frozen semen still had the potential of producing some pretty incredible offspring. The use of the frozen semen had resulted in a litter of ten puppies. Unfortunately, one of the male puppies from that litter had a significant heart murmur and it was feared he might not have a long, healthy life. The breeder was looking for a home that would provide love to this little guy and be able to handle the potential need for constant medical attention. Our friend had suggested us.

The puppy was located 1,042 miles away. To drive 15 hours to pick up a sick puppy just didn't make a lot of sense. We called the breeder and thanked her profusely for considering us for this special task, but suggested she should consider someone closer.

This conscientious breeder continued monitoring the puppies, studying their personalities, getting each one the appropriate veterinary care, and ... exchanging phone calls with us. Finally, Mel and I talked it over. It might be good to get away for a few days. It might be good to give this puppy the home he needed, however short that time might be.

Then, to everyone's amazement, the puppy's final heart check proved he was *completely healthy*! There were no concerns about his heart. In what we thought would be our final phone conversation with the breeder, we thanked her again and told her we knew someone closer needed a healthy Landseer puppy.

While the breeder had been studying the personalities of the puppies, I suppose she had been studying our personalities, as well. The more she had learned about us, the more she was convinced we could provide the right home for this particular pup. She said we had volunteered to love and care for him when his future was questionable and, now that we knew he was completely healthy, we deserved to love and care for him still. A few days later we drove 1,042 miles through some snow and ice and met the most adorable little fellow we had ever seen!

We had bought a new crate and all the items needed for a puppy, but we were a little worried about how our new boy, now named Pinkerton, would react to leaving his first home. When we lifted him into our SUV he lay right down and was soon fast asleep. He didn't bark. He didn't cry. He was practically *perfect*! Later, at the motel he slept peacefully in his crate and he pottied on leash when we took him outside. Practically *perfect*!

Wendell and Shadow accepted Pinkerton as Newfs do with a new puppy. He loved his big brother and sister and followed them anywhere, everywhere. His eagerness to stay right behind them almost ended in disaster on one occasion.

Our couch is not set against the wall, but in the middle of our living room, providing a walkway behind it leading directly to the front door. Pinkerton had grown large enough that he could easily bound onto the furniture and the leather couch was his favorite place to land. One day Pinkerton was distracted when Wendell and Shadow hurried behind the couch to head out the front door. When Pinkerton suddenly noticed he might get left behind, he decided he could just jump over the back of the couch to join them quickly.

He was too fast! I was too late to grab him! Catastrophe was pending! Over the back of the couch he went, and *splat* onto the floor! It could have been horrible. He could have broken into several pieces. But he didn't break. He picked up his head, sputtered a bit, and looked out the door. Then he raced off after his brother and sister.

Come National Specialty time, we decided to make the trip to Michigan where we could continue to socialize our dear puppy and let the breeder see how well Pinkerton was adapting to his new life.

Again, Pinkerton traveled like a pro and got on and off elevators without any hesitation. He met every Newf at the show and accepted each and every pet and scratch from their people. We went from vendor tent to vendor tent and he fit right in.

The National has all sorts of exciting activities going on and you need to keep track of all the notices so you don't miss anything. We watched as Newfs competed in confirmation. We watched as Newfs pulled carts, danced, wore costumes, and jumped through hoops. Pinkerton took it all in stride.

Researchers were conducting a genetic study that year at the Nationals and, even though we were not going to breed Pinkerton, the researchers were happy to have us participate. All that was required was a small vial of blood from the pup.

Our Newfs have always been exceptionally casual at the vet. Ephraim, our first Newf, would actually hold out his paw for a blood draw, the tech would place the tourniquet, then Ephraim would sit quietly while a needle was inserted into his Newfy-sized vein.

Pinkerton did not react the same way. The staff obtaining blood samples was located in part of a large, open building. Part of the building was set up with grooming stations, another part was curtained off for the competition of carting and obedience. Each portion of the building was quite usable and fairly well contained. But noises could easily be heard from one area to another if they were loud enough.

And Pinkerton's noises were loud enough! As the tech began to draw our puppy's blood, you would have thought we were slowly amputating his arm with a dull knife. He screamed and howled and cried at the top of his voice. We were unable to distract him or calm him down. *Everyone* in the building knew something terrible was happening and several came to see who was mistreating this poor creature. Each person was surprised to simply see a puppy with a tourniquet on his right arm. The moment the tourniquet was removed and we were no longer trying to draw his blood, everyone could see he was happy and healthy and being kissed by everyone in the area.

Guess who did not participate in the study?

Pinkerton is a handsome, 140-pound, nine-year-old now. He is very smart, usually obedient, and incredible sweet. He knows when people are sad and is always ready to make them feel better. He is still practically *perfect* in every way.

Just DO NOT try to draw his blood!

Ted Peck
Galena, Missouri, USA

Chapter 50

My Watchful Shepherd - Maxine

The day I met Maxine, I never imaged she would become my best friend.

My husband, Ian, had been wanting a Newfoundland dog since before we met. He would show me pictures of the bear-like dogs and laugh as he described the shoe-lace drool flying from their massive, loose jaws. He wanted one! He needed one! And, some day, he was getting one!

I thought he had lost his mind, but I read books and did research about the breed. Once we had our second child and our 10-year anniversary, the time was right. At last we would get our Newfoundland.

We met with a few breeders and finally found a breeder whose goal was to keep the value of the Newfoundland alive. She was not breeding for profit or because her dog was so cute. This was the right breeder. Ian and I agreed. We are doing this! We put down our deposit.

But then, while we waited for our puppy, life as we knew it came to a halt. We learned the reason our two-and-a-half-year-old son had never talked, the reason walking on carpet was like walking on fire for him, and the reason he head-butted me, screaming, anytime we went to a public place. Our son was diagnosed with Autism. It's amazing how this little word can flip your world upside down, stop your heart in your chest, and consume your whole focus.

Ian, a steel mill worker, picked up every extra shift he could to cover unexpected expenses while I threw myself at pulling our son out of the safe little world he was hiding in. His younger sister and I spent our days taking him to Speech, Occupational, and Physical Therapies. I spent every minute of my day attempting to make these two kids thrive, and it didn't matter what the personal cost was.

Meanwhile, time sped on. The day came. Our puppy was ready. Part of me was nervous. Could I handle one more thing? Part of me was excited. A Newfoundland puppy of our very own!

Ian took the day off. We packed up the car and drove the three hours to meet our new family member.

When the breeder took us into her back yard the mama dog greeted us, excited to show off her bear-cubs. Ian was in his glory, loving on this huge, furry mama-bear. Our puppy spotted our two kids, waddled over, plopped herself down between them, and went to sleep. We were off to a comfortable, relaxed beginning.

Maxine was like no other puppy. She knew to go potty outside, she picked up obedience training in record time, and she napped with the kids. Each day she watched as I dragged words out of my son, then put her head in my lap as I sat on the floor watching him walk away. Where my son lacked affection, Maxine made up for it. She was by my side every minute of my day.

As she got older, Maxine got closer to the kids. When our third child was born, Maxine slept next to her crib and got up with me at night to feed her. Our sweet bear-dog lay in the kids' toy room while they played. They rested their feet on her as they watched TV. She conscientiously cleaned their faces after each meal.

Each day, after I put the kids down for a nap, I would try to get some type of work done. One day I decided to weed the garden. I took the baby monitor with me so I could hear any noises in the house. Everything remained silent.

After half an hour my neighbor came into the garden holding my daughter in her arms, holding my son's hand, with Maxine by her side. I stood up in shock.

My neighbor smiled big and said, "Your dog came and got me. I was sitting on my porch and saw your kids. Your dog was with them. Then she came and took my hand. I thought she was going to bite me but she pulled me to the kids. Then once I picked them up, she circled me until I followed her to you."

Maxine, my heroine.

When Maxine was five, we bought an 80-acre farm. The kids loved the land, but the free space drove Maxine crazy. She spent her days following the kids around and telling them where they could and could not go. Ian and I would laugh as she stopped them from wandering away from her comfort area.

Maxine decided they could not go past the barn, the pine trees, or the garage. As long as all the kids stayed within that area, she just followed them. But if anyone tried to leave those invisible lines, she would herd them back with her massive 115-pound body, barking and circling them until they went back where they belonged. When Maxine barked at the kids, I yelled at the kids. Two mamas! Lucky kids!

Maxine could spot the new kid in a crowd and single him out. She would circle the new kid and bring him to me. Once I met our new friend, Maxine and the kids went on their way. It got to the point where people knew if they were coming to the farm, Maxine would be the first one to greet them.

When Maxine was nine years old she started to slow down. The vet found she had cancer all through her body, and my heart broke. Ian and I did all we could to save her. She would still watch the kids, but she stopped following them.

I sat with her until the very end, until her very last breath. I wanted her to know I was by her side like she had always been by mine.

At a time in my life when I thought my world was falling apart, Maxine held it all together. She let me know it was all going to be okay. She watched my kids grow. She offered them love and protection.

Maxine was more than a dog ... she was family ... she was my best friend.

Sarah Mitchell
Burgettstown, Pennsylvania, USA
Penn-Ohio Newfoundland Club
The Friends of the Great Lakes Newfoundland Club

Chapter 51

A Rescue From Above - Bear

As often happens with animal people, our friendship with Dori developed through our mutual love of rescue dogs. Dori was a fascinating, old-school Italian woman who had worked for 38 years at the township where my husband works. She gave us a fresh interpretation of the world through her photography, and when she described walks on the beach with her late husband and Bear, the Newfoundland she had rescued many years ago, she made her past sound almost magical.

Although Dori was a private and incredibly independent person, she spoke her mind on everything. She either loved you or hated you. There was no gray area in between. When she learned that I worked at an animal rescue center and Bob and I rescued dogs, our friendship was sealed. She loved us. We, in turn, grew to love her.

Shortly after we met Dori, Bob and I rescued Cvo, a Newfoundland/Border Collie mix. Dori fell madly in love with him. He reminded her of her beloved Bear. Over the next few years her bond with Cvo grew.

"He's mine, you know," she would tell me with her arms around his neck, "you and Bob just take care of him for me."

When Dori was diagnosed with cancer she quietly checked herself into a well-managed hospice facility. Only after she was properly settled did she let her closest friends know the situation. As hard as I tried, I couldn't accept this news. But Dori was positive. She reminded me that it was our devotion to rescued animals that had created our bond and told me how fortunate we were because we were able to grasp the wonder and beauty of dogs. Her next comment took me by surprise.

"When you and Bob can, will you rescue a Newfoundland in my honor?"

My eyes welled up with tears as I promised we would.

For the next few months Cvo and I traveled the 50-mile round trips to visit Dori two or three times a week. She would get tears in her eyes every time she saw Cvo. She would look up while hugging him and say "thank you" ten times in a row. Much of our visiting time was spent in silence. Just having Cvo and me next to her was enough. No words were needed.

We lost our dear friend the day after Christmas in 2016. She had asked us to rescue a Newfoundland in her honor and I had promised her we would. But it wasn't until three days after Christmas two years later that Denise, a woman who volunteers as an animal transporter, brought a rescue to our center. I talked with her about her work and told her my husband and I were looking to rescue a Newfoundland. She explained that in 15 years of transports she had only had two Newfoundlands.

She left saying, "I guess I won't be talking to you anytime soon, then."

That evening I found Denise had emailed me two hours after we had spoken. "Dawn, you are never going to believe this. I just arrived home to this message on my phone: I've got an eight-week-old Newfoundland pup with medical issues so I can't sell him. Come and get him or I will put him down."

The call had come from a puppy mill. We all know what that means—a breeding operation where profit is given priority over the well-being of the dogs.

When I told Bob about my conversation with Denise, then her email two hours later, he was as stunned as I had been.

"It's Dori!" he yelled. "She's messing with us!"

We looked at each other with tears in our eyes and agreed.

"We'll take her heaven-sent gift," I said. "We'll give this pup a loving home, whatever the medical issues."

Two and a half days later Bear arrived. The minute Denise placed him in my arms was the most emotional minute ever. Bear was covered in urine and his eyes were wet, but when he snuggled against my neck I felt only warm comfort and gratitude. My heart was so happy holding this gift from our beloved Dori.

"Little Bear," I whispered, "you have no idea how long Mommy and Daddy waited for you. We promise to do everything we can to help you, Sweet Boy."

Despite being born with several medical issues caused by reckless breeding, Bear, at one and a half years old, is 120 pounds of pure lap dog. He relishes life and lives every day to the fullest. The joy he projects has an amazing way of giving everyone he meets a lift. It's impossible not to return a smile when it comes from Bear.

Although the procedure for correcting Bear's incontinence was performed by the top specialist in our area, it did not work for him. But Bear has never objected to wearing his custom-made diapers. He doesn't even know he is different. Our other four dogs accept Bear's diapers as nonchalantly as he does. They never bother Bear's diapers. We change the pad every time there is a drip and his skin and fur are in perfect condition. Our vet has been impressed with our attention to this detail. She has told us that most dogs have issues with diapers for long-term use.

Although Bear has entropion, a hereditary disorder of the eyelids which causes them to roll inward, it is not as bad as we first thought. We are monitoring this closely and will do the surgical procedures to correct it if and when it is warranted. Meanwhile, we lubricate the eyes as needed.

A third medical issue Bear had when he came to us was an umbilical hernia. That has long since been successfully repaired and there have been no more issues of that nature.

As of April 2020 Bear is in my arms and in my heart. He is happy, safe, and thriving. Bob and I will continue our journey with Bear for all of his life. And, we will continue our mission of rescuing dogs; however, we will always believe that it was our special friend, Dori, who rescued Bear.

Bob & Dawn Steelman
Pottstown, Pennsylvania, USA

Chapter 52

Generations of Furry Comfort - Thunder & Tank

Thunder yawns and stretches across the seat of the van. As we park in front of the school, he sits up and gives an excited, "Woof!" Summer is over. It's time to go to work.

As we pass through the school doors, Thunder is greeted by a multitude of eager hands, fluffing his fur and crooning, "Thunnnnder, how was your summer, Dude?" Others yell his name and wave wildly from down the hall. Thunder does a "happy dance" as he waits for "his kids" to come to him. He licks all available hands and cheeks while doing the "total body tail wag." It's good to be back. He loves his kids.

We make our way to the main office and Thunder works the room with a purpose, making sure everything is still as he left it on the last day of school in June. The office secretary greets him with an ear rub and a pat on the head.

"Hello, Handsome! Looks like you slimmed down a bit over the summer. Low-fat cookies for you this year."

Thunder trots into the principal's office for another ear rub, then we continue down the hall. Students in the hallway are still calling out his name and greeting him.

"Thunder! Give me a high five, Dude."

"Thunder! Did ya learn any new tricks, Buddy?"

We enter a classroom and the teacher tosses a Kleenex box to the floor. A student lets loose with a fake but hearty, "Achoo!" Thunder snatches up a Kleenex and pushes it into the girl's hand. The kids squeal. Everyone is smiling. Even the kids who struggle for a reason to smile are smiling. We leave the classroom knowing we've helped give these kids a positive start to their day.

We head to the library where school pictures are being taken. Thunder climbs into the chair and poses for his staff photo. The kids giggle knowing Thunder will be in the yearbook, alongside the teaching staff.

Thunder helps students talk about tough life experiences, making him a truly remarkable teacher. Kids in a "children of divorce" group compare divorce and visitation to Thunder leaving his "dog parents," children struggling with social skills decide, "If I wouldn't do it to Thunder, I shouldn't do it to another kid," students acquiring social skills discuss the importance of good personal hygiene while I brush Thunder's teeth. Many skills seem easier to teach when using Thunder as an example.

Back in my office, Thunder relaxes and watches the doorway. He knows it won't be long before students will be visiting us. He loves the ear rubs he gets while students chat with me.

Suddenly, a student having a rough morning bursts into the room, landing in a heap on the floor near Thunder. Angry tears accompany his loud description of the mishap that resulted in his being sent to my office. Thunder shifts his position and rests his head on the boy's lap. The volume and intensity of the boy's words calm as he catches Thunder's gaze and begins stroking him. In a short time, his upset has settled enough for him to begin considering options and possible solutions to the morning's episode. He returns to class with a plan for continuing his day.

We walk down the hall towards the staff mailboxes when I see a student zipping toward his locker. He spots Thunder and stops instantly. I snap the leash onto Thunder's collar and hand it to the student. This young man's legs won't allow him to run and play with Thunder, but he feels proud to hold Thunder's leash and walk him next to his wheelchair. He explains, "It's one of the times when I feel like I'm just like other kids. Thunder never notices I'm different."

Thunder knows it's good news when a student arrives at my office door waving the "Thunder Bucks" she earned for completing her work and making good behavior choices.

"I want to cash these in," she says excitedly.

She holds up four colorful five-dollar bills with a head shot of Thunder in the center.

"Twenty minutes, right?"

I nod with a smile.

"Earning these was hard, but I kept thinking about getting to play with the big dude."

Thunder grabs his bumper from the toy box. We set the timer for the "purchased" minutes and head outside. Playtime with Thunder is well worth all the hard work.

Thunder and I return to my office to find a student standing in my doorway, tears streaming down his face. His sadness is all consuming as he describes the tragic, recent death of a family member.

"Can I just sit here with Thunder for a few minutes?"

He buries his face in Thunder's back. Thunder lies quietly as the young man cries, finding comfort and strength in the warmth of Thunder's fur. As I watch, I think about the powerful bond between animals and people. I wonder if Thunder is aware of how many young lives he touches and influences during each school day.

The bell rings to announce the end of the school day. Thunder gives a soft "Woof" to enforce that it's time to go home. As he jumps into the van, several voices from across the parking lot make me smile.

"Thunnnnnnderrrr! See ya tomorrowwwwww!"

Does Thunder know that for some of "his kids" he is the one thing they look forward to each day? He stretches across the seat and yawns. It's all in a day's work.

*****

Although Thunder passed over the Rainbow Bridge in 2016 at age 12, he will always hold a special place in my heart and in the hearts of the adults who stop me in the hallways to introduce themselves to three-year-old Tank. They often share stories about how Thunder impacted their lives and tell me how pleased they are that their child will "grow up" knowing Tank.

Now, even with our school closed as we navigate the Covid-19 pandemic, Tank, my second therapy Newf, has become a source of comfort to students and staff. Wearing his School Pride cap, he sits patiently for a photo that will comfort students while delivering the message, "Stay well! I miss you!"

The "working from home" phase of Tank's career began casually enough. Using the "My Talking Pets" app, Tank "spoke" encouraging messages to students and staff through Facebook posts, reminding everyone to "stay safe" and "wash yer paws." His talking image provided a much needed chuckle during such a stressful time. Many of my students' parents recall Thunder with fondness and tell me that the comfort they find in Tank's messages mimics the comfort they found in Thunder's companionship during their own school years.

Tank has always been a ham in front of the camera so he has been very cooperative as his mission has changed and expanded. "Talking" clips from Tank appear in text messages, emails, and the school district's staff video for the students. The contrast of the anxiety-provoking pandemic and the "talking therapy dog" elicit chuckles from Tank's adoring "kids" and their families. He is providing some much needed relief from the stress of Covid-19.

As the pandemic has continued, I have begun conducting teletherapy video sessions with students, and, of course, they want to see Tank. Many of the students have been worried that Tank could get the virus, so they are happy to hear and "see" that he is safe and healthy. Just as Thunder provided an "emotional anchor" for many of their parents, Tank is providing an "emotional anchor" for them.

We are reminded daily that "we are all in this together." This includes Tank. He has stepped right up and is doing his part. By bringing smiles and reassurances to his people, he joins Thunder and countless other loyal Newfoundlands who have served their humans before him.

Kelly Allen
Haslett, Michigan, USA
Great Lakes Newfoundland Club
Facebook: Tank Allen, Haslett, MI

Chapter 53

A Special Day - Sioux Pooh

My Newfy is Sioux Pooh, a five-year-old Landseer with the typical Newfoundland traits, who always seems to know when she needs to be more special than usual. Sometimes days are regular days. Sometimes days are special. Today was one of the latter. A special day, a remarkable day.

As Sioux Pooh and I were walking down the hall of the hospital, heading to a patient who had requested a visit from Pet Therapy, we passed a room and I overheard a woman say, "Oh, look at that dog! Wow!"

I thought, "Well, since we're so close, we can take a moment and stop for a visit." So I turned Sioux around and we approached the room where I had heard the woman. From the doorway I noticed a man, with many tubes and IV's attached, lying in the hospital bed.

I spoke up asking the woman, "Would you like a visit?"

"Oh, yes!" she replied. "It would be great if you could!"

When we entered the room Sioux was first called over by a man who was sitting in a chair at the foot of the bed. He began petting her and remarking how beautiful she is and how soft her coat feels.

The woman came over to Sioux and began petting her. As she did, I handed her one of Sioux Pooh's baseball cards that the hospital's volunteer department provides. The card has Sioux's photo on one side and her name, breed, and other biographical information on the other. The woman took the card, compared the photo on the card to the "real thing," and said, "Oh, she is so sweet."

Sioux Pooh turned to me, giving me a look as if to say, "See, they think I'm sweet."

Just then the nurse who was in the room asked the man in the bed, "Do you like dogs?"

"Oh, yes!" he replied.

"Here, let me untie your arm so you can pet her," the nurse offered.

As soon as the man's arm was free I brought Sioux Pooh over to the bed and placed a small towel next to his hand. Then Sioux placed her head on the towel.

Sioux stands 30 inches at the shoulder and weighs 125 pounds. The great thing about her size is that she can place her head on hospital beds and people don't have to strain to reach her or to see her. She's the perfect size for visiting patients in hospitals.

I watched as the man struggled to lift his hand high enough to place it on Sioux's muzzle and then struggle to place it on top of her head. I watched as his hand muscles began moving in a type of "squeezing motion" to pet her. Sioux stayed there, not moving at all, just looking up into the man's face.

When I looked into the man's face I saw tears streaming, ever so slightly, down his cheeks and I could see the joy in his eyes as a smile came to his lips. Then I noticed his wife was crying also.

She said, "Thank you for taking the time for your beautiful dog to visit with my husband."

While Sioux Pooh kept her head on the bed and the man continued petting her, the woman quietly whispered, "Last week, before he came to the hospital, we had to put our own dog down because she was so sick. He loved her so much and for you to bring your dog in to see him today, well, this is the *best medicine* he could have had."

Sioux Pooh *is* good medicine. Over and over again she has shown what an exceptional therapy dog she is. I was humbled in 2015 when Sioux and I were recognized with the Impact Volunteer of the Year Award in recognition for "outstanding service" to our community. Those present at the banquet to honor all the nominated volunteers included the Mayor of Phoenix, the Governor of Arizona, the City Council of Phoenix, and many other dignitaries of various organizations in our community. After being presented the award, Sioux was walked through the banquet hall by one of the City Council members to introduce her to the crowd. Sioux was clearly the celebrity, but I was happy to be recognized as her "driver."

And I was glad I had driven Sioux for her volunteer visits on this particular day. She was giving her *best medicine.* The two of us have been teaming up for over four years to work at John

C. Lincoln Hospital - Deer Valley, here in Phoenix. Some days are *normal* days when I know we cheered up some people, patients and staff alike. But then there are *special* days when I get a tug at my heart reminding me how much our small visits mean to some people. Today was a *special* day.

The most remarkable thing about it all was the feeling that overwhelmed me when Sioux Pooh, staying calmly in place to allow this man to pet her, looked up at me with her soft eyes as if to remind me of what pet therapy is all about. Thank God for these *special* days.

JP Bear
Phoenix, Arizona, USA
Mesquite Newfoundland Club

Chapter 54

My Almost Too Embarrassing Dog Moment - Leroy

I thought my most embarrassing dog moment was behind me. I should have known better. I mean, what could be more embarrassing than walking your champion show dog down the street and having a hot-looking motorist stop, roll down his window, and begin asking the usual questions strangers ask Newfoundland dog owners, only to have that Newfoundland dog fling an incredibly long shoestring of slobber onto your face with one end landing inside your open mouth?

That was embarrassing. That was gross. Even for me, a four-Newf veteran. However, that was not the worst of my embarrassing dog moments. I should have known while sharing my life with Leroy there were bound to be more awkward, sometimes exasperating, incidents.

On paper, Leroy was actually my husband's dog. This is remarkable because before we married, Bob was not a fan of big dogs. When we first met he literally seemed terrified of Thunder, my second Newf. In the beginning, he wouldn't even come into the house where Thunder was waiting to give him an enthusiastic greeting. But I made no secret of the fact that Newfs were part of the deal, Newfs would *always* be part of the package.

It took Bob awhile, but eventually he got hooked like the rest of us Newf lovers, and when we lost Thunder about a year after we got married he was as devastated as I was. We remained Newf-less for several months. Then it was Bob, the man who had not been a fan of big dogs, who surprised me by saying he wanted another Newf. Of course I didn't turn him down. So shortly thereafter, Sherman joined us. Bob surprised me again about a year later when he decided Sherman needed a pal. And that is why a rambunctious, 10-week-old puppy named Leroy, came to be a member of our family.

Life with Leroy was never predictable and clearly never dull. He was a handful from the start, a troublemaker and proud of it. He tried to escape the yard and investigate the neighborhood every chance he got. He was always doing silly things from talking back to eating anything and everything he wasn't supposed to, including chewing on an AA battery that ended with a vet visit. Leroy tended to do things his way or no way. Sherman seemed appalled by Leroy's puppy behavior and actually tried to avoid him for the first few weeks. But Leroy made me laugh every single day. He is the reason I started a blog, MyBrownNewfies. I wanted to share his beauty and antics with the rest of the world.

I have also shared quite a few embarrassing dog moments with the rest of the world. But the *most* embarrassing dog moment is almost too embarrassing to share. Leroy was a handsome,

160-pound, four-year old on the day he accomplished his most outrageous stunt.

We had reached the far end of our daily walk and were just turning around to head home when Mr. Leroy, for some mysterious reason, suddenly decided to jump on my back. His paw got stuck in my pocket and when he went down, he pulled my pants down with him.

Yes! Right there on Route 82! Right there in the bright light of day my derriere was exposed for all to see!

I'm pretty sure I made some truck driver's day because he beeped his extremely loud air horn as he roared by. And, I'm pretty sure he wasn't the only one who was startled by the sudden appearance of my keister in such a public place. But I didn't get an accurate count of all the other vehicles racing by. I was too busy trying to pull my pants up and feeling grateful I was wearing underwear.

Leroy passed away at 11½ years old in January 2020 after a very long battle with Inflammatory Bowel Disease. He is greatly missed by me and my family, and by all the people who loved him across the world. He was one of the most of high-spirited, lighthearted, fun-loving, fun-*giving* Newfs I've ever known. He was dearly loved and will never be forgotten.

Jen Costello
Strongsville, Ohio, USA
Facebook & Instagram: MyBrownNewfies
Twitter: @MyBrownNewfies

Chapter 55

Boulder Bear, Promoter Extraordinaire - Boulder

In 2010 our family began looking for a Newfy puppy. We lived on a lake in a small town in Northwestern Ontario. With two small children by the water, a Newfy was the perfect breed. Over the next year we searched and searched for a rescue Newf with no luck. We finally gave up and were planning on getting a Saint Bernard/Newfy cross.

The night before we were scheduled to head out on a four-hour drive to pick up the dog, I received a call from a co-worker regarding a Newfy puppy that had become available. The breeder had been involved in a car accident and was not able to properly look after the animals.

I left the next morning, after a night shift, to pick up our new family member. It was still a four-hour drive to the meeting location, but the meeting was a great success. The brown Newfy puppy was instantly affectionate and buried his head into my chest for the longest greeting.

"A brown Newfy?" is a question I didn't realize I would hear and have to answer daily for the next seven years.

"Yep, he's a purebred, and not a bear. No, I hadn't ever seen a brown Newfoundland before him, either."

Once home, two very excited children, Taryn, nine years old and Wyatt, seven, greeted their new, furry sibling. This is where the challenge of naming him began. It was to be a short-lived challenge, however, as we all agreed in short order. We are a family of rock climbers, so the name was settled on quickly. At the time Taryn had a Maplelea Doll named Taryn. The doll came complete with a back story of loving the outdoors and hiking. Little Taryn, as we referred to the doll, also came with her trusted companion, a dog named Boulder. So, from then on, our puppy was Boulder. As time passed and he developed his personality, he began to collect nicknames. The main nickname that stuck was Boulder Bear.

In 2014 our family decided to make a huge life change. At the encouragement of my children, I quit policing and we moved back to Thunder Bay where I was born and raised and still have family. The plan was to open an indoor rock-climbing gym.

After just over a year of construction, the gym was ready. So again, the naming process had to be tackled. This time there was no room for movement by Taryn and Wyatt. The name was to be Boulder Bear Climbing Centre, and that was that.

Once the gym doors opened, Boulder really came into his own and became the famous mascot he is today. Boulder is a permanent fixture at the gym. People come in and immediately ask, "Where's the dog?"

Boulder spends his days greeting people at the front door. Well, greeting them somewhat passively, sometimes. If he is really sleepy, they need to step over a slumbering Boulder to get into the gym. He can also sometimes be found wandering the climbing area, making sure all is well.

Boulder welcomes school groups and always has time for a cuddle. I have had the opportunity to watch children with autism approach him for hugs as their parents watch in tears. Boulder is also a hit when he attends summer camp. The campers love having Boulder with them on the Boulder Bus.

Boulder attends all the hikes with kids. The hike the children do ends in a large field. Once in the field we have all the youngsters try to beat Boulder back to the bus. The kids get a head start, then Boulder is released. He races to catch up and then frolics beside them. The kids scream and laugh with delight.

For a period of time a hamburger restaurant opened within the gym. Boulder took up his place in line and sat directly in front of the counter until properly acknowledged. If he was not paid the proper attention in a timely manner, he would demand attention with a short, quick, "Woof!" Everyone knew what that meant! He was going sit and stare directly at the counter server until he felt he had received an appropriate reward.

Clients on outdoor guided adventures are always glad to see Boulder lumber out of the truck to accompany them on the experience. The clients find it equally amusing to watch at the end of their excursion when Boulder is ready to get back into the truck. Everyone thinks he is hilarious when he stands at the back door waiting to be lifted into the truck while offering no assistance whatsoever.

The gym opened in 2015 and since then Boulder has been photographed thousands of times and has had thousands of interactions with clients from all over the country. He is recognized wherever we go in the community and has been an amazing addition to our family. Boulder was instrumental in creating the atmosphere at the gym and is likely the most memorable part of a visit to Boulder Bear Climbing Centre. We are happy that Boulder's loyalty and affection for our family has broadened to include his sizeable hiking and/or rock-climbing family, as well.

Dallas Markall
Thunder Bay, Ontario, Canada

Chapter 56

Almost Famous - Deacon

One of Deacon's favorite summertime activities here in Phoenix was attending baseball games at Diamondback Stadium on "Bark-in-the-Park" days. In addition to cheering for his favorite team with his loud and joyous barks, he enjoyed the attention, the cuddles, and the endless popcorn snacks he got from his fellow baseball fans.

Although Deacon had become quite famous to his regular admirers, I was surprised one day when he was given an opportunity to expand his fame beyond the baseball park, beyond Phoenix, perhaps even beyond the State of Arizona.

It happened when Deacon was noticed (all beautiful, shining, black, 200 pounds of him!) by Todd Walsh, a main sports analyst and TV announcer for the Diamondbacks. As Todd entered the baseball park he saw Deacon and immediately fell in love with him, hugging him and allowing him to lick his face vigorously enough to remove most of his TV make-up. Then he asked if Deacon could sit next to him when he did the Post-Game Show.

Wow! This was it! Here it was! Publicity! Like a thunderbolt from the blue came Deacon's big chance to get noticed by an agent, gain national exposure, possibly even become world famous! With stars in our eyes we followed Todd enthusiastically up the steps to the broadcasting booth.

It was when Todd stepped into the booth and began walking toward his broadcasting table that Deacon's chance for fame unexpectedly fizzled. Although he cheerfully followed Todd for the first few steps, he suddenly froze in his tracks. He had just noticed that the broadcasting booth hangs out over the outfield, 50 feet above the ground.

Immediately concluding that this was no place for an intelligent, self-respecting Newf, Deacon did this Michael Jackson "moonwalk" back toward the door, away from Todd's table, and out of the booth. He made it clear he that didn't want to go anywhere near Todd and his broadcasting table. He made it clear that he didn't *do* heights.

But even though the first plan didn't work out, Todd refused to completely abandon his idea of including Deacon in his broadcast. At the beginning of his show he announced he had brought his security dog with him and the camera panned over to Deacon, sitting calmly off to the side with a big, happy smile on his face, safely out of sight of the 50-foot drop-off.

Unfortunately, Deacon missed his chance for fame. But even though his bid for international recognition didn't work out, he had already achieved local celebrity status and attending baseball games continued to be one of his favorite activities. Much of his pleasure came from the children who always showered him with love, hugs, and sometimes even bites of their hot dogs.

Deacon loved kids and was great with them, but we were always extra careful when youngsters inundated him. It was because of his past experiences with children that we had become his second family.

Evidently, Deacon's first family didn't realize how big he was going to grow and, although he did very well with the three children in that family, their young friends became afraid of him. It seems Deacon would somehow knock the friends over when they came to play and they would go home crying. The first family hated to let him go, but they were at a point where the children's friends refused to visit and that was creating difficulties.

For this reason Deacon, at 1½ years old, became our "only child." Getting used to not having children around was a little hard for him at first. His ears always perked up when he heard the kids next door playing outside. We tried to compensate by never missing an opportunity for him to interact with children. He loved stopping to greet kids when we went out, and he considered his young fans at the baseball park part of his pack.

Deacon was an exceptionally smart boy and he responded well to the training we began with him as soon as he joined us. At 1½ he was quick to pick up the basic commands and he seemed to enjoy the practice. Along with learning the obedience routines he also developed uncommonly good manners.

Just three months before we adopted Deacon we had lost our first well-loved Newf, Tyson. The somewhat unusual reason Deacon came to us and the way he looked, almost like a reincarnation of Tyson, made us feel as if bringing him into our lives was meant to be. Deacon reminded us of Tyson, but he didn't replace our first big boy. Deacon created his own special place in our hearts.

Over the years Deacon had several serious medical issues, but he would always pull through. Our vet said he was like a cat because he seemed to have nine lives. We felt lucky to have had him spend most of his nine lives with us. We got to enjoy Deacon for 11 years, and for a Newf, that's pretty special.

Forrest Filippi
Phoenix, Arizona, USA
Mesquite Newfoundland Club

Chapter 57

Rising to the Occasion - Kayla

Kayla was the best baby Newfy ever! She became the best Canine Good Citizen ever, the best carting dog ever, and, ultimately, the best therapy dog ever. I visited Kayla and her ten siblings at three weeks, four weeks, and seven weeks, but making the decision to adopt her was one of the hardest decisions I ever made.

First had come Tasha, a beautiful, black puppy who stole my heart for 10 years and broke it when she passed away. Then came my sweet, loyal Josh, whom I lost at seven years old. Again, I was shattered, heartbroken.

A year passed and I waited, not knowing if I could do it again. But I stayed in my regional Newf club and helped one of my friends train his Newf. Yet even though I was missing having a Newf of my own, and I was visiting Kayla and her siblings often, I still wasn't sure if I could bring another Newf into my life.

Then came the 2004 Westminster Kennel Club Dog Show where Josh, a four-year-old, 155-pound, exuberant black Newfoundland won Best in Breed, Best in Group, and *Best in Show*. That did it! That was a *sign*. Adopting Kayla was meant to be.

So at ten weeks, wrapped up in one of my children's baby blankets, the little girl with the yellow ribbon, the little girl the breeder had called "Butterscotch," the little girl who was to bring me joy for the next 9½ years, came home with me.

From the very beginning Kayla loved training, any training. We participated in many activities with the members of our Newf club, many Fun Days. Kayla had so much fun preparing for the Canine Good Citizen test, we kept repeating the training. After she took and passed the test three times, I realized she needed a new challenge.

I had a cart made and my friend and I began her cart training. Again, she loved the fun, loved the attention, loved learning something new. At the 2008 Nationals in Rhode Island she won her Specialty Cart and Wagon Exercises Off-Lead title.

Having achieved that goal, our next challenge was mastering the requirements for a Therapy Dog title. As always, the training began smoothly. In her usual style Kayla worked earnestly to understand what she was to do. Then as soon as she knew what was being requested, she would perform the task with pleasure and pride.

Working with Kayla was always fun. True, it required patience on my part, and true, it required doling out quite a few of her favorite treats, but training her was always easy. She was a brave girl, bold, confident, courageous, willing to try anything.

Except for one thing. *Elevators*. Kayla did not like elevators. She did not like stepping into an elevator. She did not like seeing the door close on an elevator. She did not like feeling the floor move on an elevator. The only thing Kayla liked about elevators was enthusiastically stepping out of them.

At that point Kayla was five years old. We should have begun elevator training a whole lot sooner. But, other than her aversion to elevators, Kayla had all the qualities necessary for an exceptionally effective therapy dog. What to do?

Then my friend stepped in with a suggestion. She worked in a bank that had a large elevator with double doors. The door on one side was the customer door which opened into the lobby. The door on the other side was the employee door which opened into the work space. If Kayla could train with the distraction of encountering awed, surprised, and perhaps even "adoring" people, who, from their laughter and delighted behavior, were obviously *enjoying* their rides on the elevator maybe, just maybe, she would learn she had nothing to fear.

This is why Kayla and I arrived at the bank one beautiful Tuesday morning and stepped into the large elevator with a little cluster of chattering, happy people, many of whom were petting, cuddling, and otherwise reassuring Kayla that elevators were an acceptable way to travel.

Up and down we rode that morning, up and down. Sometimes we would stop off in the bank lobby, sometimes in the employee work space, but always stepping back onto the elevator with a group of people who understood what we were trying to accomplish.

I felt immensely grateful to these people. Many of them went out of their way to make Kayla feel relaxed and comfortable. As they say, it takes a village. Before too long Kayla began to feel more at ease. Participating as part of a "pack" made adapting to a new activity easier.

Although Kayla was never especially fond of elevators, she overcame her fear of them, passed the Therapy Dog test, and ultimately, became the best Therapy Dog ever. Just as I always knew she would.

Adopting Kayla was one of the hardest decisions I ever made. It was also one of the best. If only I could, I would do it all again.

Carole McLaughlin
Danvers, Massachusetts, USA
Newfoundland Club of New England

Chapter 58

The Laird of Drumnaguie - Seamas

Our brown Newfy, Seamas, was a character like no other. He kept us on our toes with his endless adventures, or as we preferred to call them, "incidents."

We live in a remote part of the Highlands of Scotland by a beautiful beach. Our house is in view of the beach car park so our boy Seamas spent his days sitting in the garden barking at all the people going to the beach. His greetings were so welcoming and friendly, many of the visitors would come down to the garden fence to say hello and/or take his picture. For some of the regular visitors, stopping by to speak to Seamas became part of their beach experience.

In his teenage years Seamas was a jumper. He would jump on everyone and, try as we might, we could not get him to stop doing it. Therefore, our days were spent making sure the gate was shut so he would not have access to any poor, unsuspecting tourists.

One day, however, when I heard Seamas giving his welcoming bark, I looked out the window and saw, to my horror, that the gate was open. My alarm was intensified when I looked over to the car park and saw an elderly lady getting out of her car.

"Quick! The gate!" I shouted to my husband.

Duncan started running to get the gate latched, but it was too late. Seamas was out and on his way!

I watched with dread as the next scene unfolded in painful slow motion. Seamas was racing, gleefully, toward the elderly lady. My husband was racing, panic-stricken, behind him, waving his arms frantically, and shouting to the lady.

"Get back in your car! Quick! Get back in your car!"

Seamas reached the car and its lady occupant and, forgoing his usual exuberant jumping behaviour, he stood at her side and very politely greeted her. Only then did my husband catch up with the escapee and secure him.

The bemused lady was very taken with our brown bear and said she wouldn't have minded being pushed to the ground by such a magnificent animal. Obviously, she was a dog lover, which was fortunate for us. In retrospect, the whole incident was like a scene from a comedy movie where things go horribly wrong at the beginning, but everything turns out okay in the end.

Unfortunately, not all of Seamas's "incidents" had such happy endings. Once when he was around a year old, my daughter and I took him down to the beach. We were still trying to train him, and since he seemed to be making great progress, and since no one was around, we decided to practice some off-lead exercises.

Seamas was thrilled to be set free. His curiosity had already been piqued by voices that had gone unheard by us. Straight away he raced down the beach, over the dunes, toward the rock pools, out of our sight. We gave chase, but soon we could hear screaming. By the time we arrived at the rock pools we found an exasperated family with their picnic in complete disarray. One member of the group, a very irate woman, then accused our big puppy of being a *hooligan* who ate their sandwiches.

Amid the lady's scolding we hurriedly snapped on Seamas's lead, attempted to apologize for his misdemeanor, and left quickly. Seamas had made one thing clear to us. He was not yet ready for off-lead training at the beach.

But with time, Seamas became a trustworthy, off-lead companion. Because we live by the beach we went there nearly every day, apart from the days of really wild weather in the winter. Although the beach was Seamas's greatest joy, we called him our fair weather swimmer, or sometimes, the toe dipper. He would swim when it suited him and would not be persuaded if it didn't. Occasionally, our daughter would jump into the water and pretend she was in trouble. Seamas would look languidly out to the waves, meander a wee bit, and then nonchalantly stroll in to "rescue" her.

However, if there were seals in the bay, Seamas was off like a shot to chase them. They would pop up and down out of the water toying with him while he tried to swim out to them. If there were no seals present he would walk the shoreline back and fore looking for them. Nothing was as exhilarating to Seamas as attempting to "rescue" seals.

Although he never rescued a seal, Seamas did once rescue a ball at a Shinty-Hurling International sporting event. Shinty-Hurling is a hybrid sport developed in the 1800's to facilitate competitions between shinty players of Scotland and hurling players of Ireland. The competition is played annually and is a very big affair.

The year of the famous rescue, we were standing behind the barrier of the sports field along with many other high-spirited fans. By mid-match Seamas had had enough excitement and was quietly lying down, taking it all in. Suddenly the ball was hit in our direction. It rolled across the line and straight to Seamas. Our big boy very casually picked it up, then looked up calmly at the player who came to take the hit.

The young lad took one look at Seamas and said to the ref, "Well, *I'm* not getting that! *You* do it! Or give me a new ball!"

The ref produced a new ball. The match continued. We had our souvenir, courtesy of our daft dog. And all of this went out live on TV. Our amusing, charismatic Seamas had given us one more of his comical, unpredictable "incidents."

Seamas was the centre of our world for ten delightful years. We miss him. We will never forget him. Newfies are just the best dogs ever.

Paula Macleod
Kinlochbervie, Sutherland, Scotland, UK

Chapter 59

Weird But Wonderful - Benny

The Kissing Bridge Ski Patrol needed to practice. They needed a victim. I stood there on that freezing New York evening and watched the members of the ski patrol go over to a huge black dog lying in the snow by the side of the trail. At their request the gigantic, inert beast got up, shook off the snow, and calmly lay down on their rescue sled. I watched in awe as the dog rode down the mountain. Wow! I was 19. I was in college. I was smitten.

I discovered everyone knew this dog. He was a local resident who was always happy to help out when needed.

I got Sheba, my first Newfoundland puppy, soon after that. My boyfriend, Steven, and I hitch-hiked with her to the university every day and never had a problem getting a ride. I took her to all my classes and got an "A" in physics *only* because Sheba enchanted my instructor. Dr. W. *loved* her.

Sheba was a wonderful girl who helped me grow up and who lived to 14½. However, this is a story about Benny, my seventh Newfoundland. Hopefully, he won't be my last.

I was always told never to get a Newfoundland from a puppy mill. But I had just lost my beloved Jude when a friend told me about a 2½-year-old male who needed a home. His first mom had suddenly died, quite young. Maybe I'd consider it. When I learned he came from a pet shop in a mall near Boston and he was from a puppy mill in Missouri, I became less enthusiastic. But we arranged a meeting between him and our female Newf, Josephine. Who knows? Maybe it could work.

When Benny arrived, Josie accepted him instantly. They celebrated their new friendship with a lively romp in the woods near our home. Josie was only ten months old at the time, but she sensed Benny would be someone she could control. And from that day onward, control him she did.

So Benny became our dog. That Benny! I loved him unconditionally, but did he ever do the dumbest things! I never knew whether it was because his executive function wasn't functioning properly or because he enjoyed creating crazy situations just to make us laugh. I merely learned to accept his nutty behavior.

For example, one day he disappeared when we were taking our daily hike in the Wendell State Forest. That was not unusual. He always rejoined us in five or ten minutes. But after 20 minutes, still no Benny. We saw a park ranger who told us he had seen some deer. Oh, great! Maybe Benny was on a chase.

Sitting by the side of the trail, I wondered how long we would be there—an hour, until nightfall, tomorrow? Then the park ranger reappeared with a strange, indecipherable expression on his face.

"I found your dog," he said, and beckoned to me to follow him to a place not far from where I was sitting.

And there, stuck in the V between two trees, was Benny. His body looked like a see-saw, front feet on the ground at one end, back feet on the ground at the other, body wedged tightly in between. I had to go to his rear end, lift it up a bit, and push him through the V to free him.

Then there was the Most Porcupine Incidents in One Season Certificate awarded to him from our vet staff. Twelve incidents. Congratulations, Benny! I was not very amused about all those trips to the vet. Actually, both he and Josephine were named on the certificate, and it was only after Josephine died and Benny never got quills again that I realized I had probably blamed the wrong dog for instigating the porcupine capers.

But the craziest thing Benny ever did happened at seven o'clock one hot summer morning. We were sleeping with the screened window open when Benny heard the neighbor dogs on the road. He went to the window and barked. I told him to be quiet and go back to sleep. Instead, he decided to jump through the window and join the other dogs. Did he not remember we were thirty feet above ground, two stories up? The next thing I heard was Benny bursting through the screen.

That shock was followed by the neighbor screaming, "He's dead! Oh, my god!"

But he wasn't. Confused, yes. He should have been! But he got up. He was okay. Recommendations from the vet report: Keep exercise restricted for seven days. No running, jumping, playing, or climbing stairs. No more jumping out of the window even if he wants to!

As for the multiple heath issues often associated with puppy mill dogs, Benny was the healthiest Newf I've ever had. No heart problems. No joint problems. His only serious health issue occurred when he was twelve. We were spending a week on an island in Maine when Benny became gravely constipated. We took the ferry to the mainland and the vet who examined him said the problem was cancer. I was devastated. But once we got home, a CT scan at the Massachusetts Specialty Hospital in Burlington confirmed that Benny didn't have cancer. They corrected the problem by operating the next day and removing three fatty tumors the size of baked potatoes.

There was one other crazy, it-could-only-happen-to-Benny, health-related gem. My husband, Steven, complained that Benny had bad breath and was drooling. I took him to the vet, who said he was fine, just a Newf. But when I got home I got a flashlight and shined it down Josephine's throat. Okay. Then I shined it down Benny's throat. OMG! The flashlight beam highlighted a stick that went across his throat and had become embedded in his gums. So, back to the vet we went. They removed the stick and said it had probably been there for months.

Benny died last year at 15 years, 10 months. He was still walking a few miles a day until a few weeks before he declined. Not a bad run. Yes, he was wacky, but I *loved* Benny and I feel it was special we could be together for so many years.

Shelley Robbins-Peyster
New Salem, Massachusetts, USA

Chapter 60

The Power of a Dog, My Dog - Jake Doyle

My whole life I have loved dogs. I always had one, mostly Heinz 57. But my dream dog was always a Newfoundland. On June, 3, 2013, I saw an ad online announcing the availability of six Newfoundland pups. Both my children were now out of school and didn't depend on me for much. Without another thought, I called and made an appointment to view the pups. I had *always* wanted a Newfoundland. This was my time!

My son, William, came with me to see the pups, and we were both mesmerized by the chubby little black balls of fur. One in particular kept coming to me so, of course, that was the one I picked.

At the time there was a TV series being filmed here in St. John's, Newfoundland, a comedy-drama called *The Republic of Doyle*. My puppy was dark-haired and extremely handsome, just like Jake Doyle, the main character in the series. Naming my puppy was a no brainer! He would be called Jake Doyle, JD or Jake, for short.

When I told my four sisters about my plan to get a Newfoundland puppy, they were shocked. They thought I was crazy. Me, being their "baby sister," they thought I couldn't handle such a large, powerful dog.

"Doreen, they are so big and strong! They could easily knock you down!"

"Doreen, they are so much work!"

"Doreen, they live for ten years or more!"

"Doreen, what are you thinking?"

Well, yes, they were right. My puppy *did* turn into a big, strong 150-pound boy who could knock me down. But he never does. We enrolled in obedience school and Jake passed with flying colours. He has excellent manners and has always been a pleasure to take anywhere.

And, well, yes, they were right. Keeping Jake neat and well-groomed *is* a lot of work. But he has such a great personality and is so cooperative, caring for him is work I thoroughly enjoy.

One thing my sisters and I didn't know about Newfoundland dogs is that they attract an enormous amount of attention. Everywhere we go Jake is a hit. Walking with him is like walking with a rock star. His popularity gets him invited to many social functions.

When Jake was a year old he was invited to a garden party at St. Patrick's Mercy Home here in St. John's. He has been invited to every one of their garden parties since. He loves socializing with the seniors and he especially enjoys the ice cream.

At one of the parties we were approached by a daughter pushing her mother in a wheelchair. The elderly lady's eyes were wide with excitement to see the dog. Jake laid his large head on the lady's lap and she stroked him, lovingly.

The mother looked up at her daughter and said, "Remember Rex, Connie? He was such a wonderful dog."

The daughter looked at me with tears in her eyes and said, "That's the first time Mom has said my name in three years."

This was a tender moment I will never forget. The power of a dog!

Another of Jake's social functions involves international hospitality. The City of St. John's sponsors a "Greet the Visitors" program every year from April through October. As passengers disembark from cruise ships they are given a joyous and friendly welcome to our city by musicians and Newfoundland dogs.

For six years Jake Doyle and I have participated in this program. We have welcomed hundreds of people from all over the world. These occasions have given me many remarkable memories, but one that still pulls at my heartstrings took place three years ago.

We were just finishing up our shift when a steward approached me and asked if I could wait a few more minutes for a husband and wife who were hoping to see us. Of course we didn't mind.

Soon, low and behold, here they came. The husband, no more than five feet high, was pushing his delicate, little wife in a wheelchair. As they approached, I could see their wide smiles. The wife was so excited.

Jake immediately approached them and did what he does best, laid his big head on the lady's lap. She laughed, she cried, and she rubbed Jake's shiny, black coat. She couldn't stop caressing him.

The husband took my hand and kissed it and thanked me. He told me his wife had dementia and this would be their last cruise. He said his wife had not been responding to anything since they boarded the ship. She had just been staring straight ahead. But that morning when she was looking out the window, she spotted Jake and got excited. She wanted to see him.

The husband said he had to act quickly. He began getting his wife ready to disembark as fast as he could. He was afraid they wouldn't get to us in time.

This wonderful man cried with happiness to see his wife so happy. I took a few pictures for him, then they headed back to the ship.

I stayed and watched them. They both waved till I couldn't see them anymore.

The power of a dog! My dog, Jake Doyle.

Doreen Moyst
St. John's, Newfoundland, Canada

Chapter 61

A Lesson in Diversity - Izzy & Elsie

My preference had led us to decide on a puppy who would become a big dog. A Newf would be perfect. My husband's preference had led us to decide not to get a black dog. A Landseer would be perfect. But after almost a year of searching for a Landseer puppy and remaining dogless (unheard of for me!), we made a call to one of the breeders we had considered earlier. She had a girl she had kept to evaluate for breeding, but had decided not to breed her. She asked if we were interested. We were.

Izzy was already eight months old, clearly not a puppy. She was black, clearly not a Landseer. But she was a Newf, and she had already become a big dog. So, even though she didn't exactly meet our original idea of *perfect*, we were pleased when she became part of our family.

Izzy is happy and loyal, smart and obedient. She is calm and easy-going and quiet. Izzy is, I am told, exactly what a Newf is supposed to be. Except for one thing. Izzy doesn't drool. Oh, maybe her mouth gets a little damp when she knows there's an apple bit or a bite of banana coming her way, but she really doesn't drool. Given the tales we had heard about Newfs and the amazing amounts of enzyme-rich liquid they produce to lubricate their food and begin the digestive process, we were delighted that Izzy didn't have this legendary Newf drool trait.

Izzy quickly developed a friendly relationship with our house cats. She is very gentle with them and allows them to rub against her and cuddle by her side, but when Izzy was almost two she tried to play with a skunk out by the barn. That's when we realized that the kitties might not be satisfying Izzy's need for animal companionship. Soon after the skunk incident we decided to find a more appropriate playmate for her.

Happily, Izzy's mom was due to have another litter, so within a few weeks we adopted Elsie. She was a puppy who would become a big dog, *and* she was a Landseer. Perfect.

Although Elsie is Izzy's half-sister, she is nothing like Izzy. Oh, she is happy and loyal, smart and obedient, but she is not calm and easy going. No, we found out right away that her energy level is always at 100%. She goes and goes and goes. Nor is Elsie quiet. Although Izzy takes her role as "kitty police" seriously, and does bark at the kitties when they do something she considers inappropriate, like jump on the table, she rarely raises her voice otherwise. Elsie, however, has something to say about everything, and I'm sure her "Woo, Woo, Woo" can easily be heard by the neighbors, a ¼-mile up the road.

This is all fine. We have had energetic dogs before, and our fenced pasture is about 12 acres so Elsie can run to her heart's content. We have even had a barker before, so Elsie's "Woo, Woo, Woo" is actually not too bad and usually sets us to laughing. But it was when Elsie was about five months old that we discovered the biggest difference between our two girls.

For years we had had a huge crock water bowl that had been the greatest find, ever. It held a substantial amount of water and was so heavy that even a large, exuberant dog could not tip it or slide it around. It had served our Golden Retriever, our German Shepherd, our Chow, our Chow/Shepherd mix, and our Kuvasz. Now it was working nicely for our two Newfs.

But one Saturday afternoon, as I was carrying that crock, full of water, from the sink to its resting place by the door, my feet suddenly went out from under me, straight up into the air. Then I came crashing down onto the kitchen floor, flat on my back, and that heavy crock, full of water, came crashing down with me. For awhile I just lay there with the wind knocked out of me, surrounded by a pool of water and a million pieces of our big, heavy, crock water bowl. What just happened?

When I was finally able to get up, I discovered I had succumbed to a "slime slick." Slime. On our kitchen floor. On the bottoms of my shoes. On the backs of my legs. Slime. *All over the place.* I was stunned, astonished.

Oh, no! Our dear, adorable, little Landseer puppy, drools. A lot! This we were not prepared for. We had heard about Newf drool. We had been warned. But we had assumed the stories were exaggerated by those who were put off by a little bit of dog saliva. Don't assume. Ever.

We learned two important lessons that first year with Elsie. One: every Newf is different, even if they come from the same bloodlines. Don't expect them to be the same and don't compare them. Two: Newfs drool. If yours doesn't, it's a rarity.

Elsie is seven years old now. Her slime slicks are much bigger now than they were when she was five months old. But we've made accommodations. She wears a bib most of the time. There are drool rags within reach of almost every place you might be standing or sitting in our home. And, heaven help you if you cannot reach a drool rag after she takes a drink.

But, drool or no drool, both of our girls have been dear to us and both have brought us many laughs and lots of pleasure. Their personalities seem close to the opposite ends of the Newf continuum, but we wouldn't have it any other way. They have constantly surprised and fascinated us. And, as different as they are, they have always been great friends.

As for that magnificent crock water bowl, occasionally, even after all these years, I still find a stray shard of it under a piece of furniture or behind a seldom-opened closet door. I sweep it up, and smile at the memory.

Kathie Norgan
Brockway, Michigan, USA

Chapter 62

The Long Road Home - Moses

"I'll take him," is not what I expected to hear myself say, looking at a Newfoundland whose face had been either stepped on or punched, and whose skin looked more like rhinoceros hide than Newfy skin. He smelled. His back legs gave him trouble when he walked.

His name was Moses, and he was being fostered by a couple who were leaving the country. He needed another foster home. The couple told me they were giving him baths with cold water in their back yard. That did it, I had to take him.

I signed the foster papers and loaded Moses into my vehicle. As I drove home, I wondered how my dogs would take this new addition. They were used to having rescues, as I have been doing this for many years, but how would they react to a broken, foul-smelling, giant dog? I had fostered Newfs before, but they were all physically sound and did not stay long, as there is a demand for young, healthy Newfoundlands. Moses did not fit that description.

I pulled into my yard, and let Moses out. He urinated, and then lay down in the grass. I let my Boxer, Hank, out to meet Moses. Hank has always been my rescue "checker." If he accepts the new guest, I know everyone else will accept it, as well. The introductions went well.

I then let Gabriel, my Newfoundland, out to meet Moses. I knew Gabe's heart would go out to Moses, and he would do whatever he could to make this boy feel welcome. Gabe went to Moses, and lay down beside him. Moses sniffed him, and seemed to relax a little more, knowing a fellow Newf lived here and was happy.

Soon we all went into the house to have a meal. Moses hobbled in. He seemed in pain. I was relieved when he was able to eat a full meal, despite his misshapen face. Later, he managed to go outside and do everything he needed to do to get ready for bed. We all slept through the night with no issues.

Before his appointment with the vet the next day, I took Moses to a grooming facility that caters to senior and handicapped dogs. After a bath with a wonderful medicated shampoo, Moses seemed to feel like a million bucks. He walked out of the facility with a bandana around his neck and a tail wagging more than before. I cheered and applauded him. He loved that, and his tail went into high gear.

Then I went to the vet to get his opinion of Moses' condition. The prognosis was not good. The vet believed Moses was quite a bit older than the four years I had been told. His hips were very bad, but due to his overall poor health and his age, the vet didn't think Moses would survive hip surgery. I left feeling a little dejected, but determined to help Moses in any way I could.

After conferring with fellow Newfoundland owners and breeders, I started Moses on several supplements and water therapy, both of which helped his general condition. Later I added acupuncture and chiropractic sessions. Within a few weeks, Moses was coming up my three front steps rather easily, which filled me with joy. Even his skin issues began improving after I implemented suggestions from specialists and experienced Newfoundland lovers.

During his months of rehabilitation, Moses showed a remarkable effort to cooperate. He attempted to do whatever I asked of him. He put his heart into every request, always responding with eagerness. He was a loving, intelligent boy with a sincere desire to please. He would have done whatever was asked of him, for as long as requested. He knew "sit" and "lie down," and during this time he learned "stay," "stop," and "speak."

Moses sometimes attempted to give me kisses, but due to his maimed face, he could not. When he tried to kiss me, I would give him a kiss and tell him he was wonderful and loved very much. He seemed to understand and was happy hearing this.

Once Moses improved as much as everyone thought he could, the Newfoundland rescue I was working with posted him on their site. I expected to hear from someone right away, but weeks passed, then months. No one seemed interested in this wonderful boy with the deformed face.

I reached out to an animal communicator to try to get more information on Moses. The details of the abuse and neglect he had endured left me in tears. The maltreatment was even more devastating because Moses' temperament was one that wanted to do the work healthy Newfoundlands want to do: draft work, obedience, water work. Whatever his person would have wanted him to do, he would have done with joy.

After having Moses for about a year, I was told that a couple was interested in meeting him. They had a senior Newf, and were hoping Moses would be a good buddy for their dog. I was ecstatic! On the day we were to meet, I took Moses to the groomer who always did a such great job with him. While we were there, I got a call from the couple. They were early, so they offered to meet us at the grooming facility.

Moses and I waited and waited. Finally, the couple arrived and got out of their car carrying a stuffed bear. With them was their senior Newf. He had issues with his legs and had his front legs wrapped to help his stability. They helped him climb out of their vehicle and slowly they walked over to us. Then we walked together, Moses next to their Newf, and the three of us behind them.

The two Newfs seemed to be fine, walking together in harmony. After about ten minutes, the couple stated that there was "no spark" between the two Newfs, so they were not going to take Moses.

Spark? Here were two senior Newfs, walking slowly together, enjoying each other's company. What did they expect to happen? Joyous jumping? Kisses? Neither dog could jump and Moses certainly could not exchange kisses. They gave Moses the stuffed bear, boosted their Newf back into their vehicle, and drove away.

I hugged, kissed, and praised Moses, telling him how wonderful he was and how well he had done during the visit. He seemed happy as I got him back into my vehicle. The last thing on this planet I wanted was for him to know he had lost his possible forever home.

That day I gave Moses a forever home, my home. In retrospect, he was a part of my family from the very first day. Welcomed by me. Welcomed by the other dogs.

Four years later Moses took his last breath in my arms at my veterinarian's office. His legs were failing him and his heart had gotten too weak to work around all his other health issues. He had suffered way too much in his life, so I let him go peacefully, knowing he was loved, knowing he would be greatly missed. I treasured my boy. His face may have been misshapen, but his spirit was flawless, perfectly formed, and radiated pure, authentic Newfoundland love.

Lisa Lathrop
Warwick, Maryland, USA
Colonial Newfoundland Club
New-Pen-Del Newfoundland Club
Newfoundland Club of America

Chapter 63

Miss Mild Meets Miss Mayhem - Taylor & Splash

Taylor was my very first Newf, and oh, was she special. For 20 years I had been flipping through my dog encyclopedia, and somehow, always coming back to the pictures and description of the Newfoundland. When the time was finally right, I got serious with my research, located just the right breeder, adopted Taylor, and immediately fell in love with my nine-week-old puppy.

From the very beginning Taylor was my sweet, adorable, loving companion, but at six months old she also became my rock, my velcro girl, my therapy dog. This was an unforeseen, unanticipated role for her. But so, too, was my ischemic stroke, unforeseen and unanticipated. I was only 36 years old.

When I was able to come home from the hospital, Taylor awed me with her amazing supportive efforts. With no formal training she simply knew what I needed and what she should do.

She walked beside me to help me keep my balance. She stood solid and strong to help me stand up from a sitting position. But most helpful of all, she was always *there*, forever faithful, and *cheerful*. It's impossible to feel gloomy or sad when a big, black Newfy is constantly giving you a big, happy smile. So began my obsession with Newfoundlands.

When Taylor was three I adopted nine-week-old Splash. Taylor valued tranquility. Peace. Serenity. She was a dignified lady, and at first she wasn't too amused with the new, little, rowdy newcomer. Happily, although it took a few weeks, the two girls eventually became very best friends.

Splash came from a Rescue in Ohio, and she was very different from calm, extremely laidback, Taylor. Splash was *energetic*. Splash was *eccentric*. She got her name due to the fact that every time she went missing at the rescuer's home, she could be found relaxing in the bathtub. She carried this trait with her for her entire 12½ years with me.

Splash grew to become the biggest, fluffiest Landseer, ever, and though she had many whimsical and unconventional habits, her favorite and most highly developed skill was counter surfing. She became a Master Counter Surfer as soon as she was tall enough for her paws to reach the counter.

I tried every trick I could think of to discourage Splash from this unmannerly, sometimes even dangerous, habit. But she seemed to rather *enjoy* toast with hot sauce, she *liked* the sound of pennies being shaken in a can, she *thrived on* using her problem solving abilities to dismantle booby traps, and she listened intently and with fascination to my clicker.

Fortunately, Splash seemed to have a cast iron stomach. One day I came home from work and was greeted by Splash, with what appeared to be chocolate around her muzzle, and Taylor, who clearly had vanilla icing all over her face.

It didn't take long to discover that Splash had not only eaten a whole, unopened bag of chocolate-covered peanuts, she had generously provided Taylor with a whole chocolate Bundt cake drizzled with vanilla icing. Because chemicals in chocolate can speed their hearts and stimulate their nervous systems, chocolate is toxic to dogs.

I called the Poison Hotline, and thankfully, due to their size and the fact that they had eaten milk chocolate rather than one of the more concentrated forms of chocolate, they hadn't put themselves in imminent danger. But they both paid for their misdeed by having diarrhea later that night.

It was at this point that the girls and I experienced an exciting life change. I got married! Taylor, of course, accepted Randy with her usual grace. Her calm, composed demeanor made adapting to new situations easy for her. But Splash, though mischievous and constantly looking for adventure, was always just a little leery of strangers and sometimes frightened by surprises. It took complete dedication on Randy's part to wait patiently for almost three months before she allowed him to pet her. It was awhile longer before she agreed to let him become her daddy.

But even finding herself in a brand new family situation didn't discourage Splash's counter surfing. Not long after Randy and I married, we experienced an event which has henceforth been known as "the day Splash ate the whole chicken." A new friend was over helping with some maintenance work so I prepared a buffet lunch including a roasted chicken which I sliced for sandwiches. We made our sandwiches in the kitchen and went into the dining room to eat. Of course Taylor went wherever I went. Splash, however, stayed behind.

Our friend was the last to make his sandwich. We had forgotten to tell him about Splash's counter surfing. He didn't know to push the chicken as far back on the counter as possible when he finished.

Later, when I went in to put away the food I spotted the empty plate immediately. The whole chicken was gone. We looked everywhere for that chicken carcass and never, ever, found one shred of meat or one hint of bone. Predictably, we did find Splash in the dog room looking very satisfied. Once again, our Newf with the cast iron stomach had no complications. Splash ate the whole chicken, Taylor had none.

The difference in personalities between the two girls was always remarkable. This difference in behaviors was never more pronounced than on one of our trips to North Carolina.

Splash and Taylor were sleeping in the back of the Explorer, Randy was driving, and I was asleep in the front seat. I was jolted awake when the vehicle began swerving all over the highway.

Randy was yelling, "I can't see the road! Help! I can't see the road!"

When I looked over at Randy I was shocked to see, wedged between him and the steering wheel, 130-pound Splash, attempting to sit on his lap. Although terrified, I was able to grab the steering wheel and guide us safely to the side of the road.

I jumped out of the vehicle yelling, "Hang on tight to Splash!"

As I opened the back of the Explorer, a burst of sunscreen was all I could smell. Somehow an aerosol can of sunscreen had exploded and sprayed its entire contents into the back of the vehicle. Taylor, in her usual undisturbed manner, was lying calmly in the sunscreen fog. Splash, being Splash, was seeking safety in her daddy's lap.

Ah, Taylor, thank you for the 10 wonderful years you were my rock. And, Splash, thank you for the 12½ wonderful years you were my silly, adventurous girl with the cast iron stomach. Even though I have had Newfs to love ever since these first two girls, and even though I have Newfs to love now, there will never be another Taylor. There will never be another Splash. Some memories are etched in gold.

Chris McSweeney Conner
Heiskell, Tennessee, USA

Chapter 64

He Sent Us Sam - Sam

As the only surviving male of his litter, our Samuel had very blessed beginnings, though I know we are the ones who have been blessed. My husband was wounded on his last deployment. His injuries resulted in his return from Kyrgyzstan, a long period of searching for appropriate medical treatments, and, finally, diagnoses of Traumatic Brain Injury (TBI) and Post-traumatic Stress Disorder (PTSD). Ultimately, this ended his military career.

Because of the TBI, Bill began experiencing falls. This is especially dangerous because TBI builds on itself. Any fall in which he hits his head can be fatal.

Thus began our journey to find a service dog. A very good friend recommended a Newf, so I began doing research. I contacted a breeder who invited us to come to her home and meet her and her dogs.

At this point Bill was very closed off to everyone and everything. His issues included falling, having difficulties speaking, a sensitivity to light, nightmares, and outbursts of anger.

I was not sure how our visit to the breeder would go, but I was sure my husband needed a service dog. So, with some concern and uncertainty on my part, we made the two-hour trip to the breeder's home.

Within minutes of our arrival, one of the breeder's dogs, Annabelle, singled Bill out. While the breeder and I talked, Annabelle refused to leave his side. She was just this soft, gentle soul who seemed to know exactly what he needed. I watched as Bill grew calmer than he had been in a very long time.

We spent almost six hours with the breeder and her dogs, and right before we left, she told us she wanted to donate a puppy to my husband, a puppy that would become his service dog.

As we were driving away, I could see the usual anxiety rolling over my husband again like a giant tidal wave. The calmness he had experienced with Annabelle by his side was gone.

All he could say was, "I need a puppy out of *that* dog. I need one from *her*." He was referring to Annabelle.

The breeder let us know she would be breeding Annabelle and we let her know we had begun praying for the puppy. She suggested we pray for a boy, as they are bigger and stronger for mobility needs, and she asked us to pray for a pup with just the right temperament.

In October, 2014, our little male pup with just the right temperament was born, the answer to our prayer. When he was three weeks old we went to meet him. I can't describe the feeling in the room when Bill held the puppy in his arms for the first time. It seemed like they bonded immediately. We knew this was meant to be.

We brought Samuel home when he was a 30-pound, eight-week-old puppy. The training began almost immediately and Sam never missed a beat. We became involved in a dog club where we shadowed multiple trainers. Sam was a dream to train. Everything my husband asked him to do, he did. After the socialization and basic obedience training was complete, the task training began. Task training involved performing tasks related to public access behaviors and disability-related work. This phase of the training seemed to come naturally to Sam. He seemed to know exactly what Bill was saying and what task he was being asked to do.

It was on one of our first public access adventures with Sam that we began to see just how incredible he would be. We were in a home improvement store and Sam suddenly started barking and pulling on the leash. At first, we thought, "stubborn puppy." But no, this was more intense. Sam was pulling my husband back toward the entrance doors.

Next we thought, "potty"? So Bill walked him outside. Sam kept pulling, and pulled Bill straight to the car. Then Sam began barking at the front passenger door. In an effort to understand Sam's behavior, Bill opened the door. As soon as he did, he fell inside onto the seat. That was the first of many falls Sam alerted him to.

When Sam was six months old, Bill began water therapy. While he worked in the pool during his first session, Sam and I watched from the side. Sam's eyes were always on my husband and the handler. Suddenly, Sam began whining. He was staring at Bill and was visibly upset. I walked him to the side of the pool so he could see that everything was okay.

But no, everything was *not* okay. Sam started barking and became frantic. Bill swam toward the stairs and, alarmingly, just as he reached them, his first seizure hit. He was helped safely from the pool and Sam lay quietly beside him until he recovered. This is how life with Sam began.

Through the years, as their relationship has grown ever closer, Sam has learned it's not necessary to become frantic when danger is imminent. He has learned Bill will respond to his silent cues. Sam can be fast asleep and will suddenly wake up and rush to Bill's side, instinctively circling him until he grabs hold of Sam and lowers himself into a sitting position. Sam is able to detect the falls and the seizures a few minutes before they happen. These warnings Sam gives my husband are invaluable.

Sam has gone on to sire several puppies and his offspring are proving to be just as intuitive as he is. They are service dogs who have warned of impending heart attacks and dangerously low blood pressures. They are therapy dogs who work in disabled adult homes and assisted living homes for the elderly.

Sam is Bill's faithful guardian. They are never apart. I prayed that God would send my husband an angel. He sent us Sam.

Liz Ishler
Arlee, Montana, USA
Trinity Newfoundlands

Chapter 65

Lex - Lex

If only I possessed the talent to write a moving sonnet or compose an epic symphony, but not even such earthly expressions of human passion could do justice to the one who saved me.

Born legally blind, I was not what my parents would have chosen for a first child. I learned quickly that security and tenderness were not rights afforded to all children. Love and acceptance were products that must be earned and paid for, and being disabled amongst so many perfect cousins and peers, I was already a step behind in the race of life. Even a connection as simple as friendship was too emotionally costly, a game of strategy I couldn't afford to play. If I wanted stability and safety, I was on my own. By the time I was 20, I was a workaholic. I was far from being driven by ambition or passion for my job. It was a primal urge to rely only on myself, because I couldn't count on anyone else.

I had nothing but money and time, so I decided to splurge both on a purebred dog. I debated between a few breeds, but one breed surpassed them all! I soon joined a club, found a breeder, and picked up my white and black Newf a year later. I thought

I was getting just another puppy, but what I received was so much more.

I don't fall in love, and I certainly don't fall in love at first sight. Love is a very deliberate choice, a choice filled with fears and doubts and hurt feelings, but that was before I held my puppy in my arms. I felt this tangible something click into place right in the center of my core. It was as though I had never seen the world in all its vibrant colors until he, Lex, became mine. All of a sudden, I began to dream, to want, to rouse from a life without inspiration. In the obedience ring, water, or trudging through mire with a cart, he earned every title. He didn't do it for ribbons or prizes, and only sometimes for cookies. He did it all for me. Our intense bond made each achievement momentous. A girl and her dog, what could be better?

Deep down, though, I wondered if I were truly worthy of him. How could I, the definition of imperfection, a being covered in scars and gashes, bruises and gushing wounds, be worthwhile in such perfect eyes? He was courageous and stable, trusting and vulnerable, everything I was lacking. He dauntlessly challenged my inner monster each and every day. No matter how low the critics in my mind dragged me down, he was always there, daring me to climb out of the darkness and face another day.

This was true love! It's not physically painful or emotionally costly, neither complicated nor terrifying. I didn't have to give back more than I received, because at times, I had nothing at all to give. The realization was shocking. I had never loved so authentically, and I had never been so loved in return. Lex was my someone when I was all alone. He wanted me when no one else did. He loved me when I didn't even love myself. He collected all my broken pieces and carried them for me. Lows and highs, successes and failures, he loved me regardless. Finally, I had someone steady to lean on. I had never felt enough until I became his. He is so much more than dog, than Newf; he is the other half of my soul.

Dana W. Kuo
Merced, California, USA
Newfoundland Club of Northern California
Newfoundland Club of America

Chapter 66

Trust—In the Midst of Chaos - Halo

"Send some HELP! In here, PLEASE!" yells the epilepsy monitoring unit nurse.

I am in the second step of being evaluated for brain surgery. I am off my usual medications. I have 10 probes on my brain. Suddenly, I have a leg shaking in the air. I am drooling and choking. I am in the middle of a bad Grand Mal Seizure.

BOING! Here comes Halo, a 100-pound, black and white Newfoundland dog, landing on the bed.

Now Halo is lying on top of me, holding me still, licking my face, keeping me from hurting myself. The poor nurse is stunned. This wasn't the response she was expecting when she called for help. Evidently, most patients don't keep their service dogs with them in the hospital. Halo's unexpected arrival has interfered with the video and the nurse's verbal observations that the doctors wanted.

As a child I was in a severe car accident that resulted in a traumatic brain injury (TBI). The TBI has led me to have seizures for the past 20 years. The seizures break through once or twice a month and I suffer the effects for a week each time.

I live in extreme fear of the seizures breaking through. Seconds before a seizure breaks through I am surrounded by an aura of doom: someone or something is coming up behind me, to stab me, kill me, eat me. When the seizure breaks through, I say over and over, "*Het komt eraan, het komt eraan, het komt eraan.*" ("It's coming, it's coming, it's coming," in Dutch, my first language.) Breakthrough seizures can progress to Grand Mals.

After a seizure, I can experience Todd's paralysis, a motor cortex exhaustion which leaves me temporarily paralyzed on one side of my body. I do not remember anything after these episodes. My seizures have never been well controlled by any of the medications that have been tried.

But now brain surgery has become a possible option, and this phase of the evaluation requires a two-week hospitalization. When we look over the brainwaves from the videoed seizure, we note that all ten probes were going crazy with activity. Then one probe channel shows something interesting. When Halo jumps on the bed, one probe goes to zero: flat-line calm. When they pull Halo off the bed, that probe indicates activity again.

Clearly, Halo being on the bed with me had an effect. It's up to the researchers to make sense of it.

We "rescued" Halo a year ago; now she rescues me.

Before surgery became an option we had talked about getting a service dog, but stopped as we learned about the two-year waiting lists and the near $60,000 cost for a certified service dog. Then, out of the blue, we came across an ad for a two-year-old, fully-trained, Service and Seizure Alert Dog being offered for only a re-homing fee. The owners needed to re-home this dog because their baby had developed an allergy to dogs. The dog's vet and vaccination records were up-to-date, and her trainer would give two free instruction sessions to the buyer.

We took a chance. We made the call.

No questions about us? Introductions in a park? Meet for the exchange at a gas station? Cash only? This is a strange and unusual situation. These are red flags.

But the next day we picked up the dog. There was no service dog vest, but we were given some paperwork.

The dog's blanket and bag of toys went into the trash before we left the gas station. On the way home we stopped at a groomer and had the knots cut out of her dirty coat. She had ticks. This dog had been seriously neglected.

There are some things you cannot unsee. This dog is sick and needs to go back to the vet!

On our second trip to the vet in the first three days she was with us, we discovered the vet records that had been provided were fraudulent, our dog had not been chipped, our dog had not been spayed, our dog had parvovirus, and the odds of her living through the week were less than 50-50. When we called the previous owner and the trainer, the phones were dead.

There we were with a giant, sick dog, with unknown, if any, service dog skills and bad odds of survival. These stresses were enough to give me more breakthrough seizures.

But four, nail-biting days, and a $1200 vet bill later, our dog made it. This was a miracle. Maybe our new dog is an angel. We renamed her "Halo."

Now what?

We looked up "service dog commands" and found that Halo seemed to know the first one: Get Busy! Okay, maybe she had had *some* training, but we hadn't had any! When she was well enough to get her rabies shots, we began making the 45-minute weekly trips to All 4 Paws Training, LLC, in Tempe, Arizona, a company that teaches people how to train their own service dogs.

"Eventually, you are going to have to trust your dog's alerting! She isn't bumping your hand because she wants a cookie," instructs Myra, our trainer.

But it's hard to get used to the fact that your dog can predict your seizures. It's a new experience to have a "boink, boink, boink" on your hand from a dog's nose mean, "Take your seizure rescue meds now!"

"I feel fine! Halo, I feel fine!"

We are in the middle of a training session. I feel fine. Five minutes later, I'm having a seizure.

"Your dog said, 'TAKE YOUR MEDS! NOW!'" from Myra. "*Trust your service dog!*"

Interspersed among the two years of testing and medical procedures to prepare for and finally undergo the brain surgery, were many hours of training for Halo and me, sometimes for Halo and Joshua, my husband, when I was unable to attend the classes. The two-week stay in the hospital became an intense

"Boot Camp Training" for Halo. But throughout her training, Halo was an angel, always passing her evaluations at the head of the class. A few months ago she re-certified and passed the Public Access Test in flying colors.

My brain surgery was successful and has brought an end to the constant seizures, although I am still transitioning off medications and still need Halo at my side.

Some of the ways in which Halo has helped me include:

- alerting about five minutes before I have a seizure ... an exceedingly rare gift only six out of 1000 dogs may have
- alerting someone and getting them to follow her to me if I have a breakthrough seizure
- pulling me to the wall with her leash in her mouth and holding me there if she thinks I am stressed because there are too many people in the area
- lying on top of me barking for help and preventing me from hurting myself or falling off the bed if I have a Grand Mal seizure
- looking into my eyes when I give a "Watch" command ... this "distraction" can stop a breakthrough seizure from progressing
- reminding me to take my evening medicine at 9 p.m. by making a fuss to get her evening treat

It can't be put into words how much Halo opens the world up for me and makes my life better. She has called for help when I couldn't. She has been there for me when I got scared that something bad might happen. She helps me feel "safe" going out of the house, despite my extreme fear of having a seizure. She often knows how my body works better than I do. I literally feel naked without her by my side.

Typically, the Giant Dog coming out from under a table in a restaurant when we are leaving is a "shock and awe" conversation starter as people can't believe a Newfoundland can fit under the table and was, thus far, unnoticed because she was so well behaved.

"Is that a Newfy?" opens conversations and makes communicating with unfamiliar people easier.

Sometimes people say, "I wish my dog was that well-behaved!"

At times I have trouble with big words and memory lapses. Having Halo at my side lets people understand my pauses or hesitations and makes me more comfortable. It makes life easier when the first impression people have is of a well-behaved dog and a talented dog handler, rather than their first impression being of my disabilities.

On October 31, 2019, I participated in the ceremony to become a U.S. citizen. Despite being in a large group of noisy and excited people, this was a happy and enjoyable occasion for me. I did not feel too nervous. I did not feel too afraid. Halo was there with me.

I named her Halo because she is my angel, my very own service dog saving me from these seizures. It took me a little time, but I have learned to *trust my service dog.*

Robin & Joshua Doremire
Fountain Hills, Arizona, USA
Mesquite Newfoundland Club

Chapter 67

Circe's Birds - Circe

The joy of the day for Circe, my great black Newfy, is our morning walk. She's right behind me from the time I get up, watching every motion, whether it's checking out the morning paper, feeding the mousers, making a cup of tea, whatever. She's like a shadow. Putting on the shoes gets her hopes up, but when the hat, the glasses, and—finally—the leash appear, then the brown eyes sparkle, the great tail goes wild, and the big paws dance.

Although our route is a little less than a mile, it takes a very long time. There is just so much p-mail to check out, so many new things to investigate, several other dogs to watch, and lots of amazing stuff to find—like morsels left along the way by children in strollers and munching adults, and, the most intriguing of all, an occasional dead bird. Dogs tend to snorp up these treasures, (yes, even the birds), swallowing stuff up before one has a chance to grab it from their jaws. Circe's skill in this snorping business is the best. She's fast. She's thorough. Except for the bird thing.

When one of these poor creatures appears along our route (which, thankfully, is not often), Circe's on it in a flash. But, instead of munching it up, she sniffs the bird intensely for a very long time. Once, many months ago, she carefully picked up a bird near the beginning of our route and patiently carried it all the way home with not one stop to sniff. I didn't try to take the bird from her as I was curious about what she planned to do with it once we were home. When we were outside our alley-side fence, she finally stopped, placed it carefully at the base of the fence, and went on inside in search of her water bowl. A bit puzzling. But that was it.

Since then, when we come upon something unacceptable, I tell her to "leave it" and she reluctantly does. Last week, we were walking on a narrow dirt road that has an irrigation ditch on its west side and, on its east side, a brick wall with various trees and shrubs growing in front of it. Under the trees is a scrabble of dumped rocks, sand, and leaves. The road is a pleasant place where people often allow their pooches the joy of running free for a little while. So, Circe was moving along, on her own, checking out things new and old when—pow!—there was a dead bird a few feet from the ditch.

She did the usual intense sniffing. I was about to tell her to leave it when she started to shovel sand on the bird with her nose. I thought that was kind of touching, so I decided to just wait and see what she was going to do. She kept trying to get enough sand from the road, but the surface was too hard and, with each nudge of her nose, her bird was pushed closer and closer to the edge of the ditch. I figured it would soon plop into the water and on we'd go.

This was not Circe's plan. When she saw she was going to lose her bird, she gently picked it up and started wandering around in search of better diggings. She took her time and ended up carrying the bird across the road to the trees. She checked out one spot. Wouldn't do. Then another, and yet another.

Finally, she chose the base of a rock where a lot of sand had collected. One great paw quickly excavated a hole, and Circe softly placed the little bird in it. Then the nose went to work. Sand from here. Sand from there. More sand. Still more sand. At last, she seemed satisfied. She finished her work with one firm tamp of her nose, then it was time to get back to the morning walk.

The next day she returned to her bird, gave the sand a little nose nudge, seemed satisfied, and went on. She hasn't returned to check on it again.

I've thought a lot about Circe's project. It wasn't so much what she did, as how she did it. Her urgency. Her effort. I couldn't help but wonder, was this a classic case of dog-saving-bird-for-weekend-snack?

Or ... had I watched a great mothering Newf needing to care for a poor, small creature?

Meg Stragier
Scottsdale, Arizona, USA

Chapter 68

Natural Born Lifesaver - Finnegan

What is all the fuss about? Isn't this his job? Aren't Newfs supposed to do water rescue? Haven't the people at this dog park heard any of those great "fisherman saved by a Newf" stories? Maybe witnessing a Newf performing a water rescue in person, in real time, is more impressive than just hearing about a Newf performing a water rescue. Whatever the reason, Finnegan, our big, brown Newf puppy, was enjoying all the hugs and praises he was getting from this group of excited and grateful strangers.

It had been a beautiful, warm afternoon, so I had taken Finnegan for some exercise at a local dog park. He was just over a year old, and although there was a huge pond at the park, he had never shown any interest in swimming. Running and playing with the other dogs was what he loved, and that's what he had been doing that afternoon as I sat on a bench watching.

Suddenly, breaking high above the lively dog barks and yips, came the frantic voice of a woman yelling, "Help! My dog's in the middle of the pond! He's drowning! He's drowning!"

Finnegan stopped playing, looked out into the pond, looked at me as if to say, "I don't really want to do this, but ...," then, very calmly, he walked to the water, strolled in, and began swimming toward the small, struggling dog. When he reached the little dog, he casually grasped him by the scruff, turned around, and with smooth, even, easy strokes, brought him to the shore.

The crowd of dog owners had watched in awe, in silence, in disbelief. To be honest, I was just a little bit awed, myself. Of course I knew all about Newfs and how water rescue is their innate, inbred, instinctive gift, but still, our big, brown puppy swimming toward the shore with a small white terrier in his mouth *was* a pretty awesome sight.

Now the grateful woman was holding her little wet dog in her arms, sobbing, hugging me, hugging Finnegan, and thanking me profusely. Several other people had joined her and were loving on Finnegan and thanking me. I tried to respond graciously, but I didn't really deserve thanks. The only part I had played in this remarkable rescue was to drive Finnegan to the dog park.

Several weeks later, a friend of ours was at that same dog park and people there were talking about this giant, brown Newfoundland that had saved the life of another dog. Our friend knew they were talking about *our* giant, brown Newfoundland. Even though we had never done any water training with him before that day, nor did we ever do any afterward, it seems Finnegan, the Newf with no interest in swimming, had become the stuff of water rescue legend.

As it turns out, the life of the little white terrier was not the only life Finnegan was to save. The next life he saved was mine.

Again, it was a beautiful, warm afternoon and Finnegan and I were outside rolling around on the ground, playing in our backyard. We had just settled down and I was giving him a belly rub when I looked down and saw, to my horror, that my entire pant leg was covered with bees.

I am deathly allergic to bee venom so my first instinct was to panic. I jumped up and began running toward the house screaming for my husband. Finnegan immediately realized I was in grave danger, but the manner in which he chose to help me still seems unusual, if not utterly bizarre. Yet his unconventional solution to the threat was incredibly effective.

Finnegan stood up, charged toward me, jumped hard against me, and knocked me to the ground. As I lay there in terror, Finnegan stood beside me barking ferociously.

Why do beekeepers traditionally wear white when tending their hives? It's because they know bees attack dark colors. Bees' natural enemies wear dark colors. Enemies like big, black bears. Enemies like ... big, brown Newfies?

As I hit the ground, every single bee left me in an instant and began swarming onto Finnegan. I could see them burrowing, fast and furiously, into his fur. But he stood his ground and continued barking while I got up and raced away.

Finnegan ended up being stung over 100 times. The emergency vet instructed us to give him Benadryl, and, within three hours, the swelling and redness around his face and muzzle had disappeared. Finnegan was completely back to normal. It was as if nothing had ever happened. As for me, on the other hand, it took me months before I could talk about this "rescue" without sobbing. My boy had saved my life that day. How can you ever thank your dog enough for doing that?

For a brief five years we were owned by a most magnificent Newfoundland boy named Finnegan. We lost him, very suddenly, four years ago. There are days when it still feels like yesterday. I loved that boy. I miss him every single day.

Michelle Forbes
Rochester, New York, USA

Chapter 69

A Life Lived on the Edge - Zulu

I've been given a not unique opportunity, but thankfully, a rare opportunity, once again, by my Newfoundland dog. I was given the opportunity to see his life through to the end, and found myself able to meet the challenge. Through this experience, I learned a few things about life, and about myself—who I have been, who I am, and who I hope I am becoming.

Friday, September 10, 2010

I woke up to find my beloved Zulu Ra unable to rise to meet the day. Unable, for the first time in a life that, incredibly, spanned over 14 years. A life lived to the extreme every day I knew him.

From Zulu I learned that even if you are a rule-follower, being a rule-follower on the outermost edge of the rule is a good thing. Don't acquiesce, don't heedlessly follow. Always test the limits! Life lived on the edge is a hell of a lot more fun.

From Zulu I learned that it is important to love, openly and completely, regardless of whether or not there is risk involved. Love given freely, without consideration of reward or return, is often returned, though not always from the place where we were seeking it. Life lived on the edge is a hell of a lot more fulfilling.

From Zulu I learned that it is important to trust, sometimes blindly, that life will be good and tomorrow will come, and that no matter what the day brings, there can be joy. Life lived on the edge is a hell of a lot more exhilarating.

Zulu's life was one of extremes. The dog never did anything in half or part measure. He ate with gusto and joy; he drank with gusto and joy; he slept intensely, resting deeply so the next adventure could be pursued with energy and passion. He loved running with the wind under his tail; he loved walking slowly to sniff out all of life's little calling cards; he loved seeing the next thing that was out there, and oftentimes, he took it upon himself to go inspect that thing, whether his humans were enthusiastic about the journey or not.

Zulu's joy in life wasn't limited by not having opposable thumbs. If he wanted to know what was in that box, tube, can, cabinet, closet, or drawer, and no one understood his need to know, he found a way to reveal the contents for himself. He was endlessly curious and always entertained by discovery, or maybe by the process of discovering.

There were people and things in Zulu's life he didn't particularly like. He chose to ignore those things rather than be made unhappy by them. He understood that life's little annoyances would either go away or were simply not important enough to interrupt his pursuit of life on the edge.

Because of Zulu I learned about compassion and sharing and being there for someone in need. I was given that gift by two friends. They were with me in spirit, supporting me while I watched my dog die. They were not telling me how or what or why, or trying to shape the experience. They were simply *there*. I learned that supporting someone in pain is the greatest gift one human can give another. I will remember that and give that gift myself.

Saturday, September 11, 2010

Zulu's last hour was a poignant experience. The vet came to our house, and it was as if Zulu knew and understood that she was there to help, there to bring him the gift of death. He wanted to go, but couldn't get his strong body and heart to follow his spirit. He licked her hand in greeting and in thanks.

Zulu loved unconditionally, and even at the end, the strength of his heart was such that when his body failed him, the last thing he did was lick the tears off my face. I choose to interpret that as our last kiss. Zulu taught me that it is okay to go, but important to say "I love you" before you do.

I am proud to say that I kept my vow to Morgana, my other precious Newf. After she told me she was done, I had let her linger on too long in the face of my loss. I promised her as I held her at her passing that never again would I put any living creature dependent on me through more days that were necessary until I let them go. My emptiness is nothing compared to giving peace and rest to a spirit who is ready to fly. Zulu only had a short time after he was done until the vet let him take wing and soar.

I am also proud to say that I didn't end his life too early because his aging was inconvenient. I lived through his aging process—the incontinence and random accidents; the change from young and able to old and feeble.

I held him up when he wanted to stand but couldn't do so on his own. I listened to his senile ramblings and followed him on his random wanderings. When he ended his journey, I listened to his last breath. That was the only "quiet" thing Zulu ever did. The rest of his life was a celebration of making his presence and his mark on the world felt, emphatically and enthusiastically.

And Zulu does leave a mark—a big one. Many people were touched by the gregarious personality that was uniquely Zulu. On the edge, to the last.

I hope it is true, the legend of the Rainbow Bridge. I hope, my Zulu, you really are young and strong and running with the wind under your tail again. I hope you find paint and canvas to strew across abundant spaces, leaves and snowflakes to name and chase, drawers to open but never close, faucets to turn on but never off, refrigerators to open and loot, counters to troll, and commotions in the distance to wonder at and go find out about. I hope you bark with *thunder* again.

Zulu Ra, January 23, 1996 - September 11, 2010. Be at peace, Master of Chaos. There is a hole in the world tonight.

Mary Belford Smith
St Louis, Missouri, USA

Chapter 70

Chief Companion - Chief

The Newf Rescue Chair called and told us about a boy who needed a foster home immediately. We were still grieving for our Baboo, who had lost her battle with Valley Fever, a fungus that lives in the desert soil in the southwestern United States, the spores of which, once inhaled, can cause lung infections. But, we agreed to provide a temporary home for this pup while the Rescue Chair found a permanent home for him.

We went the next day to facilitate the owner surrender, fell hopelessly in love with the handsome Landseer boy, realized ours would be the perfect forever home for him, and officially became another foster failure family. All this happened within the course of one single, bright, sunny morning.

Chief was our third Newf, but not my first rescue. After buying my first home, I knew I wanted a dog. My research led me to decide a Newfoundland was the one for me, and I added my name to a breeder's puppy list.

But a puppy was not to be because one evening before any puppies were born I saw a lady walking two Newfs as I was driving home from work. I literally stopped my car right there in the middle of the street and met Dryfus and Claus. The lady was fostering Dryfus. As soon as it could be arranged, I adopted that sweet boy.

Dryfus had been my special pal and protector, Baboo had been my older daughter's special playmate and protector, and now Chief, at 18 months, became the perfect protector and first playmate for our Sophia, who was about to turn two months old. These two "babies" would grow up together.

From alerting to her every whimper when she was tiny, to acting as the clean-up patrol around her high chair as she grew, Chief took his job as Sophia's main caregiver seriously. It was when Sophia began toddling that Chief's gentleness and patience truly began to shine. Sophia would grab big tufts of Chief's fur with her little fingers, use those tufts to pull herself to her feet, then, strongly attached to her big playmate, teeter along beside him while he took small, carefully calculated steps. Chief taught Sophia to walk.

One of Chief's best canine friends was Sioux Pooh, who visited often and spent time with us when her family went out of town. One of my favorite memories of Sophia's younger days happened during one of Sioux Pooh's visits. With a dog escort on each side of her, a tuft of Newfy fur in each hand, Sophia was prowling through the grass and lantana ground cover in our backyard.

Suddenly a loud cacophony of barking arose as both normally quiet dogs signaled alarm, danger, "Mama, you need to get out here quick!" I rushed to the window to see two kids riding mountain bikes on the hillside trail up behind our house. And there, pinned between her two big protectors, was little three-year-old Sophia, the human filling in a giant Landseer sandwich.

"Thank you, Newfs! I see the kids. Trust me, they won't come anywhere near Sophia with you two on the job. Everybody can go back to inspecting the ground cover now."

When Sophia was about six years old she went through a phase where she loved to play dress-up, and Chief was her favorite playmate. She would dress him up in tutus, flower hair pins, pantyhose with holes cut out for his feet and tail, necklaces, fairy costumes, and anything else her imagination would contrive. Lucky for Sophia, Chief was always up to the task. He would cooperate with just about anything for a treat. She would have the treat container nearby, and the understanding was that with each additional piece of bling she added, he earned an additional yummy treat. But really, I think he just liked making Sophia happy.

Somehow Chief was able to go along with most any outrageous antic and still retain an air of righteousness and respectability. One of his best displays of dignity and decorum happened one holiday season when Sioux Pooh was visiting.

Chief and Sioux were roaming around in the kitchen while I was preparing my traditional pot of ham and bean soup, guaranteed to bring prosperity and good luck if eaten on New Year's Day.

That evening we went out for dinner to celebrate New Year's Eve, leaving Chief and Sioux Pooh at home. When we returned a couple of hours later we were enthusiastically greeted at the front door by Sioux Pooh. Around her neck she was wearing the lid of our "swing-top" kitchen trash can. Chief, with his usual air of poise and propriety, was lying nonchalantly on his bed in the corner, in full support of his dear friend Sioux's priceless attempt to project an "everything's totally normal here" atmosphere.

We had no way of knowing whether or not Chief had played a role in the ham bone retrieval attempt, although I feel certain he must have participated. However, even his excellent show of normalcy was not enough to rid his friend of the evidence of *her* involvement in the caper. Innocent Newfies do not have trash can lids attached to their heads.

Newfies have been a part of my life now for the past 23 years. They have been pals, playmates, and protectors. They have been loving and loyal through thick and thin. They have made me laugh. They have helped me raise my daughters. When I did my research all those years ago and decided a Newfoundland was the one for me, I have been shown, countless times over, that I made the right decision.

Susan Nicolson
Phoenix, Arizona, USA
Mesquite Newfoundland Club

Chapter 71

A Life in the Limelight - Pirate

Twenty-five years ago, my wife and I acquired our first Newfoundland after a bad experience with a different breed. We had been looking for a quiet new member for our family, but instead we had gotten a "wild thing" who ultimately became a "dangerous thing." The experience had left us shaken, but we still longed to add a dog to our family, a quiet, gentle dog.

Bethany began doing research. She referred to a few books and took a few "dog personality" tests. Newfs kept coming up, so we contacted the local Newf club. After meeting several genial, good-natured Newfs, we were hooked. Our 14-year-old son and 10-year-old daughter especially liked the idea of participating in Newf water activities.

One of the club members had a litter so it wasn't long before we had our big, black boy, Admiral. And it wasn't long before Admiral and our whole family were involved in water rescue training.

After enjoying Admiral for a year, we decided to get a Landseer from the same breeder. She had an entire litter of little black and white balls of fluff. After observing the litter from age three weeks on, we settled on a little boy who was the most laidback of the entire litter. Hampton Hills Li'l John Silver came home with us at nine weeks. He was named, in part, after our son, John, who was integral in choosing him. We called the puppy Pirate.

Pirate took to our family the day he came home, although it became obvious that he was low man on the totem pole. But he loved it! He had no responsibilities and he always got fed without asking.

One thing Pirate learned quickly was the bedtime routine. We put our boys to bed at 10 p.m. each night. Pirate would lie on the floor while we watched TV. But at about 9:50 he would get up, come over, and stare at us like he was trying to tell us something. Why? He wanted outside because as soon as he came back in, he received a treat and went to bed. Treats and sleep—these were two of his favorite things.

When he was about six months old Pirate developed a slight limp in his rear leg. After a visit to an orthopedic vet, we were told he had hip dysplasia and would need a hip replacement in about two years when his skeletal system was fully developed. We were advised to keep him exercised and not to overfeed him.

Since we were doing water training with Admiral, Pirate was always along at training sessions. Although he didn't begin formal training until the following year, the vet said swimming would be a good exercise for him without stressing his hip joints.

Pirate took to the water right away. He loved it! But Pirate and Admiral were very different in the water. Admiral was the high-speed ski boat zooming past the shore pulling water skiers. Pirate was more like the pontoon boat with a family grilling hamburgers as they cruised casually around the lake. Both boats reached their destinations, but at much different paces.

Pirate went on to earn his Junior Water titles in the US and Canada. A year later he earned his Senior Water titles in both countries. Even though Pirate was relaxed and easy-going, he was enthusiastic about participating in all kinds of activities. He simply liked doing things with us. So over the years Pirate earned many titles: Draft, Team Draft, Canine Good Citizen, Companion Dog, and Therapy Dog. He kept busy. And, he kept our children busy.

In his "off time," Pirate, along with Admiral, made more than 50 visits to local elementary schools. Part of the Pennsylvania 4th grade reading curriculum was the book, *Hugger to the Rescue.* Admiral played Hugger, a black Newfy trained in Search and Rescue. Guess who got to play his sidekick, Panda, a black and white Newfy? As the visits came to a close, we would permit the students to come up and give the dogs a hug if they wanted. Since Pirate was a "lover" and a "licker," we warned that he would give kisses and he loved to lick ears. At one visit we noticed a little boy visiting with Pirate and holding his ears up to Pirate's head. Pirate obliged and gave them a good lick. Of course, this resulted in lots of giggles.

Once the news of our Newfy boys' school visits got around, they were invited to audition, along with approximately 20 other dogs, for a series of performances with the Pittsburgh Symphony Orchestra. Pirate was one of the five dogs chosen for a role in a "hunt" piece where the dogs provided the "barking" for the hunt. Pirate was completely comfortable with the instruments and the conductor. He had a knack for understanding what was wanted and was always more than happy to provide. And since he loved treats, training was easy.

Not to stop with his stage life, Pirate later performed with the orchestra of Butler, Pennsylvania, and went on to show great stage presence in 11 performances of a local Summer Stock Theater. That role required him to ignore a bowl of food, answer to a different name, carry a newspaper to a designated spot, and, of course, share the final curtain call. He always hit his mark, taking center stage every time.

During the Bicentennial of the Lewis and Clark Expedition, a reenactment was held in Pittsburgh as it was the original port of departure. After several black Newfies were used to represent Lewis's dog, Seaman, Pirate was honored as the only Landseer ever permitted on the expedition replica keelboat. He participated in this celebration with his usual charm and charisma.

As we relay some of these stories to friends and acquaintances, inevitably we get the question, "When did he have his hip replaced?"

We smile and say, "He never did. We just didn't tell him he needed a hip replacement."

As I write this, it brings a smile to my face, a tear to my eye, and a twinkle to my heart. Pirate managed to be a star without ever seeking the limelight.

He died at 12½ years old, having made a huge impact on almost every human life he encountered. There will never be another Pirate.

Bruce & Bethany Karger
Allison Park, Pennsylvania, USA
Hampton Hills Newfoundlands
Penn-Ohio Newfoundland Club
Newfoundland Club of America

Chapter 72

Alaska Luke - Luke

An old dog thundering through this brutal Alaskan forest scares me, but at 10, Luke still feels the need to protect his territory from threats unseen by us but clearly obvious to him. A couple of nights ago he sensed "something" alarming and charged off after it. I heard him crashing through the woods, then saw him racing down toward Whiskey Creek, splashing through the water, then disappearing into the forest on the other side. He sounded like a clip from Jurassic Park in his endeavor to catch The Thing, and nothing I said would make him come back. I am thankful he can still race through the wilderness though, and I was especially thankful when he finally succeeded in driving off the unseen menace and returned to the cabin in triumph.

Luke is my protector in the forest when we are alone. He has halted me on many occasions when he sensed a bear or a wolf nearby, only allowing me to proceed down a trail after the threat has moved off. Sometimes *I* see these animals, as well, and I am struck by Luke's ability to realize he needs to stay with me rather than challenge them.

Several years ago I developed a balance issue and as we hiked one day, Luke sensed I was about to fall. He ran back to my side and just intuitively braced himself against me. With more specific training he became my service dog. This has allowed me to continue doing the things I love and the things we love doing together.

Luke thoroughly enjoys his role as our champion protector and helpmate, but fishing is still his greatest passion. He is happy to get up at 4:00 a.m., out the door by 5:00. As soon as we turn the corner to the dock where one of our boats is moored, he gets excited and starts trying to hurry us along with his encouraging comments.

Luke lies patiently on deck while we're getting underway, but as soon as we've reached our destination and the lines are down he is alert and watching the tips of the rods, especially Gary's, for the slightest tug. He knows, even before we do, that we're getting a bite. And once the rod tips, the game is on. Luke's barking begins! He knows it's a fish and he knows it's part of his future meals as well as ours. He does not stop this racket until the fish is in the fish box.

We learned recently that Luke seems to be known throughout the area. When Gary went over to the other side of the island to work on one of our boats, all the dock people were asking, "Where's the big boy?"*(No one asked about me!)*

After Gary finished with the repairs he took the boat out for a test drive, then over to the fuel dock to gas up. All the dock people over there were asking, "Where's the big boy?"*(No one asked about me!)*

Then Gary got a clue about Luke's reputation as a fisherman when a big charter fishing boat came in and docked near our boat.

As soon as the charter guide saw Gary he asked the inevitable question, "Where's the big boy?"

Then he asked if Luke *always* barks when we get a fish on. "Does he bark *every* time?"

Gary explained that Luke seems to know a fish is on even before we do and apologized for Luke. He told the guide he hoped his fishing clients weren't bothered by the barking.

The guide replied, "No, actually, it's quite entertaining for them. Plus, the big boy lets everyone know exactly where the fish are biting."

Even though Luke has been giving away all the good fishing spots, he takes catching fish very seriously. Heaven forbid that a fish gets off or that we bring one in and toss it back because it doesn't comply with regulations. When either of those things happen he gives us a look of disgust, then thumps back down on the deck and shuts his eyes. Humans are just too *stupid*!

Eight hours on the ocean is exhausting for all of us, but Luke loves every moment of it, although he is not fond of whales or sea lions. He jumps up and barks at both, but seems especially irritated by the stink of whale blow if they come too close to the boat. However, he is tolerant and completely undisturbed by the eagles that swoop down to pluck a fish or our discarded baitfish out of the water. Perhaps he sees eagles as part of his family since they are all over our beach at home.

On our way back home from our fishing trips Luke watches closely for the road that takes us to the ice cream cones. Luke and I share a cone while Gary hogs most of his. But Luke stares like a vulture at Gary's cone, knowing he will eventually get his share. The second Luke gobbles the last bite of Gary's cone, he thumps down in the back seat for a nap. Luke has completed another great fishing trip. All is well and right in his world, and we're all happy.

We will admit, Luke is a barker. But he barks for a reason. Always. Fish on! People coming to the cabin! Minks in the woodshed! Bear under the cabin or at the back door! Skiff sinking because *somebody* forgot to bail the rain water out.

And Luke sings. To opera (he loves a good tenor and *Il Divo*). To commercial jingles that strike his fancy (Fiji Water, 1-800-EMPIRE). To "Say a Prayer for Peace"(Wounded Warriors). To Etta James (*At Last*). Luke throws his big, ole head back and issues forth all the joyful sound he can muster. It's a thing of beauty.

And now Luke is teaching our puppy, Amazing Grace, the things she needs to know in order to be a successful Alaska Newfy, and she is learning quite well how to get along and survive here. But, she doesn't bark at the fish. Yet.

Oh, my gosh, how I love this boy!

Lin Holt
Prince of Wales Island, Alaska, USA
Facebook: linda.holt.1213/

Chapter 73

Nana and the Old Guy - Nana & Moses

Poor Nana! She searched every room of the house. She stared through every window. She investigated every acre of the yard. But she couldn't find him. Her big, black friend was *gone*. She was so heartbroken she stopped eating.

Nana is our first Newf and her reaction surprised me. We had been fostering Ready for almost three months and had felt so fortunate when we found a lovely home for him. Since Nana had been a happy only dog before his stay, I thought she would be glad when the intruder was gone. I was wrong.

Nana finally stopped searching for Ready, but her happy-go-lucky attitude disappeared. She began sleeping more. She lost interest in food and in play. Our girl was depressed.

When I mentioned Nana's predicament to our Newf Rescue Chair, she told me about an old boy who had just come in. Her information indicated he had spent most of his life alone in a backyard. He was nearly deaf, he would require vet care for the usual geriatric problems, and like all rescues, he would need copious amounts of reassurance and love. His name was Moses.

I thought about my sad little 1½-year-old girl. She was lonely. She needed a friend. We would adopt that old guy! Without even meeting Moses, we made the three-hour drive to pick him up.

Nana was delighted when we brought Moses home. Showing perfect Newfy hospitality, she immediately took him on a backyard tour of the most desirable water puddles. Happily, he sloshed through each one.

Next, she introduced him to her little plastic wading pool and invited him in. He *adored* it! He absolutely went nuts. The slow and sluggish Moses actually began *bouncing* up and down in the water.

His actions and demeanor led us to believe he had had very little experience being a Newf, but playing in the water seemed to awaken his ancient racial memories. He just couldn't get enough of that pool! He would splash in, splash out, then turn around and splash back in again. His excitement over the wading pool brought us real joy.

All the action created by the water play attracted our llamas. Since llamas are highly curious and inquisitive, they were immediately fascinated by the new dog in their pasture. They ran toward him to investigate. Llamas generally leave the dogs alone, but they just *had* to sniff out the new guy.

Poor Moses! He had probably never before seen a llama, much less had four, large, wildly curious, adult llamas trying to get a good whiff of him. He was scared! He ran from them! Naturally, they ran after him. The more he ran, the more insistent they became to sniff him.

Suddenly, Nana assessed the situation and rushed to defend Moses. Placing herself between him and his perceived terrorists, she began barking at the llamas. Since this was startling, unprecedented behavior on her part, the surprised llamas skittered to a halt. Then, forgoing their curiosity, they thundered off toward the other side of the pasture and took cover behind the barn.

Moses was visibly relieved and grateful for Nana's help. He had also learned a useful lesson.

"Hmmmm ... so, if I *bark* at those creatures, they go away!"

Now, every time Moses goes outside and sees the llamas, he barks at them. Even if they are minding their own business in the distance, he barks at them. Evidently, he likes reassuring himself, and barking at them makes him feel safe.

Our new family is working out beautifully. At first Nana was rather puzzled because Moses wouldn't play tug-of-war and other puppy games with her, but now that she's gotten over that disappointment, she is satisfied simply to enjoy his company. The two of them spend most of their time side by side.

As for Moses, he has really warmed up to us. He appreciates having a family. He loves to be loved. And he's a smart old guy! After only a few days, he understood that I don't like the TV, sofa, recliner, piano, tables, or doors squirted. While mostly deaf, he could definitely hear me hollering at him to "stop that and go outside." So that's what he does now.

"Hmmmm ... so if I go *outside*, my new mom stops hollering at me."

Nana has also taught Moses other indoor behavior that he, previously being an outdoor dog, had never been able to learn on his own. For example, she has taught him our nighttime routine. Although Newfs are notorious for waking their people up requesting to go in and out throughout the night, I no longer have this problem. Having concluded this disruptive behavior is simply the result of boredom, I have learned to provide my dogs with a variety of enrichment activities for their wee-hours entertainment. As a result, Nana and Moses are content to stay inside, and our sleep is never interrupted.

These enrichment activities include, but are not limited to, leaving the garbage compactor unlocked so coffee grounds and rice can easily be removed. Our Newfs particularly enjoy spreading these items on the living room carpet. If I provide an adequate amount, they can also cover the tile floor in the kitchen, and if they engage in this activity early in the night and squish hard with their big paws, the rice will adhere permanently to the tile.

Another enrichment activity I provide involves reminding our children to put juicy portions of leftover spaghetti and meatballs in the garbage can in the evening. If the children make sure the spaghetti has lots and *lots* of sauce on it, the Newfs will be able to do paw painting throughout the house. This will amuse them for quite some time.

A third Newf diversion involves asking the children to scatter their homework and backpacks all over the living room floor before bedtime. They are to make sure no one picks anything up. This is a special treat for the Newfs as they relish hiding these items where the kids will not be able to retrieve them before the school bus comes at 7:05 a.m.

These are just a few of my recommendations for keeping Newfs fully amused and happy inside all night. These activities also keep them out of our bedrooms where they might snore or otherwise bother us. We have found these activities especially effective if company is coming early the next morning.

In spite of the extra hours required to clean up after two Newfs instead of only one, we are glad we adopted Moses. Until they met, he and Nana had both been only dogs for most of their lives. Now that they have each other, they are almost inseparable. These two Newfs seem as happy to have each other in their family as we are to have them.

C. Janel Croy
Payson, Arizona, USA

Chapter 74

My Heart and Soul - Mojo

My father was the man who would pick up stray dogs on the side of the road and rescue dogs in poor situations. Therefore, we always had a potpourri of canines in our home. I grew up loving them all and, like my father, appreciating the loyalty and companionship they so generously gave.

When I was nine years old, my father and I went to the Kennel Club of Philadelphia's National Dog Show, and it was there that I saw my first Newfoundland. I loved looking at all the dogs, but as we walked, hand-in-hand among the dogs, I remember my big "Wow!" and the huge smile on my face as I spotted the Newfoundland. I remember pulling Daddy to a stop so I could watch the "Black Bear." My passion for Newfoundlands had begun.

That year for my birthday I requested a Newfoundland dog. The time was not right for a real Newfy, but I treasured the figurine of the black Newfy I received. For the rest of my childhood I kept my little clay Newfy by my bedside, knowing that someday I would have a real living, breathing, flesh and blood Newfoundland.

My love of dogs, all animals really, led me to do a research project on Pet-facilitated Therapy (PFT) when I was in nursing school. With the help of my cat, Kahlua, and 100 volunteers, I was able to show that blood pressure readings could be reduced simply by allowing subjects to stroke an animal in their lap. I have been a fan of this therapy modality ever since.

Fast forward to love and marriage, a home of our own, and my opportunity, at last, to have a living, breathing Newfoundland. We picked up our little Mojo when he was 10 weeks old and weighed 35 pounds. We saw his parents that day, and were promised clearances of his heart and hips. The clearances never came, and that, along with several other disappointments, taught me that I should have done a more thorough investigation of this breeder than I had done.

However, Mojo was a soft love, and after seeing the size of his sire and knowing the importance of a well-trained giant breed, I began working with him on basic obedience when he was still a young puppy.

I adored our training time, our bonding time, really. It would be just the two of us outside in the crisp air, working on "heel, slow, sit, down, right, left, and easy." Mojo seemed to enjoy our training sessions as much as I did.

When Mojo was about 15 months old, we were in a park, walking, training, and enjoying the children who came over for a Mojo hug. After watching us train and interact with the children, a lady approached us, introduced herself as Andrea, and told me she was a Therapy Dogs International (TDI) Evaluator.

Then she asked if I had ever considered certifying Mojo to conduct therapy visits.

The timing was perfect. I suppose Mojo and I had been working towards this goal all along without realizing it. The next day we met Andrea at the park and Mojo and I passed the evaluation.

Andrea took us under her wing and we began the next step in the certification process. This consisted of logging 100 hours of therapy visits along with three or four other TDI trainee teams.

Completing these hours was great fun. We would begin our visits to senior centers by walking into a room where residents would be waiting. Eyes would brighten, smiles would spread. Everyone wanted to touch Mojo, to pet him, hug him, love him up.

We enjoyed this part of the visit, but the most special time was when we walked the hallways and residents who were confined to their beds would ask us to come in. It was a joy to watch the interaction between these residents and Mojo as he rested his head on their beds. His size made it perfect for both of them. The resident, smiling ear to ear, could reach to pet him, while Mojo, tail wagging side to side, could stand comfortably to enjoy the attention.

In no time at all, Mojo and I completed our 100 hours of training, passed the TDI test, became a registered team, and could do independent visits wherever we were invited.

I work at the Thomas Jefferson University Hospital in Philadelphia as the Clinical Research Nurse Project Manager for The Department of Surgery. A few years ago, a co-worker told me her husband was in our hospital, and was not sleeping well. She thought a visit from their dog might help and she was about to request permission to bring her in. But she was concerned because their dog is not well trained.

Without thought to myself or my proposed evening, and clearly without thought to where this would eventually lead, I told her I had three Newfoundlands at home, all certified therapy dogs, and offered to bring one of them to the hospital for a visit.

She accepted my offer and I made the 45-minute trip home to collect one of the dogs. I took all three Newfies outside to decide which one would be best for this visit. The Peach is my love, my heart. Millie is my party girl, my soul. But Mojo is my first Newfoundland and my first therapy dog. Mojo is my heart *and* my soul.

I groomed Mojo for the visit. Then the two of us drove to the hospital, valet parked, and walked through the ER down the hall to the elevator. A big, brown, 170-pound boy is quite the showstopper, so our walk to the elevator took forever. Mojo is a Rock Star. Everywhere he goes takes forever.

We finally arrived at the room where my co-worker and her husband were. As he always does, Mojo laid his head on the hospital bed and stood there waiting to be loved. It was magical to see both my co-worker and her husband light up with laughter and joy. Soon staff members began coming in to meet Mojo.

After awhile, the attending physician asked us to visit some other patients and their families. For the next few hours Mojo put smiles on everyone's face. When it was time to leave, Mojo refused to get on the elevator or descend the stairs. He was not yet ready to leave. He had more visits he needed to make.

After another hour of inspiring smiles, laughs, hugs, and love, Mojo and I were both tired, and finally, we were both in the elevator. But just as the door began closing, a family member stopped it to request a visit for her dad who had been in our hospital for five months.

I felt so bad about declining. I explained I was afraid Mojo would not get in the elevator again. But I told her we would visit her dad the next day.

As promised, we returned the next day and visited the daughter and her dad. Then we visited many others who were eager to meet my brown bear.

My spur-of-the-moment offer to bring Mojo to visit a colleague's husband led to the discovery that my own hospital did not have a therapy dog program. With all my focus on my clinical responsibilities, I had overlooked the value of providing an ailing patient with some Newfy-created moments of comfort and optimism.

The next day I wrote a plan for a Pet-facilitated Therapy Dog Program and received approval. In no time at all, Mojo and my two girls started daily visitations.

I take the "dog for the day" with me to work, and the very happy "chosen one" stays in my office during the day. After work we do our hospital visit.

My dogs brighten up the hallways of the Medical College Building where my office and the offices of the surgeons are located. By special request, the dog of the day accompanies me to all the surgeons' meetings. As a healthcare worker, I know the value of stress relief and I know the surgeons truly enjoy the therapy visits themselves. Surgeons, as well as patients and their families, appreciate Newfy-created moments of comfort and optimism.

Mojo, with his gentle, natural love for people, led me to the Therapy Dog International program. His enthusiasm for meeting new people brings joy to him, to me, and to everyone who reaches out to him. I am grateful to my boy for creating this amazing part of my life. Pet-facilitated Therapy is a win-win for everyone.

Jamie Jay Rothstein, RN
Medford, New Jersey, USA
New-Pen-Del Newfoundland Club
Newfoundland Club of America

Chapter 75

Turned Around By Love - Leia

Stitch, a Jack Russel Terrier, and Poocho, a Pit/Lab mix, were two of my best friends. In April, 2018, I lost them both within a week of each other. It was heartbreaking, but both boys had lived long, happy lives and had fairly peaceful departures.

Now, suddenly, after 30 years of having dogs, I found myself dogless. I took a deep breath and let the vague, ambiguous idea that had been buried in my brain take shape. I would travel. I would see the world.

But when you've always shared your life with dogs, an empty home seems, well, *empty*. And quiet. Quiet when I walked in the door. Quiet when I ate my meals. Quiet when I talked to the mailman.

So, I did not travel. I did not see the world. Instead, within three months I rescued Ziggy, a three-year-old terrier mix. No more quiet! Two months later, my phone rang again. Leia, a two-year-old Newf, needed help. Immediately!

Two years earlier I had become interested in Newfoundlands and had begun learning more about them. I joined the local Newf club, met the members' dogs, helped re-home a couple of Newfs, and became guilty of severe Newf envy. I couldn't wait to foster, maybe to adopt, a Newf. Now, my turn had come.

We met for the exchange in a park and the first things I noticed about Leia were that she was thin, her coat was terribly matted, and she had a sadness about her that was unlike any Newfoundland I had seen. But driving home, I felt confident and optimistic. I had my first Newf to foster, maybe to adopt. Maybe I was driving Leia to her forever home. Oh, happy day!

My expectations were badly shaken when Leia showed immediate and utter disdain toward Ziggy. Leia want to shred him to pieces. She followed one aggressive attack on him with another, and another. Oh, happy day?

Records showed three-month-old Leia was acquired from a retail store by a young couple who saw her playing in the window. The couple then followed all the steps new puppy owners take: agreeing to love and care for her; creating a relationship with a vet; getting her micro-chipped; buying appropriate food. They were all set.

Leia was in her new home for a month when the couple learned they were going to have a baby. The new puppy was no longer the center of attention. For the next few months Leia spent several hours a day in her kennel while the couple was at work. Even when they were home, their new focus didn't include a big pup who was growing bigger every day. Leia was given no training and her "socialization" consisted of rather limited contact with her owners.

Leia was allowed out of her kennel less and less. As a result, she became more and more aggressive and unruly. At one year old, she crashed into the pregnant owner causing her to fall. That was it. Leia was out.

A 21-year-old girl responded to the "Free Newfoundland to good home ..."ad. The owners didn't check on the girl's situation or make sure she was able to care for an 80-pound puppy. Clueless to Leia's lack of training and aggressive behavior, the girl was thrilled with the idea that she had gotten a free Newfy.

The girl's family consisted of her parents, her one-year-old baby, a Basset hound, and a Chow. Leia was now fourth in the food chain and was once again kenneled because she was aggressive toward the baby, the other dogs, and people in general.

After 10 months, the young girl waved a white flag and reached out to a Newfoundland rescue group. That's when my phone rang and the peaceful life Ziggy and I had been enjoying came to an abrupt halt.

During our first few weeks together Leia's aggression was almost unmanageable. I honestly was beside myself thinking there was something permanently wrong with this big dog I had brought into my home. Many people told me she was dangerous and suggested I should simply put her down. I knew they were wrong, but I wasn't sure what to do.

Then it hit me. With everything I knew about Leia, one thing was certain. No one had ever shown her love. No one *could* show her love! I could. I would.

We spent the first few weeks just trying to learn silence and calm. Not knowing where to start, I began by trying to get her to maintain eye contact. At first, she wouldn't look me in the eyes for more than a second. Once she was able to hold eye contact, I moved on to holding her paws.

After a few weeks of attempting to gain her trust, I called for support and had a trainer come in and teach us the basics: how to play, how to walk on a leash.

After six months of hell and my near-admittance of foster failure, Leia started responding to me and my efforts to train her. However, we continued to have many days of frustration because her default was to attack and tear things to shreds. These setback were devastating. Afterward, hours would pass before I could get back to calm.

I cried. I got hurt. I got bitten. But, I absolutely fell in love with this dog.

It took over a year and it makes me sad to remember how hard it was and how discouraging it was to have people constantly telling me to put her down. But finally she was at peace with Ziggy and me. Eventually, she even became nana to my two-year-old grandson and three-month-old granddaughter.

Sometimes I think Leia remembers our early days when life was such a struggle. She will sit next to me on the couch and quietly reach out her paw. This is my cue to hold it, just like I did in the beginning. Then we make eye contact. My heart melts every time.

Leia will be four in December. All she needed was love.

Julie Tuttle
Gilbert, Arizona, USA
Mesquite Newfoundland Club

Chapter 76

Faux Motherhood - Maple

To spay or not to spay is an easy question for mindful dog owners to answer. No responsible person wants to add unwanted puppies to an already overwhelmed homeless dog population. However, the answer to the question "when to spay?" is not as clear. The research we did on giant breeds led us to decide that waiting until the dog finished growing and developing before spaying would be the better course of action for our chocolate Newf, Maple. However, waiting until she was two years old was much more stressful than we thought it would be.

When Maple was six months old she went into heat. She began eating like a cow and gaining weight. Were we worried that she had accidently become pregnant? No, not exactly. But, why did she suddenly seem so restless?

Maple didn't stop at overeating and gaining weight. The next thing she did was to crawl as far back under our deck as she could go and dig a huge hole. Was she making a den? Was she preparing a place for her babies? Maple's "mothering" behavior was beginning to look too real. Now we were officially becoming worried. There had been a few times when she had been in the yard without our supervision. Had she had a visitor?

A few days later, Maple carefully chose three stuffed animals from her toy bin and began moving them from room to room. Since she seemed to be creating a family with selections from her stuffy collection, we relaxed a little. By then we had learned that false pregnancies were fairly common with female dogs.

But Maple's make-believe was very convincing, very authentic. After she had selected her "babies," she became very protective of them and would get a little anxious when we gave them too much attention. She spent about a week moving her false family from room to room. She spent a lot of time cleaning them, and pretending to feed them. She was even secreting liquid from her nipples.

Her next idea was to move the babies to the den she had prepared outside. We weren't exactly thrilled about her taking them to her outside den because they would get dirty and impossible to retrieve. But she stood at the back door with a stuffy in her mouth and whined and cried and paced until we finally gave in and allowed the transfer.

The mothering behavior continued for several more days with Maple spending time with her babies under the deck, checking on them, cleaning them, and "feeding" them.

Finally it was over. Maple's false pregnancy had run its course and she returned to her usual normal puppy behavior. Our young niece crawled under the deck and retrieved the three stuffed animals. We washed them, dried them, and returned them to the toy bin.

Maple was our first Newf and the false pregnancy had been a learning experience for us. There had been more than a few anxious moments when we feared she had actually become pregnant. There had been worries when she was begging for extra food and gaining weight. There had been inconveniences when she made multiple dens in multiple rooms of our home. However, we had been patient with her and tried to keep her comfortable and content, but to be honest, we were glad when her false pregnancy was over. The days of being uncertain about her condition had been unsettling.

But within a few months, Maple went into heat again. She followed her previous routine of overeating and creating an outside den. Now that she was an experienced "mother," this pregnancy seemed even more convincing than her first one. So, once again, we followed our previous routine of worrying and wondering and feeling anxious. We kept our fingers crossed until she selected the same three "babies" and began caring for them. At that point, we relaxed. A little.

And so it went. In the two years while we waited for Maple's growth plates to mature, she went into heat five separate times. Although she always selected the same three stuffies to serve as her puppies, she added two extra babies to her fourth and fifth pregnancies. And every single time she experienced a false pregnancy, her mothering skills became ever more credible. It was impossible not to worry.

But no more fake pregnancies. Maple has been fixed. Hallelujah!

About a year ago Maple's Saint Bernard big sister died. Maple was devastated. She had loved Milly from the day we brought her home as an eleven-week-old puppy. When we couldn't bear to look at Maple's sad, lonely face anymore, we got a puppy for her, a cute, little, eight-week-old chocolate Newf. At only seven and a half pounds, it was the runt of the litter. But no more false pregnancies while we wait for growth plates to mature. Marshall is a boy. And he's growing like a weed!

Kaycee Meracle
Dousman, Wisconsin, USA
Facebook: Meracle Acres

Chapter 77

My Veteran Show Dog - Dante

Dante was blessed with what we've come to call the "dog show gene." From the day he began walking he was always most comfortable moving in a perfect "show trot," never a walk, never a gallop. He was most comfortable standing in a perfect "show stack." He found it almost impossible to move with his head down. With his first step he would throw his shoulders back, lift his head, and "move out," tail wagging merrily behind him—a perfectly-tuned machine.

In 2000 Dante was three years old, ready to begin campaigning. When we met Sam Mammano, the man who would become his handler, Dante locked eyes with him, approached him enthusiastically, and seemed to say, "*Finally!* I've been waiting for you all my life!" Dante had found his *soulmate*.

Dante spent a year with Sam and his wife, Karen. He enjoyed traveling, showing, winning, doing endurance-building walks and jogs, and playing with an endless supply of Wiggly Giggly balls. Dante played with each ball for one month, then, like clockwork, he would destroy it, forcing the Mammanos to buy him another.

I have a wonderful memory of arriving at a show site in the early morning and spotting Sam and Dante off in the distance—Sam in a baseball cap, Dante jogging along at his side, looking up at him occasionally, tail swishing happily. This scene—a boy and his dog—is frozen in time in my mind, like a Norman Rockwell painting.

Dante was not very happy to come home after his year with the Mammanos. He spent the first three weeks at the kitchen door, moaning and howling mournfully. He was grieving. He slowly settled back into life at home, running in the fields, playing with his family, sleeping at my bedside, waking me every morning with a gentle kiss.

After a few years I took Dante along with me to a show where I knew the Mammanos would be working. He was very excited when we entered the grounds.

But when I located the Mammanos' set-up and approached to greet them and show them "our boy," Dante would have none of it. He pretended he had never met them, did not know them, and did not care to be introduced. He absolutely refused to acknowledge their existence.

I could read his mind, "You told me I was the *best*. You made me feel like I was *special*. We were having the *best* time of our lives. And then *you sent me back!*"

I tried again a year or two later. This time Dante was pleased to see Karen. He leaped into her arms, joyfully greeting an old girlfriend. He made little whimpering happy sounds, hopping up and down.

Sam approached the set-up, coming from another ring with a terrier. Dante stopped rejoicing and deliberately turned his back. Sam tried to talk to him, and Dante, again, pretended he had never met the man. He was still not ready to forgive.

Another year, another show, another trip with Dante. Once again he was thrilled to see Karen. This time when Sam approached Dante hesitated. Then he gave a little shiver, and finally, relented. He leaned into Sam and melted.

Dante looked up at Sam with soulful eyes, rested against him, and said with every quiet gesture, "I do still love you, Sam."

I believe in my heart that Dante loved dog shows, everything about them, more than anything else in his life. I believe he thought every show was held just for him, and that every person in attendance came just to say "Hi!" to him and to applaud him.

After he retired from the ring and was our beloved house dog, when guests arrived, even if it was just the cable man to install some new wiring, Dante would jump onto our coffee table and stack himself, head up, tail swishing, so people could get a better look at him. He had, after all, become a Champion in 2006, been one of the two Top Dogs who sired the most puppies that year, and been on the cover of *Newf Tide*, the magazine of the Newfoundland Club of America (NCA), in 2007.

By the time of the 2008 NCA National Specialty, Dante was over 10 years old and had never looked better. As I filled out the show entry forms, I had glorious dreams of Dante winning Best of Breed from the Veteran Class.

Between the time I did the entries and the week before the show, Dante began to slow down, lose weight, and get the first powdered sugar dusting of gray on his chin. I knew in my heart that no dog loses 25 pounds unless something terrible is happening. But the vet couldn't find anything except a small tumor which he removed. I left for the National with Dante, carrying the sick knowledge that this would be our last show.

Dante was tremendously excited when we reached the site. He wanted to go from set-up to set-up, as though he were reuniting with old friends, both human and Newf. People kept remarking how wonderful he looked for a 10+-year-old. This tore at my already broken heart because I knew what he had looked like just one month earlier, and I knew that this show would mark the end of our amazing journey together.

At the Mammanos' set-up Dante was rejuvenated. He wanted to spend all his time on the grooming table with Sam touching and trimming and talking to him. When Sam put another dog on the table, Dante barked incessantly.

"*HEY!* Don't trim him! I'm your Top Dog! *Remember?*"

When the time came for Veteran Sweepstakes, Sam slipped the show lead on Dante's neck, and off they went. I was transported in time as I watched Sam (with a little less hair) and Dante (with a little less weight and a little gray on his muzzle) walk off to the ring together.

From his first step Dante moved into his "show trot" and looked up at Sam with pure joy in his eyes. I saw Sam brush away a tear, and I could barely speak. They stood waiting for their number to be called, Sam reaching down occasionally with a comb to smooth some fur, petting Dante under his ear, talking quietly to him.

The steward called their number and Sam said the words Dante loved and had waited so long to hear again, "Ready, Buddy? Let's go."

Dante threw back those magnificent shoulders, lifted his head, and trotted into the ring. Their "down and back" was a little shorter than it used to be. Their "go around" was a smaller circle. But the magic was still there. Dante heard the applause. He was with his best friend, Sam. He was once again young and happy. And he was a *Show Dog*.

Patti McDowell
Briar Creek, Pennsylvania, USA

Chapter 78

Days With Dundee - Dundee

Looking back, we now think adopting a six-month-old Newfoundland is probably not the best idea. At that age their behavior tends to fluctuate between the terrible twos and the terrifying teens. And, although the breed standard states that "sweetness of temperament" is the most important single characteristic of the breed, no mention is made of how lively and rambunctious a sweet-tempered *juvenile* Newf can be. Think high-powered, ball-of-energy Border Collie puppy, only much, much bigger.

But Dundee came from excellent breeders who had decided to reduce the number of dogs they considered for their breeding program, he would be our second Newf so we were familiar with the breed, and he was a flashy Landseer. I was in love with Newfoundlands, especially Landseers, and, at first sight, especially Dundee.

And Dundee *loved* me. As soon as we got him, he attached himself to me. I couldn't even go to the loo or vacuum the stairs without his close supervision. He was right there for anything and everything. I spent a lot of time with him in obedience and showing classes, and we walked every day. We took long quiet walks in the woods behind our townhouse and long, sometimes noisy, walks in our neighborhood.

Dundee wasn't the one making noise on our neighborhood walks. The ruckus was caused by a little tan dog we would meet. He would come down the sidewalk barking his little head off at Dundee. After this had gone on for several weeks, the day came when Dundee had had enough. As we walked past the little dog that day, Dundee reached over and calmly picked him up by the scruff of the neck. Then he spit him out. This didn't hurt the little dog, but it seemed to have taught him a lesson. He never barked at Dundee again.

My husband had started a new business and we had an office in the high-rise complex of Crystal City in Arlington, Virginia. Considered avant-garde at the time, Crystal City was the first total "urban village" in the state. It included offices, residential apartments, hotels, shops, and restaurants. It was possible to walk from one end of the complex to the other without ever leaving the underground. This was a particular plus in inclement weather.

I was acting as the receptionist at our business during this time and Dundee, by then well-trained and quite mellow, was acting as my assistant and bodyguard. We would park in the underground garage, walk up some spooky stairs, navigate a series of elevators, and eventually make our way through the maze to our office on the 4th floor.

This was in the early 1970's and people weren't taking their dogs everywhere like they do now. A big, handsome Newfoundland surprising people in elevators was unprecedented, so Dundee always attracted lots of attention.

When we got to our office, Dundee would lie quietly behind my desk. People wouldn't see him until he stood up and looked *over* the desk at them. A giant dog appearing suddenly and waving his tail in greeting caused quite a shock, but he was just so striking and well-mannered he was almost always well received.

Driving with Dundee in the back seat of my sporty, two-door Grand Prix was always somewhat hazardous because people were constantly pulling up too close to take a look at him. But one winter morning, as the two of us participated in the mad dash down Interstate 95 with the rest of the huge, commuting community in the Northern Virginia/Washington, D.C. area, my classy Pontiac decided to give up. Since this was many years before cell phones became common, I showed my distress in the way we showed car problems in those days. I pulled to the side of the road and raised my hood. Dundee, though a bit concerned, continued sitting, tall and alert, in the back seat.

Finally, an eighteen wheeler pulled off behind me and the driver offered to call for help on his CB. He also invited me into the warm cab while I waited, but I couldn't leave my Dundee alone. The trucker was kind enough to wait in his cab until a police officer arrived to rescue me.

Dundee and I sat in the back seat of the police cruiser and, looking often into his rear view mirror, the nice officer laughed all the way to our place of business. I was very grateful to Dundee that cold morning. He had made a potentially frightening event less stressful for me, and he had given the police officer a positive start to his day.

Landseers are said to have tighter mouths than black Newfs, but they still slobber. We had towels everywhere and Dundee wore a bib. When we dressed for an evening out, we had to plan carefully and sneak away before we could be slobbered on.

However, since it was Dundee's custom to greet us and welcome us home by putting his front paws on our shoulders and drooling profusely while looking us in the face, we had to devise a creative re-entry strategy. If we didn't have a doggie bag from dinner, we would stop at McDonald's and get something for Dundee. Then we would pass delicious snacks to him through the mail slot in our front door. That kept Dundee busy while we unlocked the door, hurried inside, and got prepared for our face-to-face homecoming encounter.

Even though our Landseer boy has been gone for many years, little Dundee memory bubbles often pop up and make us smile. We miss him still. Newfoundlands are wonderful dogs.

Francie Chenoweth
Darien, Georgia, USA

Chapter 79

A Swedish Teddy Bear - Nalle

"I know you wanted a female Landseer," Diane said on the phone, "but Nalle is really a nice, gentle, 18-month-old, black male."

Nalle had been rescued from the tarmac at Sky Harbor Airport in Phoenix. He'd been ready to board for a trip to Sweden. All his paperwork was in order in English and Swedish, his inoculations were up-to-date, he was approved for travel. Yet, his humans had walked away from him. Abandoned him.

Rescue had prepared Nalle for adoption by having him neutered, having his teeth cleaned, and having surgery to correct his entropion, an abnormality in which the eyelid rolls inward.

Previously, I'd had two boys from the time they were puppies. Thoughts of their puppyhood flashed through my mind. The puppy breath. The budding personality. Alex was my first Newfy adventure, Noah, my second.

And it was Noah who had fit into the palm of my hand when he was a few days old, who had been my love for nearly 13 years, and who had made me promise not to loll around mourning too long for him. He had advised me to open my heart, adopt a Newfy, and give it the love I'd given him. He'd told me my heart was too big not to share it with a Newfy in need. But was I ready?

"So, Sue, will you at least take a look at him?"

This *was* a Newfy. A *rescue* Newfy. I'd made that promise to Noah.

"Okay," I replied with a heavy, uncertain sigh. "I'll take a look."

A few hours later Nalle met me at my front door, Diane and Rick in tow. He was a big boy, taller and bigger in bone than my other Newfies. He had a full, black coat and lots of Newfy slobber. He walked right in, greeted my three little Lhasas and my Peke mix with a sniff, and proceeded to lie down.

You know how there are times when you're *certain* you're receiving guidance from somewhere else, and you *know* you have to listen and follow it? I felt Noah smiling all around, a sensation only Nalle and I could feel.

Nalle stayed. I wasn't about to send him anywhere but his new back yard with the huge pool or his new house with its many comfy corners. This boy would complete Noah's request. Promise kept. Nalle was home.

Our next few months together were wonderful. We were getting to know each other and learning the boundaries with my small dogs. Nalle was well-behaved, but he only knew Swedish. +Babbel to the rescue! Giving him a crash course in English became the challenge. I gave myself a linguistic challenge, as well. I learned "sit," "stay," and "down" in some sort of Scandinavian dialect. I also learned that the word "nalle" translates to "teddy bear." What awful thing could have happened to cause someone to abandon the dog they had called Teddy Bear?

Each evening my bilingual Newfy and I went for a long walk. He was helping me heal from some emotional losses; I was helping him understand he had a forever home. When we returned from our walks we would sit together on the floor, his head on my lap, while I stroked his beautiful, dark fur. We were a team. We were going to be okay.

I have a dog massage practice that involves several modalities, and my goal was to study Tellington-Touch, a marvelous healing technique developed by Linda Tellington-Jones. A week-long course in T-Touch was being offered that fall in Camp Verde, a town in the high desert mountainous area north of Phoenix.

Nothing could have been better than heading up north with Nalle, seeing the beautiful autumn leaves, enjoying the cool weather. Nalle loved the long drive in my awesome Honda Accord Sport with the moon roof open, the wind blowing his fur. His eyes glowed with happiness. Nalle and Mom, conquering the world!

Then it happened ...

On Friday, the week before Thanksgiving, Nalle was lethargic and began vomiting. Since all dogs have their not-so-good days, I decided to give it some time. But the next morning found him weak and cold. We headed to Emergency.

After an examination and a frantic call to a previous vet, she and the ER vets concluded that Nalle had Addison's, a disease of the adrenal glands which, as in Nalle's case, can appear suddenly and lead to life-threatening shock and cardiac arrest.

I was devastated. I have suffered with borderline Addison's most of my life so I had a limited idea of what Nalle was going through. Choking back tears, I realized I'd nearly lost my Nalle.

Nalle remained in hospital for five more days, then was released on a formulated medication with prednisone as a backup should he have another crisis.

Gradually, Nalle became stronger, but he had changed. He was cautious now about exploring new things. He seemed more deeply aware of everything. He'd take his time observing, thinking everything over carefully before he made any decisions.

But Nalle had not lost his Newfy humor. He still gave me a hockey-type "body check" before he raced out, caught his Frisbee, then tossed it in the air. He still took every opportunity to make me laugh during training when, on long sits, he would show me a "stink eye" glare, then give me a Newfy grumble under his breath as he took a bounce and headed in for a "front and finish."

Two years later the housing crises arrived, making the next few years difficult for many landlords, and requiring me to relocate several times. I felt incredibly guilty about all the disruptions, knowing how bad stress can be for those with Addison's disease. But Nalle seemed to take the changes in stride.

No matter where we lived, we were always able to find a park nearby and take our ritual walks. But gradually Nalle began moving more slowly and having Addison's crises more often.

Our walks became shorter. Denial was not an option. My Nalle was not doing well. My heart was breaking.

As time slipped into the spring of his sixth year, I lost my Nalle, my Teddy Bear. You know what it's like when they leave you. Memories come flooding back. Funny things, serious things. Images so vivid you are living them again.

Nalle was my first rescue Newfy and I know Noah was smiling and watching us all the while. Nalle and I needed each other, we loved each other, we laughed, and we cried. We will always be together in our hearts—all of us. That is how love is. Love never leaves us.

Susanne Davis
Phoenix, Arizona, USA
Mesquite Newfoundland Club

Chapter 80

A Cautionary Tale - Ellie

Nothing prepared us for Ellie, our tumultuous, Newfoundland puppy. We had read up on the breed, talked to Newf owners online, had in-depth discussions with breeders, and most importantly, engaged in serious family conferences. We wanted a loving addition to our family and a companion for our six-year-old Golden Retriever, Benson. The Newfoundland was described as "a gentle giant, loyal and strong, with a calm, docile nature and a sweet disposition." That was exactly what we wanted.

So off we go to Nottingham on Boxing Day, very excited to collect our lovely puppy. We were introduced to two little, eleven-week-old Newfy girls, both of whom were bombing around, seemingly identical in looks and personalities. After spending some time with them, Ellie was the puppy we chose. Then away we went with our little bear cub and a good advice sheet of what to do to continue her care.

We adored Ellie straight away. What would be different from any of the Goldens we had taken on? We were used to dog hair and muddy paws coming through the house, and we were aware that puppy training takes time, and teething would likely lead to some damage. We knew it was up to us to make everywhere safe.

Ellie landed at our home, and life as we knew it changed, forever. Everything she saw, she assumed was a plaything of hers. After several frolicsome chase games focused on retrieving Christmas decorations from her mouth, we introduced her to our garden.

At the time, we had several rescue hens that the Goldens had always been a little scared of. Ellie spotted them at the far end of the garden and instantly thought they must be toys. After a lot of squawking and flapping, the hens had to take refuge behind a fence for their own safety.

But feeling confident after having trained several Golden pups, off we went to puppy training with our little bear. Ellie looked comical being so much bigger than the other puppies, but everyone loved meeting her and watching her socialise and play with the others.

Ellie took to puppy training with great enthusiasm. Sometimes she complied with the commands. Sometimes, in a normal, short-attention-span puppy way, she got distracted and got creative. But, along with the other puppies, she enjoyed the interaction and the positive reinforcements.

For a lesson meant to teach the puppies to "leave it," the trainer put a treat on the nose of a big, soft Scoobie-Doo toy and proceeded with the instruction. Off the pups went in turn, some being good and leaving the treat, some not being able to resist a small snack. When it was Ellie's turn, not only did she eat the treat, she grabbed the Scoobie-Doo, gave it a thorough shaking, then raced off with it in her mouth to join in with the other pups. Playing with toys and puppies was much more interesting than obeying a "leave it" command. After devouring the treat and killing the toy, Ellie did not graduate at the head of the class that evening.

But as Ellie's training progressed, she became very consistent with the recall command. Convinced she would always respond appropriately, down to the park we went, Ellie off leash.

I suppose it was our fault. We used to throw empty lemonade bottles for Ellie to play with. Therefore, in her view, all plastic bottles were hers. Unfortunately, Ellie spotted a lady with a plastic water bottle in her hand. My heart sank as Ellie froze, stared, ignored my command, then took off like a freight train toward the poor lady.

"Throw your bottle! Please throw your bottle!" I shouted.

But it was too late. Ellie flattened the lady, grabbed the bottle, and ran. Thankfully, the lady wasn't hurt and, once over the shock, this understanding dog lover doubled over in fits of laughter.

I did not learn my lesson. Months passed, training continued, and Ellie became brilliant at recall. Away we went to another lovely park, Ellie off leash. Regrettably, Ellie spotted a family having a picnic, all nicely set out on a blanket. Déjà vu, with the addition of sandwiches flying through the air. Ellie's assault included stealing a pair of sandals and depositing them in a muddy swamp.

There was no laughter this time. Sometimes you just have to remove the culprit from the scene, as no amount of "sorrys" will make any difference.

There were *many* more Ellie disasters and near disasters. The blue light flashing in her mouth quickly became the remains of my Bluetooth earpiece. The awful smell of burnt fur was the result of a big, fluffy paw on the gas cooker. The vacuum cleaner care advisor's assessment that I'm a giggling nut job was the aftermath of being knocked flat on the floor during a help call. The terror of meeting death by stabbing was a consequence of being chased around the garden by a puppy brandishing a bread knife. The sound of a crack on my nose followed by blackness and blood was the outcome of a sharp-eyed young canine retrieving a chew stick from a fireplace mantle.

When Ellie was three years old we had to let our lovely, old Benson boy go. Ellie became very depressed. Our whirlwind dog completely lost her spark. As the weeks went by, she just wasn't the same. Although there had been times when I would think how nice it would be when she calmed down, it was heartbreaking to see her so unhappy.

Finally, we took Ellie around to visit a Newfy breeder. A small, three-year-old, gingery-brown girl called Hope ran straight into my arms and something just clicked. Ellie loved her, we loved her, and she loved us. Hope adapted to our home without any stress, and Ellie gained a lovely companion who had a calming influence on her.

We have continued taking on adult Newfies. Once Hope's breeder saw how much we treasured our dogs, she felt ours was the perfect and right home for Newfies. After Hope, she has entrusted us with five more adults, none of whom were ever used for breeding, all of whom were just waiting for the ideal home. Every one of these dogs has been sweet and loving, and every one we have lost has left a tender memory. At the present time, Kodie, Dora, and Lola have been entrusted to us. A Newfoundland dog, *once it has passed the puppy stage*, does fit the description of being "a gentle giant, loyal and strong, with a calm, docile nature and a sweet disposition."

While Ellie easily wins the award for the most energetic, exuberant, ebullient Newfy puppy *ever*, her story needs to be told. Before taking on a giant breed, prospective Newfy owners should understand that giant breed puppies can have giant amounts of energy, and, as in Ellie's case, might have minds of their own, overflowing with independent opinions and ideas. The puppy side of a giant breed can hit your home like a ton of bricks.

The saving grace is that giant breeds, even as irrepressible puppies, are capable of giant amounts of love. Ellie will be 13 next month and is still going strong. Although her puppyhood was fraught with hair-raising incidents and seemed to last for six years, I'm so glad we have had her in our lives. She is treasured, the apple of our eye, source of countless welcome and wonderful adventures, enormously loved.

Paula Wooldridge
Meir Heath, Stoke-on-Trent, Staffordshire, England, UK

Chapter 81

Welcome Home - Miska

It was time to take Juneau, our 10-month-old Newfy, to the vet for her shots and yearly check-up. Our first thought was to take all four of the children with us, but the idea of four kids and a giant-sized Newfy in the backseat of a truck wasn't all that appealing to Angie, eight years old, and Jane, almost nine.

Maybe because she's the oldest, and because the younger children are only five and three, Jane feels she is almost a "grown-up." In the last few months she has been eager to become more independent and frequently asks for opportunities to practice new responsibilities. I have tried to support her bids for independence in a safe way, and it has been a pleasure watching her confidence and self-reliance develop.

Several times Jane has asked to try staying home when we go to Helena. I had never allowed this, but today, with just a little hesitation, I agreed. So, after reviewing our numerous discussions of ways to stay safe, naming which of our trusted neighbors to call if she needed help, and providing her with my cell phone, my husband, the two little kids, Juneau, and I began our thirty-mile trip to the vet, leaving the two older girls at home to practice the ultimate "grown-up experience"—staying home alone.

In truth, the girls weren't completely alone. They were in the company of Kenai, the four-year-old German short-hair/lab escape artist, Sasha, the 12-year-old lab/unknown mix rescue, Jack Daniels, the eight-year-old blue heeler/collie rescue, and Miska, the 10½-month-old, happy Newfy.

Although he is the youngest dog we left at home, Miska *is* the Newfoundland, so he is the one I knew I could rely on to maintain the normal routine and back up the girls' courage and morale while we were gone.

Miska had been chosen with great care and we had gotten it exactly right. We had talked with breeders in various parts of the country and asked tons of questions to make sure we selected the right dog for our family. Finally, about eight months ago, we located just the right breeder with just the right puppy in ... Ohio? *Ohio?* Ohio is a state more than half-way across the continent from Montana.

Originally, we had arranged for a pet courier to deliver Miska, but then came Covid and travel restrictions. The restrictions would have delayed his arrival for at least a month, possibly longer. I considered flying to Ohio to get him, but we were unable to find reliable information on flying with a dog, and I was not going to trust my pup to an airline employee. In the end, after arranging for a friend to take care of the older dogs, my husband, all four children, Juneau (who was too young and too new to our family to be left behind), and I all piled into our truck and drove to Ohio.

The 27+ hour one-way trek in a truck filled with humans and one Newfy pup on the way there and two Newfy pups on the way back was an adventure in itself, but well worth every fun-filled mile. Long before we got back home we knew we had chosen the perfect puppy. Miska fits into our crazy family like a hand in a glove. He is bright, enthusiastic, and loving. He quickly bonded with all of us, especially the children. At night he makes the rounds, lying on the feet of first one child, then another, keeping their feet warm and adding to their sense of security.

It is Miska's attention to the children that made me think the girls could handle being home alone. With him at their side they would feel safe. Therefore, on this beautiful summer day, under a perfect Montana Big Sky, Jane and Angie stayed home, and our trip to Helena unfolded normally. I called home a couple of times to check with Jane. Juneau was her usual, cooperative self at the vet's office. And, before long we were headed home. All was well in our world.

About twenty minutes before we reached our driveway, we were amazed to see red lights flashing in the distance behind us. We pulled over to let a highway patrol car fly by. This is rural Montana. We rarely see red flashing lights. We rarely see highway patrol cars flying by. We were curious. We wondered where the car was going in such a hurry. In just a few minutes we were going to find out exactly where that car was going.

My husband's cell phone rang. It was Jane. Was she hyperventilating? I could tell she was extremely distressed.

"How far away are you?" Jane blurted.

"About ten seconds. What's wrong?"

Between gasps and what might have been a few half-sobs, Jane began telling me what had happened. She had left my phone on the kitchen counter. Miska, in an attempt to sneak some snacks, had climbed up on the counter. Jane didn't notice that one of his big Newfy paws landed on the phone's emergency call button.

In an effort to get Miska off the counter, Jane had begun yelling, "No! No! No!"

Meanwhile, the 911 dispatcher had picked up the call, heard the frantic yelling, and notified the emergency responder. And the police officer, having no way of knowing that Jane was just yelling at a counter-surfing Newfy, raced to our house as fast as he could, flying past our truck along the way.

The unexpected appearance of a police officer, inquiring about the presence of weapons and the necessity of calling for paramedics, was just a little bit overwhelming for Jane. Then it had taken a while to determine what had instigated the 911 call. Adding to the drama, Miska had greeted the officer at the door—according to the officer, "very affectionately"—but had then almost knocked him over in an attempt to join Kenai who had suddenly dashed out, seizing an opportunity for a jail break.

Now Kenai, who can jump the fence, has escaped. Miska, who can't, has come back inside.

Jane gave us a complete explanation so when we got out of the truck a minute later and greeted the officer, we were already aware of the situation.

Now that the officer has determined no one is in danger, he seems to find this whole episode amusing. This is the first time he has been summoned by a giant dog.

Now that Jane has had the experience of staying home alone, it may be awhile before she asks to try it again. I will look for other ways to help her practice being independent.

Now that Miska has his whole family back home, he is demonstrating his usual exuberant welcoming behavior. For some reason he appears to be very pleased with himself.

Now that I've caught my breath, I'm not sure how I want to react to this incident. It might be funny ... tomorrow.

On this beautiful summer day, under a perfect Montana Big Sky, Kenai remains at large.

Kristyn Vandyke
Basin, Montana, USA
Facebook: miskathenewfie

Chapter 82

Jude Takes Manhattan - Jude

Jude had never been in a cab before, and he was nervous to the point of hyperventilating. This would not normally be cause for serious concern, except for two things. First, our cab driver knew very little English, and even less about the city. He had to ask my mom and me how to get from lower Fifth Avenue to upper Fifth Avenue. And second, Jude is a 150-pound Newfoundland dog. When the going gets tough, Jude starts drooling and just now, in the backseat of the cab, a four-inch strand of drool slapped across my face and dangled from the end of my nose.

Jude may not be easy to travel with, but he deserves the extra effort because he is sweet and never complains. He is also spectacularly handsome, which makes people want to talk to you when you are among strangers. That is one reason why I decided to bring him to New York City from our home in rural Massachusetts. The other reason is that I was eager to find out where I could get away with taking him.

The first thing we needed in New York was a hotel where Jude could stay with my mom and dad and me. The Motel 6 near my little town won't even allow dogs in its lobby, so what would be our chances of finding a comfortable Manhattan hotel that would allow him to sleep in a room? But after searching the Internet for information on pet-friendly hotels, we discovered a site called petswelcome.com which actually listed a few options for Manhattan. The one that caught my eye was the SoHo Grand Hotel.

When I learned that the SoHo Grand was a popular place for rock stars and actors to stay, my mind became flooded with scenes of Jade giving his paw to Mick Jagger and being hugged and petted by Gwyneth Paltrow. I also learned that the SoHo Grand offered dog-walking services, dog-sitting, room service for hungry pets, and even a limo service that ferries pets around town with or without their human companions.

Yes, staying at the SoHo Grand would definitely be classier than those budget motels that we always had to sneak Jude into on our way up to Canada every summer, and it would make an excellent base camp for Jude's assault on the Big Apple.

In front of the SoHo Grand Hotel, we were greeted by a bellhop who bowed and offered Jude a liver-flavored jerky treat, which he promptly devoured, then washed down with a slurp of cold water from the stone tub the hotel calls the Dog Bar.

Jude's needs and our baggage having been taken care of, we all went inside to check out the lobby. What impressed us most was the cast iron and bottle glass staircase whose treads let the light shine through from above and below, just like the front steps of hundreds of 19th-century SoHo loft buildings, which were designed to let sunlight down into their basements. Jude, however found the bronze Dobermans and Greyhounds that lounge at the top of the stairs more to his liking.

A place where we all found something to like was our room. Although it wasn't very big, you could lie on your bed and enjoy views of the Empire State Building and the Hudson River. For Jude, it offered a cool tiled bathroom floor where he could catch up on his beauty sleep and rest his tired feet after we had completed adventures such as crossing the Brooklyn Bridge and trekking through SoHo, Little Italy, Chinatown, and the financial district.

I must admit that my first day with Jude in New York City was only a partial success. Jude tasted hot dogs, falafel, and empanadas, bathed in the fountain at City Hall, and drew crowds of admirers everywhere we went. Still we were unable to go into some stores and restaurants, and we were thrown out of the lobby of the Woolworth Building.

The next day we were determined to do better. With the help of another web site, DogFriendly.com, we were able to plan a day that offered Jude better access to the finer things the city has to offer.

We started at Tiffany, where we had trouble right away. No, we weren't kicked out, but Jude couldn't fit through the revolving door. However, with the help of a smiling security guard pushing Jude's rump, we made it in to enjoy the shining silver and diamonds.

That wasn't Jude's last glimpse of luxury that day. An hour or so later at Ralph Lauren, he was treated to a porcelain bowl of water and a silver tray of gourmet biscuits. A dog's life!

As if that weren't too much already, we took him to the William Second Gallery which specializes in 19th and 20th-century dog portraits. We humans were impressed, but then we noticed Jude, lying on the floor, surrounded by scores of framed masterpieces, sleeping soundly. We supposed he wanted to conserve energy for his evening rendezvous.

At 5 p.m. in Washington Square Park, we met Art Zuckerman, the owner of a computer systems company who has developed a second career as a tour guide for dog owners and their dogs. With him were his wife, his 11-year-old son, and his Golden Retriever, Tawny. I was thrilled when he handed me a Razor scooter. That made the "walking" tour especially fun for me.

With Jude and Tawny in tow, we visited many notable places in Washington Square and the West Village. When the tour was over, I thanked everyone and reluctantly handed back the scooter. Jude, exhausted from all the miles and overwhelmed by all the information, collapsed on the pavement. It may have looked like New York had finally conquered him, but we were all certain he would wake up hours later in Massachusetts, a wiser and worldlier pet.

Jonathan Peyster
New Salem, Massachusetts, USA
Another version of this story appeared in
Diversion Magazine, June, 2001

The Ninety-nine MORE Newfies

(in the order in which their story was completed)

1. Joey, 2. Murphy, 3. Bailey, 4. Blackie, 5. Ophie, 6. Scooter,

7. Yogi, 8. Noah, 9. Truffles, 10. Nana (Ciandrini), 11. Rosie,

12. Ruggles, 13. Mariah, 14. Seamus, 15. Abra, 16. Shiloh,

17. Molly (Ball), 18. Annie, 19. Rowdy, 20. Seven-of-Nine,

21. Lulu, 22. Shandy, 23. Mandy, 24. Heffalump, 25. Jack,

26. Cree, 27. Bear (Brown), 28. Molly (Daulton), 29. Kahlua,

30. Osa, 31. Mamut, 32. Susy, 33. Harley Bean, 34. Coda,

35. Gummy Bear, 36. River, 37. Malcolm, 38. Cassiopeia,

39. Jeter, 40. Taz, Tiny (debuted as a puppy, #82, in *Ninety-nine Newfies*),

41. Wendell, 42. Shadow, 43. Gabriel, 44. Gus, 45. Brandy,

46. Mercedes, 47. Maverick, 48. Henry, 49. Kona,

50. Cheyenne, 51. Angus, 52. Duchess, 53. Jackson Brown,

54. Maggie Mae, 55. Norman, 56. Rudy, 57. Lily,

58. Lexi-Bear, 59. Penny, 60. Sage, 61. Juno,

62. Miley, 63. Pinkerton, 64. Maxine, 65. Bear (Steelman),

66. Thunder, 67. Tank, 68. Sioux Pooh, 69. Leroy, 70. Boulder,

71. Deacon, 72. Kayla, 73. Seamas, 74. Benny, 75. Jake Doyle,

76. Izzy, 77. Elsie, 78. Taylor, 79. Splash, 80. Sam, 81. Lex,

82. Halo, 83. Circe, 84. Finnegan, 85. Zulu, 86. Chief,

87. Pirate, 88. Luke, 89. Nana (Croy), 90. Moses,

91. Mojo, 92. Leia, 93. Maple, 94. Dante, 95. Dundee,

96. Nalle, 97. Ellie, 98. Miska, 99. Jude.

Acknowledgements

Organizing *Ninety-nine Newfies* was a profound learning experience, an amazing example of community cooperation, and enormous fun. It was published in 2001. That was that, and I thought the job of sharing stories about our Newfoundland dogs was done. But then came a report of how Abra gained a competitive edge at a KFC drive-thru window. It made me laugh out loud. Maybe our job of sharing Newfy stories wasn't quite done.

Thank you, *Ninety-nine Newfies* authors who said, "Yes! There are ninety-nine MORE stories! Let's go for it!" then contributed stories.

Thank you, new *Ninety-nine MORE Newfies* authors who said, "Yes! I'll participate in this adventure!" then contributed stories.

Thank you, Newfy regional club members who said, "Yes! Let's show our team spirit!" then urged each other to contribute stories.

Thank you, friends and family members who said, "Yes! I know someone who has a Newfy!" then encouraged him or her to contribute a story.

And thank you, Mr. John P. Seawell, who said, "Yes! Once again I will remain incredibly patient and supportive throughout this project." then critiqued all of the stories and created many of the titles.

Ninety-nine MORE Newfies is dedicated to all of you, and to all of our precious Newfies, past, present, and future, with gratitude, love, and many hugs.

www.ingramcontent.com/pod-product-compliance
Lightning Source LLC
Chambersburg PA
CBHW051707160426
43209CB00004B/1051